Denzel Washington
His Films and Career

Denzel Washington
His Films and Career

DOUGLAS BRODE

A Birch Lane Press Book
Published by Carol Publishing Group

A Birch Lane Press Book
Published by Carol Publishing Group
Birch Lane Press is a registered trademark of Carol Communications, Inc.

Editorial, sales and distribution, rights and permissions inquiries should be addressed to Carol Publishing Group, 120 Enterprise Avenue, Secaucus, N.J. 07094

In Canada: Canadian Manda Group, One Atlantic Avenue, Suite 105, Toronto, Ontario, M6K 3E7

Carol Publishing Group books may be purchased in bulk at special discounts for sales promotion, fund-raising, or educational purposes. Special editions can be created to specifications. For details, contact Special Sales Department, 120 Enterprise Avenue, Secaucus, N.J. 07094.

MANUFACTURED IN THE UNITED STATES OF AMERICA
10 9 8 7 6 5 4 3 2 1

Library of Congress Cataloging-in-Publication Data

Brode, Douglas, 1941–
    Denzel Washington : his films & career / by Douglas Brode.
        p.   cm.
    ISBN 1-55972-381-5 (hc)
    1. Washington, Denzel, 1954–   —Criticism and interpretation.
    I. Title.
PN2287.W452B76   1996
791.43'028'092—dc20   96-42254
                                                       CIP

For
Kathryn
with appreciation and admiration

Contents

Acknowledgments

Scott Lecleau and Peter Violas, for their many hours of research work; Jerry Ohlinger's Movie Material store in New York and Cinema Collectors in Los Angeles; the Academy of Motion Picture Arts and Sciences Library and the Lincoln Center Library; NBC-TV Publicity Department, Avco Embassy Pictures, Hemdale Leisure Corporation, RKO-Radio Pictures, Columbia Pictures, Lorimar Pictures, 20th Century-Fox Distribution, Universal Pictures, Marble Arch Productions, Atlantic Releasing, Working Title Films, Metro-Goldwyn-Mayer Pictures, Tri-Star Pictures, New Line Cinema, Warner Bros., Samuel Goldwyn Releasing, Buena Vista, Hollywood Films, and Paramount Pictures.

Introduction: Deconstructing Denzel

I am who I am," Denzel Washington once told a reporter eagerly interviewing him for a story. "What people write about me is who *they* are, and what they *think* I am." An intriguing point of view from an actor who once considered a career in journalism. And an interesting starting point for a study of his films and career. All of what follows should be taken, as Denzel himself would insist, for what it is: one person's perception of an elusive human being who remains, regardless of what anyone writes, his own man.

That said, while Denzel Washington may be many things to many people—writers and the general public alike—there is one thing he is not. He adamantly insists he is *not* the Sidney Poitier of the 1990s. Sir Richard Attenborough, diehard liberal crusader as filmmaker and person, learned this the hard way. "Dickie," as he likes to be called, believed he was paying his *Cry Freedom* star the highest compliment when he compared the two thespians; instead, Washington complained, "I think that's the most racist thing." Why, of all the popular stars from previous generations, should he be compared to Poitier? Is it simply because both men happen to be black?

Another director, Alan Pakula, while working with Denzel on *The Pelican Brief,* was struck by his similarity to another established performer. "You remind me exactly of Robert Redford," Pakula blurted out. "You have that look of the romantic but masculine gentleman." This time, Denzel was flattered: "No one ever said that to me before," he responded. That is, no one had overlooked his race to precisely note what Denzel's particular charisma is about.

Set color aside and it's obvious Denzel has far more in common with Redford or Paul Newman, both of whom project intense masculine sex appeal despite a clean-cut aura. Martin Stellman, who directed Denzel in *For Queen and Country,* notes: "He has a very still quality, like (Clint) Eastwood. He's almost minimalist in his expressions and gestures and movement. Yet he still manages to be powerful on the screen." Then there's James Stewart, whom Denzel admires for being "so wholesome and honest. A regular guy who overcomes" in Frank Capra's topical comedies.

"First of all," Denzel Washington explained in 1990, "I'm a *man.*" It would be wrong to assume he was talking gender; he meant Homo sapiens, a human being, and an *individual* human being at that. "As an actor, ask me how I feel about things. But [too often], the questions are always, 'As a *black...*' I'm very proud to be black, but *black is not all I am.* That's my cultural, historical background, my genetic makeup, but it's not the basis from which I answer every question....I don't think I should be talked to only as a black actor." It's absurd to assume that since he happens to be black, his own perceptions speak for the entire race. Once, when questioned by the press as to how he thought the black community would react to his latest film, Denzel retorted: "I don't know. The black community doesn't get together at my house on Wednesday nights."

"It's not that he speaks for no one," Peter Richmond noted in *Gentleman's Quarterly.* "He speaks quite eloquently, when pressed, for *himself.*" When, in the late eighties, endless reporters hailed Denzel as "America's finest young black actor," he bridled. Why should the word "black" be brought into play at all? Back in the sixties, no one referred to Paul Newman as "the best young *Jewish* actor" around. Sidney Poitier, on the other hand, was immediately segregated in print as his era's best young *black* actor. Attaching such a limiting label to Poitier was as unfair to Sidney back then as it is to Denzel today.

Nonetheless, we live in America during the 1990s, when issues of race are unavoidable. Social critic Hilary De Vries was correct when, at the decade's onset, she noted that Denzel "is a leader among a handful of artists—a list that also includes Morgan Freeman and Danny Glover—who are redefining how black Americans are portrayed on film." As actors who happened to be black and who greatly appeal not only to ethnic audiences but to the entire moviegoing public, their roles—in particular, Denzel's—impacted on the general perception of African Americans.

The responsibility weighs heavily on Denzel's shoulders, and his words suggest he'd prefer the weight to be lifted: "People say, 'You're the guy that's gonna carry the torch for history.' But I'm not that guy. I just want to do the things I want to do.... I'm not antiblack or shunning my own blackness. But if we are making any progress, if Hollywood is getting any better, it has to start with each one of us." Each of us as an *individual*; Denzel's past and present words make clear that he favors "rugged individuality" over any sense of "community loyalty." When other blacks complain that their race has been consistently slighted in historical films made by whites, Denzel retorts: "*Don't* say [to the white Hollywood Establishment], 'Tell my story for me and make it good, 'cause if it's not, you're a racist.' *Tell your own story!*"

Understandably, he came to hold such values as a result of his life's unfolding journey.

Denzel was born on December 28, 1954, the second of three children. He was named after his father, who embodied the American work ethic. All week long, Denzel senior rushed back and forth between two jobs, at the S. Klein department store and the water department, following his own true calling through additional work on Sundays as a Pentecostal preacher. In addition to the Washington family, there might be only two or three people listening to his sermons, but that didn't hold Denzel senior back from sharing his strong beliefs with whatever congregation he had. Denzel, his older sister Lorice, and younger brother David, didn't see their dad much other than at those sermons. Weekdays, he was gone when they got up; they were asleep before he arrived home.

The family lived in Mount Vernon, New York, an area Denzel would later recall as a "buffer zone" between the mean streets of Manhattan and those wealthy, largely white suburbs to the north. Mount Vernon was, philosophically as well as physically, somewhere in between: a middle-class haven bordering the Bronx, interracial in its makeup. That allowed Denzel to associate with young people from diverse backgrounds. His childhood friends were

West Indian, Irish, and Italian, as well as black. "I learned a lot of different cultures," he recalls today. Such boyhood experiences suggest why, later in life, Denzel would not automatically identify with black issues.

Perhaps surprisingly, the child did not become a great movie fan. His morally conservative father only gave his blessing to religious epics like *The Ten Commandments* (1956) or *King of Kings* (1961), along with selected Disney films. As a budding teenager, Denzel often sneaked out to catch the controversial fare then making the rounds, including the legendary black-exploitation flick *Superfly* (1972). Aside from such minor infractions, Denzel was a good kid, and the family's lifestyle remained relatively calm until the parents divorced when Denzel was fourteen.

What ensued thereafter is a subject about which Denzel remains guarded. "I guess it made me angry," he reflects. "I went through a phase where I got into a lot of fights. Working it out." Family and religion had been the basis of Denzel's existence; now, with a firm sense of the former dissolving, he purposefully rejected the latter. "I don't think there was a conscious effort to reject religion," he later admitted, "but I rejected it," though the mature Denzel adds: "I've come around since then!"

The breakup also made him vow to someday be in a solid marital situation; today he and singer Pauletta Pearson are the rare Hollywood couple who live quietly with their children. "My parents' divorce made me want to make my marriage work," he now admits. "I guess I felt a responsibility to marriage." A responsibility, perhaps, to his own children so they wouldn't experience the alienation that follows a divorce.

There is no question that the teenage Denzel was negatively effected by the divorce. At school, he went from being the brightest student to a chronic underachiever. Denzel interrupted teachers with endless variations on one recurring question, "Why?" He was referring, perhaps unconsciously, to his parents' breakup as much as to the academic material at hand.

Following the split, his father returned to his home town of Dillwyn, Virginia, continuing his religious work until his death at age eighty-one in 1991. Denzel's mother, a former gospel singer born in Georgia but raised in Harlem, supported the family as a beautician.

Mother Lennis, a first-rate businesswoman owing to her natural abilities and sudden financial necessity, soon owned and operated several area shops. Hanging out after school, Denzel experienced his first taste of dramatic performance: "My mother's beauty parlor is her own stage where she performs matinees on a daily basis," he recalled. At age twelve, Denzel worked part-time in a barbershop in which his mom owned half interest, whisk-brooming people, hustling their clothes to the cleaners. He learned to like the tips: "Everybody looked like a dollar bill to me."

Mostly, though, he acquired an appreciation for life-as-theater. "The lives and the lies you could encounter there every day were unbelievable." Long before opting for a dramatic career, Denzel was intuitively aware of what Shakespeare noted some four hundred years earlier: "All the world's a stage, and all the men and women, merely players."

A popular high school jock, Denzel excelled at football, and considered a pro career. Always, though, there was an element of the artist in him; he played piano in a local soul band called the Last Express, which imitated the briefly popular Grand Funk Railroad. Also, he tried his hand at theatrical performance while attending YMCA summer camps, where Denzel was tagged a natural leader in both plays and athletics.

Though he now resided in a one-parent home, Denzel was fortunate enough to have a strong mother who insisted on a tightly controlled environment, an attitude he would later adapt to his own life. "She was a very tough disciplinarian," he recalls. At age sixteen, other guys were hanging out until midnight, but Denzel was expected to be in the house when the streetlights went on. He always did so; otherwise, "I knew my mother would kill me!" Soon some members of the Last Express were doing time; one landed in the morgue. One former band member, Charles McCutchen, now resides in the Westchester County Medical Center in Valhalla, victim of liver and kidney damage from a lifetime of drinking and drug abuse. Denzel's onetime best pal, "Cutch" provides insight into why Denzel made it big: "He always had goals—things he wanted to do in life."

In part, Denzel escaped the fate of many of his peers by spending most of his nonschool hours at the local Boys Club, where he found alternative father figures. And thanks to his mother, Denzel was already on the high road, morally and culturally. "She saw to it I was exposed to a lot of things," he recalled. "She couldn't afford [life's finer things], but she was very intelligent. She is basically responsible for my success."

Lennis sensed her son's potential talents while also fearing the dangerous lure of the streets. So she conferred with a guidance counselor, who likewise sensed that Denzel was a special youth. They urged him to apply to New Windsor's Oakland Academy, a private upstate boarding school where most students were "very rich and very white." He was accepted on partial scholarship, the remaining funds scraped together by his mom. At Oakland, Denzel held his own with classmates thanks to natural abilities in sports and scholastics. Still, he remained an underachiever, winning decent grades without excelling, though he obviously had the ability to do so. If only he could find a point of focus.

One teacher wrote in Denzel's Oakland yearbook: "Keep your individuality...but maybe cut down on the noise."

Following graduation in 1972, Denzel attended Fordham University. It was his third choice; his grades weren't good enough to win the scholarship necessary to attend Boston University, and he hadn't been accepted into Yale. So it was off to the Bronx, pulling together enough money from several loans and augmenting that by running an after-school program, baby-sitting children of single working parents at a Greek Orthodox church in Upper Manhattan. His major was premed; once more his grades were less than spectacular. Denzel sensed that however noble the profession, medicine was not for him. The only class he really enjoyed that first year was an Introduction to Communications; he considered changing his major to either journalism or political science.

For one semester, he dropped out of school when his grades were poor. Denzel floundered about, working at the post office, then with the sanitation department, collecting trash. It wasn't a pleasant experience; as soon as possible, he was back at Fordham. Denzel still adored sports, effectively competing with guys attending on athletic scholarships. He was a walk-on in basketball and football and was at one point coached by the well-regarded P. J. Carlesimo. Denzel had begun to dabble in the arts, writing a great deal of poetry, inspired by recordings of Minnie Riperton. Though they would never meet during Minnie's brief lifetime, Denzel was deeply moved by her work as well as that of Patti LaBelle and Angela Bofill; "Female singers touch me more than anybody else," he later admitted, adding with a wink: "I married one, you know." He might have added that he was the son of one as well. Denzel considered sending his verse to Minnie, but was too shy to ever put anything of the sort in the mail.

It happened that, one summer, Denzel earned much-needed money by working as a counselor at the same YMCA camp he'd attended in Connecticut. The people in charge invited Denzel back to coach kids in athletics as well as stage talent shows. Everyone praised Denzel's innate gifts as a director, making it a point to tell Denzel that when he stepped out onstage, excitement rippled through the audience. He had the gift of presence; it was something they suggested he really ought to follow up on.

Back at Fordham, open auditions were announced for a student production of *The Emperor Jones,* and Denzel showed up. Knowing nothing about the complexities of "serious" drama, he bluffed his way through the audition process and was cast in a role the legendary Paul Robeson once made his own. Denzel didn't, at this point, know enough to be nervous on opening night; peering through the scrim at the audience, the star-to-be felt no intimidation, bounding out onstage as if this were yet another summer camp show. In good time, that attitude would change: "I'm more afraid now. I know what can go wrong!" In the meantime, something finally excited him. Denzel had stumbled upon his niche; the moment he did, college took on new meaning. Then it was on to an even more difficult part, after winning the lead in Shakespeare's *Othello*.

In no time flat, Denzel was out of premed and enrolled in journalism, eventually graduating with a dual major in journalism and drama. During his junior year, Denzel signed up for a theater workshop taught by Robinson Stone, a veteran actor best remembered for a supporting role in *Stalag 17* (1953). Denzel "was easily the best Othello I had ever seen," Stone recalled for the *Chicago Tribune* years later; impressive words, coming from an actor who had played Brabantio in a production headlined by Paul Robeson.

Stone encouraged old friend José Ferrer, the villainous Iago in that same touring company, to visit the campus and catch Denzel. Ferrer did so, agreeing that this young man could be one of the greats. "He played Othello with so much majesty and beauty," Stone says, "but also rage and hate." Stone became Denzel's mentor, helping the young actor find an agent.

While still in college, Denzel won a role in the 1977 made-for-TV movie *Wilma*. Once more, he bluffed his way in, improvising a full verbal resumé suggesting he'd appeared in a whole host of independent films. "Maybe they cast me because I cared enough about it to lie to get it," he later said, laughing. A run-of-the-mill "disease of the week" feature, *Wilma* featured Cicely Tyson as Wilma Rudolph, who overcame polio to win three gold medals in track and field at the 1960 Rome Olympics. Denzel was cast as the boyfriend Wilma eventually marries. He later confided to interviewer Gary Ballard: "I'd never been a real broad [stage] actor, so I didn't come across as too big on film, but I kept playing the scenes with my head down. Every few minutes, they were telling me, 'Get your head up. We can't see your expressions. We're losing your face.' I was afraid of the camera. I didn't know how to relate to it. I caught on to it pretty quick, but I also knew I wasn't ready for this quite yet. I needed to learn more."

If he'd felt completely comfortable in front of the camera, Denzel might well have dropped out of school to pursue films. So he remained, for the time being, at Fordham. "People have gotten away from the *work*," he would later insist when asked why so many young actors burn brightly for a brief time, then fall out of favor. In his mind, they were not sufficiently prepared, hadn't paid the necessary dues. "They don't put in the *work*," Denzel admonished.

Doing *Wilma* had introduced Denzel to something more important than screen acting. His first day on the set, Denzel briefly met Pauletta Pearson, an attractive young classical pianist and Broadway singer (whose credits include the *Jesus Christ, Superstar* revival and *Sophisticated Ladies*). She was exiting the production, having completed her role as runner Mae Faggs. The two exchanged polite conversation, though he'd been too awestruck at being in a movie to later recall the details of their meeting.

On the night when *Wilma* aired, Denzel wasn't even able to watch; he was busy busing tables at a San Francisco restaurant, augmenting the scholarship money he'd received to continue his education. Following graduation, Denzel had been granted admission to the American Conservatory Theater (ACT), one of the forty-five applicants who had been chosen out of many thousands of hopefuls nationwide. At ACT, he put in fourteen-hour days, studying acting, dancing, and scene design. One class focused on sense-memory exercises, while another emphasized an actor's awareness of his physical movements; a third dealt with the famed "Method" for emotionally immersing oneself in a role. As an alternative, there were studies in "technique," the intellectual approach to a part. While some aspiring actors locked into one particular theory, Denzel—as always the individualist—picked bits and pieces from each but embraced no one of them entirely.

Throughout his career, Denzel would maintain a similar balance between time-tested theories and his own innate instincts. "Mastering those basics is so important" is his best advice for young performers. This belief stems from an early experience. While a high school track star, Denzel felt threatened when a new kid appeared who was faster than he. Sensing this, Denzel's coach took him aside, insisting: "Don't worry. He's fast, but he don't know how to run."

In fact, what transpired was akin to the legendary tortoise-and-hare bout, Denzel carrying the day. He never forgot the coach's words, later applying them to every aspect of life: "He meant that technique can outperform raw, untrained talent every time, which is true in *any* endeavor, so you should learn your craft. It's like I believe musicians should be classically trained even if they're never going to play a note of classical music, because it makes the music they play so much richer." Likewise, actors should be familiar with the classics, even if they only perform contemporary material; mastering Sophocles and Shakespeare ultimately enrich modern work.

At the conservatory, Denzel was awarded more than his fair share of work. In large-scale productions, he carried the proverbial spear onstage, also winning key roles in *Man and Superman* and *Moonchildren*. The forty-five members of his class were whittled down to twenty in even tougher competition for sophomore-year study. Again numbering among the fittest, Denzel was invited back.

But the lure of the silver screen beckoned. Upon enrollment, Denzel had been given an option of going for a degree or merely studying; he chose the latter. Onetime teacher Joy Carlin notes: "Some people who, like Denzel, are naturals pick up the techniques quickly and incorporate them into their own kind of technique." Carlin also recalls that as the year progressed, Denzel was "frequently absent" from class. "I have the feeling he learned what he had to learn and then got a little bored." Perhaps now, Denzel believed, he's acquired the necessary background his instincts told him had been missing while shooting *Wilma*. There was only one way to find out. Denzel left the conservatory following completion of the first phase of its three year-program and, headed down to L.A. to "test the waters."

A cousin put Denzel up while the would-be star searched for jobs. Competition was frightfully stiff; Denzel realized that even if he'd been right about having all the education he needed, he still required more hands-on experience. If he returned to the stage, he might acquire a reputation that would precede him to Hollywood. Failing to land a single film role, he returned home to begin searching for employment, moving back into his mother's Mount Vernon house.

At a Manhattan party, Denzel was approached by Paulette, who reminded him of their brief encounter two years earlier; Denzel sheepishly admitted that he couldn't recall the incident. The following night, the two bumped into one another again, at an off-Broadway play each happened to be attending. Pauletta later recalled being impressed that in New York's rough world here was "a true gentleman" who "treated women with so much respect." An old-fashioned southern woman with values as traditional as his, Pauletta was more impressed by Denzel's gracious manner than his striking looks. Shortly, Pauletta moved into the Washingtons' Mount Vernon home. The two broke up briefly, largely because countless other women also found Denzel irresistibly attractive and he was not immune to their charms. Shortly, though, each realized the other was a born soul mate.

Soon they were a couple once more. Denzel attended endless auditions, painfully learning that the New York theater scene is surfeited with a talented, aspiring actors, each of whom wowed his college drama professor, all these gifted hopefuls now vying with one another for the coveted parts that had once been theirs for the asking at their respective schools. "I was so frustrated," Denzel later recalled, "ready to quit" several times during the 1970s. He would have, except "my wife kept me going." Denzel and Pauletta literally wore out their unemployment books and had to pick up new ones. "I still have mine," Denzel admitted long after success had come his way, adding: "I don't want to forget."

All the while, he remained true to his code. Close friend and occasional costar Robert Townsend (*The Mighty Quinn*) recalls: "I remember when we were unemployed actors hanging around the Actors' Equity lounge in New York, desperate for work. Denzel was telling me he had just turned down a movie role. I couldn't believe it. He said, 'It's not going to do anything to further my career.' It was something stupid, playing a junkie, I think. And I realized he was right. You can't just take some role, pick up one hundred thousand dollars and hope nobody will notice. He was always thinking of his longevity."

He did appear in one film, the ambitious social comedy *Carbon Copy*. But it flopped at the box office and did not lead to other parts. The day that movie opened in Manhattan sans fanfare, Denzel couldn't catch the matinee because he had to stand in the unemployment line for his desperately needed $125 check. Though Pauletta kept pushing him to continue, Denzel, during his darkest hour, felt that his dream of being an actor had died. So he accepted a job at an urban recreation center; even if it wasn't his first choice, Denzel knew he could find satisfaction in teaching sports and theatrics to kids. One week before he was to begin, word reached him that the role of Malcolm X in a play he'd auditioned for—*When the Chickens Come Home to Roost*, at the Henry Street Settlement Arts for Living Center—was his. Denzel started rehearsing and never looked back.

He still cites playing Malcolm at the Federal Theatre as his personal-favorite stage work, though he was paid a meager seven hundred dollars for twelve performances. An off-Broadway Obie Award for his role in the Negro Ensemble Company's production of *A Soldier's Play* allowed him the satisfaction of knowing he'd truly arrived. Most of the work he found was with small, impoverished black theater companies operating off Broadway; Denzel appeared in Richard Wesley's *Mighty Gents* and Lonne Elder's *Ceremonies in Dark Old Men*. He also played a supporting role in a Shakespeare-in-the-

Park production of *Coriolanus*. Acting accolades aside, the six-footer could hardly glance in the mirror and fail to notice that in addition to talent, he was movie-star handsome.

So it was Tinseltown time again. He took the first major step toward stardom with some TV work, *License to Kill* and *Flesh & Blood*. He rejected several movie offers, pimp and druggie stereotypical roles that seemed to reinforce negative clichés. Producer Bruce Paltrow, who had caught *Carbon Copy*, felt the young man playing George Segal's illegitimate son was precisely what he had in mind for an NBC series he was developing. Paltrow offered Denzel the ongoing role of Dr. Phillip Chandler on *St. Elsewhere*, ironic considering that Denzel had dropped out of premed. In fact, doubly so: Chandler is a Yale graduate, and Denzel had been disappointed about not winning admission to that university.

Denzel previously had turned down several TV series, terrified of what he called "the J.J. syndrome," referring to actor Jimmie Walker, so associated with his popular *Good Times* character that no one could imagine him in any other role. Denzel agreed to do *St. Elsewhere*, but with reservations, signing on only because he'd had it with being a starving actor and longed for a steady, lucrative paycheck. At least playing a doctor allowed Denzel to provide a positive role model for young blacks; thankfully, though, the character as written was something other than an idealized cliché that replaced older, negative ones. Megan Rosenfeld of the *Washington Post* noted: "Chandler is an intelligent and ambitious young man, portrayed not as a black paragon, but as a human being with all the flaws and problems of anyone else."

Denzel harbored mixed emotions about his newfound status, aware of how limiting it might be: "I can't do this part for forty million black people. On the other hand, I'm not going to do anything to embarrass my people." He puts himself and his integrity as an individual actor first; though racial loyalty comes in second, personal pride is never out of mind. This would be Denzel's attitude not only toward this one character but for his career.

Thanks to *St. Elsewhere*, he enjoyed name recognition. People now waved to him on the street. That was nice in a way, but when they called out, "Hi, Dr. Chandler," he knew it was important to stretch. Rather than play a Chandler-like lead in a feature film during the summer hiatus, he wisely accepted the supporting role of a villain in Sidney Lumet's *Power*. The more different parts he played, the more difficult it would be for the public to pigeonhole him.

Denzel had already emerged as something of a "company man": loyal to those who gave him his big break while simultaneously planning his own rich, full future. "The television series has been very good to me," he said in 1985, adding: "I *do* want to expand creatively." He was too canny to make the same mistake David Caruso would ten years later, walking out on *NYPD Blue*: "They're going to have to kick me out," Denzel laughingly insisted. They weren't that stupid; Denzel remained with *St. Elsewhere* for its full run (1982–86). During breaks, he appeared in various movies, *For Queen and Country* and *Cry Freedom* among them, always in non-Chandler roles.

After two years with the series, Denzel and Pauletta felt financially secure enough to expand their family. The first of four (to date) children, John David, was born in 1984; shortly thereafter, Denzel allowed the infant to "play" a baby in a maternity-ward scene in *St. Elsewhere*. At aged two months, the budding thespian had four hundred dollars earning interest in a bank account. Halfway through his show's run, Denzel fulfilled a longtime ambition, buying his mother a beautiful new Buick, placing hard, cold cash on the counter. Perhaps surprisingly, he was less than impressed with his Hollywood-sized paycheck, which by the final season had climbed to nearly $30,000 an episode.

"I am not making as much money as I thought I would," he insisted. "There's so much money in the world, I figure at least twenty billion of it belongs to me." That may sound like unbridled ego; rather, Denzel insisted it expressed self-worth: "I think people play themselves cheap. Real cheap. I don't. Whatever's coming to me, I expect. As a matter of fact, I try to create that for myself mentally. I'm pissed off that I wasn't a millionaire by age twenty-five." No wonder his wife once said: "He's a very impatient person. He wants everything yesterday." However much Denzel talks about wanting a million bucks, the ambitious American Dreamer represents only one side of him. The other side is the man of personal integrity. In 1986, Denzel was offered that elusive cool million to do a film which he sensed was wrong for him. "He wouldn't do it," Pauletta recalled. "I said, 'I agree with your decision, Denzel. But... *the money.*' He just shook his head. It's all about principle with him."

Principle is the reason Denzel also turned down one of the great films of the 1980s, *Platoon.* Impressed by this young actor's TV work, Oliver Stone sent the script to Denzel, offering him a role as one of the black characters. Denzel read it and expressed his desire to play the part that eventually went to Willem Dafoe. Denzel determined to meet Stone and convince the filmmaker he could do it. Stone only shook his head, explaining he'd originally pictured a Native American in the part.

"I got Indian [blood] in my family," Denzel insisted. "Let me play that part." But Stone would not bend, and neither would Denzel.

"All the black characters in that film, I thought, who are they? Nobody I knew. A couple of scared black guys and one guy who cleaned toilets; [then they] left before the fighting started. That's how we were represented, either afraid or cleaning shit." When reminded that Stone did serve in Vietnam, basing his script on the reality he'd experienced, Denzel wholeheartedly agreed with Stone's artistic right to portray his vision on-screen. That didn't mean, however, that Denzel had to participate: "*My* reality is different."

Denzel would reach his much-desired millionaire status at about the time he reached age thirty. By then he was making major waves in the entertainment industry. Still, success—the money and fame he hungered for—took a backseat to what he sagely viewed as the anchor in his life: family. In March 1987, Denzel at last achieved a show-business pinnacle: A major magazine wanted to feature him on the cover. All set to do the interview, Denzel realized that there was a scheduling problem. For years his wife had put her singing career aside, first to support her husband, then to raise their children. She was now scheduled to perform in concert at precisely the same time Denzel was to meet with the journalist.

This was, suddenly, one of those moments in life when an individual must choose, and beyond practical considerations, the decision is of a moral order. Denzel canceled the interview, first to care for John David while Pauletta rehearsed, then to be at her side before showtime, helping her overcome any nervousness following a long absence from the stage. Her concert was a success; at the end, she interrupted a standing ovation to thank "the best husband anyone could ever have," asking him to join her onstage for a kiss. Beaming with both pride and embarrassment, he did. That was a reward for his choice, though in fact he would brush his sacrifice aside, claiming: "It really *wasn't* a choice. Family *always* comes first."

There would be other magazine cover stories and the consequent attention. Following an Oscar nomination for *Cry Freedom,* he believed that roles in sought-after pictures would come his way. The phone rang only once, for the independent feature *The Mighty Quinn.* Rather than sit around the swimming pool or take up that old Hollywood perennial, golf, he reconnected with his roots in New York theater, making a belated *on-*Broadway debut in *Checkmates.* When that unsuccessful play swiftly closed, Denzel returned to Hollywood, where, rather than patiently wait for the studios to call, he searched out projects being assembled by smaller companies attempting to launch worthwhile projects on tight budgets. He participated in the 1988 art film *Reunion,* partly out of respect for its worthy ambitions, partly because he wanted to work.

At last, there was *Glory*—and the Oscar. It would have been easy for Denzel to slip into a star persona, but he would have none of it, continuing to choose each role based on its unique challenge. "It's ground that hasn't been broken," Denzel told the press. "That's what I'm here to do." His *Mighty Quinn* producer Dale Pollock adds: "He works out of an interior process. He's [always] looking inward."

Meanwhile, major changes were taking place in Hollywood. At last, black writers and directors were carving out a niche for themselves. Spike Lee was the first, his *Do the Right Thing* rating as one of the great films—black or otherwise—of the late eighties. Soon John Singleton (*Boys N the Hood* [1991]), Ernest Dickerson (*Juice* [1992]), and Denzel's old pal Robert Townsend (*Hollywood Shuffle* [1982]) were turning out a new kind of film, influenced by the black-exploitation flicks of the seventies they'd watched while growing up. But their own films would be very much of, for, and about their own time, the emerging decade of the 1990s.

This would be an era when a rare few black Americans, Denzel among them, made enormous strides at assimilating into the main-stream, while the great majority of African Americans, still reeling in the aftereffects of the previous decade's Reagan Revolution, with its drastic cuts in spending for social problems, were forced back below the poverty line.

In describing the cinema that reflected this greater social reality, Henry Louis Gates Jr., W. E. B. Du Bois Professor of the Humanities at Harvard University, said: "The politics of black identity, and the determined quest to reconcile upward mobility with cultural 'authenticity,' is a central preoccupation." Gates dubbed these films "guiltsploitation," noting some that Denzel had appeared in: *Carbon Copy, For Queen and Country, The Mighty Quinn,* and *Ricochet.* In the latter two, his character appears to achieve success within the white world, only to discover that he's betrayed his culture in general and his best buddy (Robert Townsend in *Quinn*; Ice T in *Ricochet*) in particular by "going white." Humbled, he returns to his roots, where he is resanctified. Gates, who himself had successfully integrated into the upscale Establishment, took umbrage at such cinematic portrayals of successful blacks. In a 1992 *New York Times (Sunday)* "think-piece," he wrote: "These films argue that to be upper middle class is to be alienated from the 'real' black community. Why is the supposed tension between class and race—no matter how subtly resolved—such an attractive premise?"

Gates chose to end his article with that question, one with which Denzel must have occasionally grappled. Despite his most memorable characters' self-assurance, as well as the confidence he personally exudes, more than one observer has noted in Denzel an element of self-contradiction. "As he talks about his experience as a black actor in white-run Hollywood," Patrick Goldstein noted in the *Los Angeles Times,* "Washington begins to sound like a man still wrestling with his own beliefs, still developing a personal strategy for matching realism with idealism." When Denzel talks to reporters (something he does as rarely as possible), he insists he's attracted to racially nonspecific roles in films which avoid the issue of racism. Here's Denzel praising a movie he didn't appear in: "Look at the successful buddy films that are black and white, like *Lethal Weapon* (1987). There's nothing in it about the 'black experience,' and you notice that about sixty-five million dollars' worth of people went to see it." This is Denzel the American capitalist dreamer, the Denzel who was "pissed off" that he hadn't become a millionaire by age twenty-five. "I just think people are tired of hearing about racism. Give it a rest. *Do* something positive. Don't just show it."

Strong—perhaps surprising—words! In another context he provided more of the same: "I've never chosen a role for political or social reasons. That would be stupid." In fact, though, such statements belie much of his best work. Denzel has appeared in films— *For Queen and Country, Cry Freedom, The Mighty Quinn, Glory,* the underappreciated *Mississippi Masala,* the social-epic *Malcolm X,* even the lamentable *Ricochet*—which openly address racism. He's turned down lucrative offers to appear in escapist films, instead, doing modestly budgeted, socially conscious projects. While he has appeared in commercial action films (the excellent *Crimson Tide*; the dreadful *Virtuosity*), he agreed to do so only when assured that his part would be positive in nature, casting him as a lawyer or a scientist. And when he received the NAACP Image Award for *Glory,* he proclaimed that it was "more important" to him than the Oscar he'd won, though he had received the latter award in a racially nonspecific competition, as an actor rather than as a black actor.

Pauletta has commented, "Denzel is a messenger. He chooses his roles very carefully." On the issue of race, Denzel's personal attitude appears to be that of an old-fashioned Martin Luther King Jr. integrationist, demanding acceptance as an equal into society at large. Explaining his willingness to appear in *Glory* after having turned down earlier offers for what he derisively refers to as "slave films," Denzel said: "Unlike other films dealing with racism, there's a payoff. It shows how [black and white soldiers] come together, work together. That's why I did it."

In contrast, one thinks of a key scene in the later *Malcolm X*: A well-meaning white girl approaches the black leader, sincerely asking what she can do to help; "Nothing!" he replies, cold and aloof. In the movie, Denzel delivers the line so perfectly, one might momentarily think that the actor shares his character's sentiments, employing the film as a mouthpiece for his own personal thoughts. The opposite would appear to be the case: a brilliant actor giving full-blooded life to a philosophy, with which he himself disagrees. "I'm *not* Malcolm X," he insists, nor does he necessarily accept Malcolm's views. "But," he adds, "the same God that moved Malcolm can move me."

That same God moves men of different color. So Denzel was thrilled to return to New York and play the title role of *Richard III* at Joseph Papp's New York Shakespeare Festival. Or on film, to portray Don Pedro in Kenneth Branagh's *Much Ado About Nothing.* Whereas *Othello* is generally considered the great challenge for an African-American actor, Denzel seeks out Shakespearean roles originally written as white. Doing so allows him to prove, through his talent, that such parts can be handled as well by black actors, the issue of color dissipating if the viewer is as willing as the performer to relegate it to insignificance. As an individual actor, Denzel wants to face the challenge of Shakespeare and succeed (as he did in *Much Ado About Nothing*) or fail (*Richard III*) on the basis of his interpretation; he does not want to be confined by playing only Othello, which is to segregate him within the Shakespeare canon.

"He does this amazing thing," Denzel's *Philadelphia* costar Tom Hanks has marveled, "of completely crossing over." Entertainment lawyer Nina Shaw adds: "There's something about Denzel people identify with, something that allows people to look at him and see themselves reflected in him." Perhaps we see an idealized vision of ourselves, the hero we would all—black or white—like to be. Such actors as Laurence Fishburne and Wesley Snipes do not touch a general audience that way; while ethnic moviegoers may experience a surge of black pride while watching those performers, a largely white audience, however enlightened and nonbigoted, remains aware of such an actor's color. Nonetheless, while Denzel's parts in movies like *The Pelican Brief, Crimson Tide,* and *Philadelphia* were not race-specific, the actor playing them did happen to be black. Even in plays and films that have nothing to do with racism, he implicitly struck a blow for civil rights, of the integrationist order, by helping, via drama, to make American color-blind.

Denzel did the same in his private life. In June 1988 the mailman delivered an invitation requesting that he compete in a celebrity tennis tournament at Windsor Green, a fund-raising function for the prince's trust. Denzel had already planned to be in England at roughly that time for a benefit concert at Wembley Stadium in support of Nelson Mandela. Momentarily, the situation seemed a perfect balance between his two ambitions: at Wembley, he'd make a statement as a black man; at Windsor Green, he'd be acknowledged as a star, regardless of race. So Denzel altered his flight plans to accommodate both events.

In New York two days before his scheduled departure, Denzel attended *Sarafina!*, a musical inspired by Mandela. He noticed with horror that, among the actors onstage, a young female was visibly scarred from torture she'd experienced while in South Africa; when, after the show, Denzel went backstage to congratulate the performers, they hugged him and called him Biko. Then it hit him: "At the tennis tournament I would have to meet all those lords and ladies and ministers who refused to attend the premiere of *Cry Freedom*, who refuse to support antiapartheid. I said the hell with that, I ain't going." The following day, he changed his travel plans back again, flying over for the concert and skipping the tournament.

No wonder Diane K. Shal noted: "The question of who he is and what he should be is one he must grapple with constantly." For millions of adoring fans, however, there is no question at all: Denzel Washington is a sex symbol. He has achieved something no previous black actor had done, at least outside of films designed specifically with an African-American audience in mind. Denzel Washington is undeniably a *romantic* leading man. In *Vogue* magazine, Elvis Mitchell commented: "He manages to be both supple and brittle... perhaps the first black man to be taken seriously as an earthy and sexual presence on-screen." Veteran actor Ossie Davis describes Denzel as "a respectable lover" rather than the dangerously sexual, dark male of movie mythology: "Denzel is the only performer, *purveyor,* of sexuality whose blackness is not an extra cause or a negative" but simply a matter of physical fact.

As to the precise nature of that sex appeal, actress Vanessa Bell Calloway summed it up thusly: "He has this cool confidence that's totally devoid of arrogance." Actress Halle Berry added: "As good-looking as he is, he doesn't seem egotistic." However successful Sidney Poitier's career may have been, such romantic status was the one thing the handsome and charismatic man never achieved. Poitier always excelled in sexless, almost God-like roles (*Lillies of the Field* [1963], *To Sir With Love* [1967], *In the Heat of the Night* [1967], even *Guess Who's Coming to Dinner* [1967]), whereas his rare flops (*A Warm December* [1975]) were attempts to do romantic movies.

Denzel achieved his romantic-hero quality despite, by his own admission, being "just not comfortable with love scenes." No wonder he regarded the sexy sequences in Spike Lee's *Mo' Better Blues*, between himself and African-American actress Cynda Williams, as "the most embarrassing thing" he has ever had to do on film. A bigger hurdle to his acceptance as a romantic lead is the lack of love affairs between himself and white women in *The Mighty Quinn*, *The Pelican Brief*, and *Devil in a Blue Dress*; each script's sexual encounter was eventually eliminated. According to some sources, Denzel is less the victim of racial nervousness than the instigator of those cuts. He was scheduled to play opposite Michelle Pfeiffer in 1992's *Love Field* but dropped out; it was rumored that he did so to avoid an interracial love scene with the blonde actress.

"That's not true," he insisted to interviewer Veronica Webb. "It was as simple as this: Michelle had a great character, really strong; my character was weak [undeveloped in the script], [he] wasn't saying anything. He was just there to help the story along, [so] it just wasn't something I could do." When pressed on that point—confronted with "word on the street" wisdom that he'd backed out because he had never kissed a white woman before and was nervous—Denzel replied: "See, if you get a white person and you get a black person, that's what everyone's going to talk about. Folks don't know what the movie's about. Gossip is gossip." Perhaps; yet it's worth noting that he sidestepped, rather than flat-out denied, the charge.

Not surprisingly, then, he passed on the chance to do the 1995 film version of Shakespeare's *Othello*, letting the role of a black man who marries, then murders, a white woman go instead to Laurence Fishburne.

When asked about the lack of romance in general, interracial romance in particular, Denzel flatly told *Time* in 1995: "Is [romance] being kept from me? I don't know. I can say that a love story within a film has never been a reason for my doing or not doing a film." That statement exists in contradiction to what Denzel told the *UCLA Daily Bruin* in February 1990, while still actively involved with *Love Field*: "I am working on a film at the moment with Michelle Pfeiffer, and with me and Michelle in a film, you can imagine what is going to happen between us sooner or later! I'm *struggling* with that, whether I should even *do* it, because the interracial thing is still a big deal."

A big deal to producers who fear it, unenlightened audiences who won't accept it, or Denzel himself? Let's momentarily grant that producers eliminated the interracial love scenes. Whining about such stuff is not Denzel's style; "I'm a positive thinker," he insists, refusing to grow bitter. To the contrary, he sounds like a black Republican when he claims: "People ask about the lack of work for black actors. I say, 'What about the lack of work for white actors?'" Denzel is an actor, period; if you care to notice, he's an actor who happens to be black. Again sounding conservative—refusing to wait for someone else to fix things for everybody, following an individualistic approach to solving one's problems—he continues: "I think if you're not happy with what's happening for you, go out and make something happen."

Some black artists complain that important white filmmakers, such as Woody Allen, fail to create strong roles for blacks, going so far as to picket Allen's sets. Denzel, on the other hand, insists: "You can't make a picture that covers everything. I mean, there weren't any good roles for [fine white actors like] Willem Dafoe in *Hollywood Shuffle*. Do there have to be?" His answer is clearly no. Denzel does not accept the reverse racism of such a double standard.

So how to, as Denzel put it, "make things happen"? One possibility is the formation of a black-owned studio, run by black producers, which would allow black directors to bring the work of black writers to life. Though the idea always creates excitement when discussed among Hollywood's African-American artists, Denzel harbors doubts: "I don't know about that," he told *Interview* in 1990. "A studio is just a group of people making films." Far more important, as far as he's concerned, is distribution: "You still have to have a theatre to put them in. What you gotta do is, you got to own theatres. I'm not talkin' about the million or so dollars it takes to make a movie; I'm talkin' about the hundreds of millions it takes to buy the theatres so people can see the movies. . . . If you have the best popcorn in the world and no place to sell it, then ain't nobody gonna buy it."

It shouldn't be surprising, then, to learn that Denzel's greatest personal heroes among men ("God," he insists, "is my only *real* hero!") are not legendary actors he admires but entrepreneurs. "I keep up with guys like Donald Trump," he once claimed. "And

Garth Drabinsky [owner of the Cineplex Odeon conglomerate]. People like Lew Wasserman [former chairman of MCA]. I guess there's a business side of me. It's respect for their guts. Or their egos. They go for it, and it works. I like that." Likes it in part, perhaps, because how his own instincts drive him in that direction. John Masius, who wrote and directed *St. Elsewhere,* recalls that Denzel turned down leading roles in other series to become a supporting actor on the medical show, picking up a weekly paycheck and national exposure without committing himself to a grueling sched- ule that would have left no time for coveted movie roles; "I think Denzel is a very smart man. When the opportunity cards are turned over, he knows exactly what to do with them."

Not surprisingly, then, Denzel moved into production. By 1990 he was head of his own production company; he and his partner, Flo Allen, developed projects for Tri-Star Pictures on a nonexclusive basis over the following two years. As to the ambitions for such possible films, Denzel—as always—wielded a verbal double-edged sword, emphasizing the primary importance of audience-pleasing entertainment without ruling out the possibility of social statement: "The first thing is to try and make good movies. As for what the significance of [those films] will be, we'll see."

He suspects he wouldn't be in his current position of power were it not for the fact that he fought for and received roles originally written as white. The *Los Angeles Times* reported in 1995: "Among African-American actors—Washington is virtually alone in making the transition to the big-grossing, mainstream dramas that play equally well with urban audiences and the mostly white suburban- triplex crowd."

Denzel didn't let stardom affect his priorities. He passed on several lucrative movie offers to do live theater virtually on an annual basis, for a minuscule fraction of the $10 million he now commands per picture. "I like to get onstage once a year," he admits, although fully aware that the big bucks are how he buys freedom to indulge in plays: "I had to get back to work and make some money [doing a movie] so I could [afford to] get out onstage again." Even for a superstar, everything in life is a trade-off; without junk like *Ricochet* there would have been no *Richard III.* Whenever he's been asked to name his own favorite actors, he mentions theater-trained people who balance movie stardom with returning to the stage: Dustin Hoffman, Meryl Streep, Gene Hackman, Al Pacino, and Robert De Niro. Occasionally, he also includes James Earl Jones on his short list but he feels no compunction to mention an African American.

Denzel's paradoxical nature can be seen even in such an unlikely detail as one of his homes. Some years ago, Denzel bought a house in fashionable Beverly Hills, the ultimate sign of making it in Hollywood. Notably, though, it was a home built by a black architect of the thirties, Paul Williams. "It's true that I've seen white actors shoot past me when they may not deserve to," he has admitted, quickly adding, "but I always say to black people, 'If *we* were running Hollywood, would *we* necessarily be looking out for other races?'"

For Christopher J. Farley of *Time,* the two sides of Denzel seem less a contradiction of opposites than a perfect yin-yang coming together of complements: "He is a black actor—proudly, fiercely so— who has succeeded in making that term merely descriptive, not professionally limiting." As to Denzel's personal life, there exists what screenwriters like to call a through line: Family and religion remain the essence. "The base that keeps me solid" is how he describes his family, and—like a good Shakespearean scholar—he senses that appearance is as important as reality. "I always try to have my family with me when I am out in public," he has claimed, not only because he loves their company but also as "one small attempt to show that black people can have families." Since he's a celebrity, the Washingtons are regularly photographed for newspapers and taped for TV; such images send a visual message to contradict negative stereotypes of the one-parent black family—a cliché, certainly, though too often a reality he once survived, apparently with some invisible scars.

When he took his family to visit Africa in the summer of 1995, he and Pauletta renewed their wedding vows in a ceremony conducted by Archbishop Desmond Tutu. On that trip, the family also went on safari in Kenya.

"Well, I guess you're leaving the jungle," their guide said to them when it was time to fly back to Hollywood.

"No," Pauletta corrected, speaking for her husband as well as herself. "We're leaving civilization. We're heading *back* to the jungle."

The only newspaper Denzel religiously (no pun intended) reads every day is the *Daily Word*. As for stardom, he works hard at keeping a level head about the accolades, particularly those emphasizing sex appeal over talent: "People heap attention onto you, and most of it is hype. I struggle to resist it in order not to be affected by it." Denzel remains traditionalist in his values. When asked about recent attempts by politicians to censor the popular arts, his response at first sounds liberal—"You do have the right to your [artistic] freedom . . ."—only to change philosophical horses in midstream—"though I think you also have an obligation to a certain amount of taste."

Denzel continues coaching Little League and serves as national spokesperson for the Boys and Girls Clubs of America. Could he truly be as straitlaced as he sounds? If there's a darker side, it was suggested in his appreciation of what would seem a notably non-Denzel movie: "I like *Blue Velvet* [1986]. I would have wanted to play some of the parts. Something about that film got to me on some weird, kinky level." So there's more to the man than is at first obvious. He can become obsessive and moody, as on the day when he drove through a red light at the corner of Beverly and Gardner in Los Angeles, ramming into a passing car. Denzel wasn't paying attention; rather, he was fuming about a just-concluded Little League game in which he felt that the referees had robbed his team owing to his celebrity status.

If there is another side to Denzel, it's doubtful he'll choose to reveal it following the fiasco of an interview on a 1993 Barbara Walters show, broadcast just before the Oscar ceremonies in which he was a nominee for *Malcolm X*. When questioned about his marriage, Denzel insisted he'd never leave his wife, then unguardedly blurted out: "I may give *her* reason to leave *me*. . . . Being a star and all that, temptation is *all around,* you know, and I haven't been perfect. I'll be quite candid about it." He was naive enough to believe there'd be no repercussions.

"You try to be honest, and you get stepped on," he later said with a sigh. A year later, *People* magazine cited him as one of Hollywood's *least* faithful husbands!

Certainly, he's at least a little less perfect—and less confident—than he always appears; he is, after all, human. Denzel has achieved that longed-for millionaire status numerous times over, now giving away millions every year to charities like the Gathering Place, a South-Central haven for HIV-infected people. Nonetheless, he hoards pennies in jars, drawers, and shoe boxes. Why? "Because I'm convinced that [someday] the only money I'll ever have is my penny collection," he admits. Although he has millions in the bank, he cautions his children not to set their sights on that nest egg; when asked in 1994 if John David were aware of all the money, Denzel reminded the interviewer, "It's his *Dad's*." Then he added: "He's going to *work*; no doubt about it." The family may be rich, but the kids will learn the same work ethic Denzel grew up with.

His attitude about Hollywood? The town is essentially color-blind, to the degree that it's less interested in white or black than in a single shade of green. "The bottom line is that someone like Spike Lee takes six million dollars and comes back with forty million, so there's a whole lot of people in Hollywood who are prepared to let him say whatever he wants to, with that kind of return." Today, Lee has trouble getting financing for films because of box-office disappointments, not race.

It should come as no great surprise that Denzel's latest project is *Preacher's Wife*, a remake of the 1940s fantasy, *The Bishop's Wife*, about an angel who provides positive direction in people's lives, with Denzel cast in the old Cary Grant role. The original—about retaining one's religious values while under pressure from a world that appears increasingly unresponsive—is not so different from another of that era's classics, Frank Capra's *It's a Wonderful Life* (1946). "I don't know if you can get away with that anymore," Denzel says sadly, recalling the beacon of light James Stewart once provided by playing a common man who perseveres in the face of awesome obstacles and, through the sheer determination of his spirit, eventually wins. "It's hard to believe in the American Dream he was always fighting for."

If Denzel's right about that then we are in serious trouble as a people. Certainly, it *is* harder to believe than it once was. But if we stop believing, then we stop being Americans, in the best sense of what that term has always meant. Certainly, Denzel's onetime costar Tom Hanks provided just such reassurance in *Forrest Gump* (1994). If any actor is the ethnic embodiment of that image, and in a position to prove that obstacles can be overridden, enemies conquered, and the American Dream made real even by those formerly locked out, that actor is Denzel Washington.

His decision to appear in *Preacher's Wife* proves that he is at least willing to try. In his own life, Denzel always acknowledged that the odds were against him, then overcame and won what he wanted while maintaining what he calls "an ongoing conversation with God." Today the estate where he, his wife, and their children reside is in the Toluca Lake section of Los Angeles; William Holden once lived there, hosting the wedding reception for Nancy and Ronald Reagan, with James Stewart in attendance as prominent guest of honor.

Does this suggest that Denzel is a traitor to his race, having sold out for Republican-style luxury? Or, to the contrary, do he and his accomplishments mark a stunning victory for African Americans, proving that the American Dream can indeed be achieved by people of color who follow their inner voices, develop their God-given talents, and refuse to let the issue of race limit them? Like the proverbial glass, half full or half empty, it comes down to how you choose to interpret the situation.

So the divided Denzel juggles the extremes of his life, currently balancing his professional time between running Mundy Lane Entertainment, his own film company for developing racially non-specific projects, and helping friend Douglas Turner Ward revitalize the Negro Ensemble Company to ensure the survival of black theater. Perhaps Denzel, in his life partnership with Pauletta, will always find himself torn between two equally strong magnets: the dog-eat-dog demimonde of predominately white Hollywood, where he has survived as an equal, perhaps even a superior, and the alternate world of the black community, land of his roots and the source of his social conscience.

Ebony magazine, attempting to put a finger on the uniqueness of Denzel's appeal, insisted that it is derived from the remarkable way in which "he somehow manages to combine regular guyness with an aura of celebrity, mystery, exclusivity." According to the simple philosophy he learned from his mother, life comes down to four things: "the grace of God, the will of man, the hand you're dealt, the way you play it." Success or failure derive from a combination of destiny, free will, blind luck, and native intelligence. Ultimately, though, it's that divine decision coupled with personal integrity. "I am where I am by the grace of God," Denzel says, "but I haven't had to do anything [other than] just work hard to get where I am. I didn't get here from partying with the right people or doing *anything* other than working hard." God helps those who help themselves.

Clearly blessed with his God's grace, Denzel should continue to live and act for decades. Eventually, though, what would he like to have inscribed on his tombstone? That's an easy one to answer: "Hard work *is* good enough."

Denzel Washington
His Films and Career

1

Carbon Copy

1981

AN AVCO-EMBASSY RELEASE

CAST: George Segal (*Walter Whitney*); Susan Saint James (*Vivian*); Denzel Washington (*Roger*); Jack Warden (*Nelson Longhurst*); Paul Winfield (*Bob Garvey*); Vicky Dawson (*Mary Ann*); Parley Baer (*Dr. Bristol*); Edward Marshall (*Freddie*); Angeline Estrada (*Bianca*); Tom Poston (*Priest*).

CREDITS: Director, Michael Schultz; screenplay, Stanley Shapiro; cinematography, Fred J. Koenkamo; editor, Marion Segal; music, Bill Conti; producers, Shapiro and Carter De Haven; rating, PG; running time, 91 min.

T he director told me even though I read better than anyone else, I was all wrong for the role. He said, 'You're too big. You're too tall. You're too dark.' I said, 'I'll get thinner. I'll grow shorter. I'll lighten up.'" The quote is not by Michael Jackson but Denzel Washington, recalling in 1985 the behind-the-scenes encounter that led to his theatrical film debut four years earlier. "After I got the part, I blocked out his negative comments and concentrated on the work. I felt the pressure was then on him. I knew I was going to do my part. It was up to him to get what he needed."

In *Carbon Copy*, Denzel played Roger Porter, a seventeen-year-old black youth who, without warning, stops by the office of thirty-nine-year-old Walter Whitney (George Segal) and announces to the

3

stunned middle-aged executive that he, Roger, happens to be Walter's son from a long-ago three-year love affair with a woman of color. Roger's mother has recently passed away, a fact which distresses Walter terribly, since their intense romance and overall relationship occurred during the most exciting and creative period of Walter's life. He loved the woman—sexually, emotionally, intellectually—far more than his current wife, Vivian (Susan Saint James), the frigid WASP princess and daughter of his wealthy boss, Nelson Longhurst (Jack Warden). As chairman of Unilectron, Nelson holds Walter's career in the palm of his hand and isn't above meddling in Walter and Vivian's domestic affairs.

Roger comes armed with letters and diaries that prove he is indeed illegitimate and not a con artist. But this wealth of information panics Walter, who fears it may threaten his comfortable, if unsatisfying, lifestyle: a company Rolls-Royce at his disposal, membership at an exclusive golf club, and more credit cards than he can count, in addition to a mansionlike home. These luxuries are important enough to him, at this stage in life, to make him tolerate the fact that his wife thinks of nothing but her rigorous social schedule and his stepdaughter Mary Ann (Vicky Dawson) has never acknowledged him as a father figure. Still, there's enough decency left in Walter that he wants to help Roger, who initially appears as the embodiment of "the stereotype," wearing a Black is Beautiful T-shirt and claiming to be a high school dropout.

To retain what he's earned by a daily piece-by-piece surrendering of his soul, Walter concocts a deal that, to work, must proceed from a debatable assumption. Walter chooses to believe that during the past decade of social change, Nelson Longhurst and his family must have finally come to accept integration. Now, in what is hopefully a more enlightened age, even such dilettantish types may be willing to make a stab at civil rights activism. Walter attempts to convince Vivian that shortly, her friends will be competing with one another, each one trying to prove she's more liberal about racial issues than the next. Vivian will be able to leap forward in the upcoming racial race by announcing plans to adopt a black orphan (Roger) for the summer. Walter's hope is that things will go so well that Vivian will accept Roger, then ask him to stay on permanently.

But when, at a dinner arranged to introduce Vivian and Roger, she expresses deep doubts concerning the arrangement, Walter reminds her that, after all, he's accepted Mary Ann as his own. Vivian counters by insisting that if he had a son of *his* own, she'd have done the same. Walter, made vulnerable by too much white wine, blurts out that that's precisely what Roger is. Bad move: Vivian explodes, calling Daddy to announce that her latest marriage is over. So is Walter's world, as he's come to know it. Everyone, from the family doctor (Parley Baer), who treats Vivian for shock, to the family priest (Tom Poston), who tries to provide moral guidance, berates him. His supposed best friend, a lawyer, announces that he'll represent Vivian in the legal proceedings.

Walter is forcibly removed from the house, his overpaid job no longer exists, and everything from the Rolls to his credit cards are confiscated by security guards. Worse still, his personal bank accounts, listed under the company's name for tax purposes, are no longer available. The situation reaches tragic proportions when Walter, owing to Nelson's power, realizes he won't be able to find another executive job. Shortly, Walter and Roger are sharing a sleazy motel room; before they're finished, they will have sunk even lower, landing in the worst section of Watts, Walter hurtling all the way down from the top of contemporary society's financial heap to the bottom: He is the ambitious Jewish male who aspired to WASP security, only to experience black poverty. But during this unpleasantness, Walter realizes that Roger is anything but the racial stereotype in sneakers and Afro hairstyle he first encountered. Far from a dropout, Roger is actually a highly qualified scholar, studying for a degree in medicine. Roger simply assumed he'd have the best chance of locking into a relationship with Walter, thereby joining the posh life, if he presented himself as precisely what the white Establishment expects him to be; like Walter, Roger thinks in stereotypical terms.

Gradually, Walter realizes that his son is a unique human being and a distinct individual rather than some living symbol of African-American youth; that's the first necessary step toward accepting and acknowledging Roger, who likewise comes to see Walter as something other than an elitist snob, now that Walter is a bearded street person.

Comedy, at its most intense, always exists on the edge of full-blown tragedy, and that's certainly true in *Carbon Copy*. Walter is the "king" of his immediate domain, though through a combination of fate (a long-forgotten incident from the past) and character flaw (his hubris in believing that Vivian will accept anything) falls in the worldly sense but rises spiritually.

A "very delicate subject" is how producers Carter De Haven and Stanley Shapiro described their project after deciding to invest their own time and $6 million on a satire of race relations in America, circa 1980. *Carbon Copy* was planned as one of the first social comedies of the 1980s. It had the potential to be a movie that, under its surface guise of light and breezy entertainment, would delineate substantial social situations. "A good comedy," Shapiro said, "tries to say something serious with laughter.

Though Shapiro wrote his initial draft in the late 1970s, he did so with an eye on the shifting social scene of the country in general, and Hollywood in particular, as America approached the upcoming decade. Even as Shapiro scribed his initial screenplay, *Superman* (1978) was vying with *Star Wars* (1977) as most financially successful film of the time; audiences were flocking to escapist works, which took Action Comics characters and Saturday morning space-fantasy serials from the thirties and forties, re-creating them in state-of-the-art fashion, with stunning special effects that really did make an audience believe a man could fly.

Traditionalist Americans who had briefly embraced hippie values and fashions in the late 1960s and early seventies, who had been flocking to post–*Easy Rider* (1969) movies that expressed just such philosophies, glanced around and realized that the sweet dream of *Alice's Restaurant* (1969) had long since degenerated into the darker realities of *Mean Streets* (1973) and *Taxi Driver* (1976). In the late seventies, the pendulum was swinging once again, back to the right.

That's precisely the situation with Walter. Even the character's changing his name from Weisenthal to Whitney conveys his desire, however unconscious, to assimilate, divesting himself of ethnicity and disappearing into the mainstream. His personal desire crystallized in this work of entertainment as a broader but similar desire on the part of so many people who had been observed by Shapiro. That approach fit in nicely with Denzel's views on art; he has said, "I've always believed that through the specific comes the universal."

Roger, though like Walter a singularly drawn character, represents the young black of the 1980s, an entirely different young man than we might meet in a 1970s film. Roger shows up at his father's residence for one reason: not to discover his roots but because he wants "in." Like his father, he's out for himself; like his father, he wants the good life. Roger does not act or speak out of social consciousness; indeed, on those few occasions when he does express social attitudes, he does so to play off white guilt (or, more correctly in this case, Jewish guilt) in hopes of getting the best possible deal for himself. This would be a considerably different film if Roger were presented as honest and pure in comparison to the corrupt Walter; but Roger lies whenever it's in his best interest to do so. The film does not simplistically imply that the black character, as an outsider, is more closely in touch with decent basic values than the Jew; what it says, rather, is that the black has had to wait longer for his acceptance than the Jew and that he perceives the Jew's apparent assimilation as an opportunity to work his way in.

Importantly, the decision was made early on that this film, written by a Jew, ought to be directed by a black to achieve the kind of balance behind the cameras that was also taking place between the characters. Which explains why Michael Schultz was brought onboard. Though he'd originally planned to become an astronautical engineer, Schultz had been bitten by the theater bug early in life and had headed for Manhattan, where, in 1964, he became only the third black director to stage a play on Broadway. After winning a New York Drama Critics Award and a Tony to boot, Schultz then pursued his dream of becoming a Hollywood director, moving to the West Coast and mounting a play at the Mark Taper Forum. Critical acclaim brought Schultz to the attention of the studios, which were, during the civil rights sixties, belatedly courting talented black artists. In short succession, Schultz directed the interracial high school drama *Cooley High* (1975) and the ensemble interracial comedy *Car Wash* (1976), proving that his talent was broad and deep enough to allow him to develop white characters who were as believable and fallible as his blacks.

However, Schultz's subsequent work disappointed: The superficial Richard Pryor vehicle *Which Way is Up?* (1977) and the universally panned *Sgt. Pepper's Lonely Hearts Club Band* (1978) hardly

advanced his reputation. If he were to in fact become what support-
ers claimed he had the talent to be—an African-American Frank
Capra—he needed to find a comedy of substance, precisely what
Schultz hoped *Carbon Copy* would be.

An immediate and unanimous decision was to cast an unknown
as Roger, and a national talent search was instigated. Shapiro later
recalled, "We spent three or four months looking for the right young
man. We saw something like four hundred or five hundred actors.
They had to act and [also] be able to do comedy." Early into the
preproduction process, Schultz started jetting cross-country to
check out all the talented young black actors who were then
performing on Broadway. He was immediately struck by twenty-
two-year-old Denzel Washington, who had no movies to his credit
and only a little TV work but whose New York stage roles were
establishing him as a charismatic newcomer.

The casting of such an unknown was risky; behind-the-scenes
people sensed that the dynamic that did or did not happen when
Segal and Washington ultimately came face-to-face would make or
break this movie. "The picture hooks on the relationship between
Segal and the young man," Shapiro admitted. "The best actor got the
part. He and George make a nice-looking twosome." The notion of
"nice-looking" goes deeper than is apparent. *Carbon Copy* would be a
different film if an African-American actor whose screen presence
expressed anger and hostility (say, a Wesley Snipes or an Ice T)
played the part. Such casting would shape the film's sensibility,
which movie people know is true of *any* film. Denzel's agreeable,
clean-cut persona made the WASP family's choice much easier for
them. Their subsequent refusal to accept such an assimilation was
due to lingering prejudice, not personality conflict.

In this light, De Haven added while filming interiors at the
Goldwyn Studios: "Credibility is very important in this story. The
boy has to have a sense of humor, and he has to come across with a
sense of innocence." Considering Denzel at work in a scene with
Susan Saint James, De Haven added: "Denzel will be a real star." Of
course, every producer says that about every newcomer picked for a
key role in his major movie; in this case, the prediction would ring
true. As an actor, Washington's cool, calm air of professionalism was
obvious to everyone who visited the set, including journalist Ralph

Kaminsky. In *Box-Office* magazine, Kaminsky reported on the young performer's dedication during a going-away bash for Susan Saint James, who played out her final scene on the twenty-eighth day of filming: "While the party was still in full swing, young Washington moved onto the set in which he and Segal were to be filmed, and like an experienced professional, ignored the hubbub all around him and went through the entire scene, rehearsing the reactions to the lines that Segal would speak when the camera would roll." Segal, who not so many years earlier had been just such a notable newcomer, now took on the role of the old pro, whispering to those around him: "One good one comes along once in a while. He's so good!" Then, considering the worldliness of Denzel and his seen-it-all, done-it-all generation, Segal sighed: "They know so much more nowadays. He knows more than I ever did when I was starting."

The Goldwyn Studio interiors concluded a largely on-location shooting schedule that made as much use of the Los Angeles area as possible, taking the film crew from Leo Carillo Beach to a luxury mansion in Pasadena as well as to the run-down Watts area. Shapiro's concept was to make Southern California a character rather than a mere backdrop. To do this, he employed twenty-five diverse locales, hoping that as the characters played out their own little story, the settings would interact with them, treating the viewer to a vivid sense of the highs and lows of modern Los Angeles. In order to accomplish this, Shapiro and Schultz hired Jack English, a highly experienced location manager who had worked with Francis Ford Coppola on the monumental *Apocalypse Now* (1979). Owing to his D day–like experience on that picture, English now approached the unique difficulties of each new location as a "situation" to be dealt with rather than a "problem" to be solved, thereby transforming what could have been a negative (if perceived as such) into a positive. During the first twenty-five days of shooting, English had Denzel and other cast members rushing from middlebrow Pasadena to a sleazy Sunset Strip motel, from ultra-upscale Bel Air to the worst black ghetto areas in Watts, from fashionable stables in Glendale to the actual jail that sits atop the Hall of Justice building.

Considering the racial orientation of the film, no location proved as memorable as a schoolyard, located a mere two blocks from the studio. The sequence required Washington to play basketball against a white kid, with surprising results. To achieve that moment and to capture it in the proper lighting so that the scene would look its best on film, the crew would have to visit the playground during school hours. To receive the necessary accommodations from the Los Angeles School Board, the film company made a generous contribution to the school's student council.

Throughout the movie, there is evidence that the filmmakers wanted to make a complex rather than a simplistic film, and the school-playground sequence is a case in point. A destitute Walter, desperate to scrounge up some money so he and Roger can eat, comes up with what seems a clever scheme. Without bothering to inform Roger first, Walter makes a five-dollar bet that his son (hiding around the corner) can beat anyone on the basketball court. Walter's assumption—his "benign" racial prejudice—is that as a black male, Roger can massacre any of these white kids; the supposed ace up his sleeve is that the ballplayers won't consider the possibility that this Jewish guy's hidden "son" might be black. Having made the bet, he'll produce Roger, who'll then win. The problem: Roger does not conform to the stereotype, sheepishly admitting that he may be the only black teenager in America who can't play basketball. The gag is an attempt to subvert the stereotype from the inside out, making clear that even such nonthreatening prejudices as Walter's aren't always true. Sadly, this gag backfires on the filmmakers, since Roger's line—however comical in context—implies that the stereotype generally *is* true, that Roger is a *rare* (indeed, the only!) exception.

A problem arises when the filmmakers' lofty ambitions lead to ambiguous gags that can be taken either as put-downs of racism or as examples of racist thinking. To put it another way, for the film to work with total effectiveness, there must be a notable distinction between the point of view of the Jewish character, Walter, and the Jewish writer, Shapiro; the problem raised by the basketball gag suggests that Shapiro has no greater insight than his character.

No wonder, then, that while *Carbon Copy* received almost unanimously lukewarm reviews as to its effectiveness as a work of entertainment, it was alternately hailed and damned for its presentation of "delicate" racial material by those who felt that the film damned or defended racist thinking.

In the *Amsterdam News* (New York), critic Billy Graham, who saw the film with an off-the-street audience, reported not only on the film but on his experience watching it: "The film goes in directions from [nearly] semi-racist to blunt inferences of a society dominated by the ruling class: 'White' people. The mixed audience in the theatre where I saw *Carbon Copy* hissed, booed, and at times yelled out snide remarks to express their disapproval of some of the dialogue." Perhaps Graham's hesitant, self-contradictory language ("nearly semi-racist") suggests that although he himself understood the filmmakers' intention to take racism to task, he was also impacted by the audience's missing this entirely, interpreting racist implications by certain characters (characters offered up for ridicule and scorn) at face value.

A critic who watches the same film in an entirely different circumstance will come away with an alternative view. Janet Maslin of the *New York Times*, who attends special advance previews in posh Manhattan screening rooms, wrote that *"Carbon Copy* is by no means a sparkling comedy, but neither is it the uneasy mélange of racial stereotypes that it might have been... [what] might well have been the occasion for apoplexy, double takes and a very broad and dopey brand of comedy or a prelude to mutual understanding and saccharine sentiments all around, [instead] keeps the cheap gags to a minimum." Yet she complained that the film "remains uncertain in tone and somewhat overpowered by its gimmick's implications."

A balanced approach was taken by *Variety*'s Len Klady, who noted that one of the "strongest assets of the film" was "director Schultz's evenhanded treatment of the touchy material." Intellectual critic Philip French saw some of the same qualities, though he argued that they did not redeem the entire work: "There is real savagery in *Carbon Copy*, but like everything Stanley Shapiro writes, the thin satirical edge precedes a heavily compromised wedge." The general consensus that, despite honorable intentions and major ambitions, this was indeed the case helps explain why the movie did not emerge as the desired contemporary equivalent of a topical Capra comedy of social import.

An entirely different aesthetic allows a critic to forgive some obvious weaknesses if a film fulfills some social responsibilities; during the dawn of the Reagan era and its concurrent craze for escapist fare, *Carbon Copy* was lauded by Seth Cagin of the *SoHo Weekly News* for what it attempted rather than what it achieved: "The near-abolition of blacks from the screen lends *Carbon Copy* distinction, even a sense of adventure, despite its thoroughly middlebrow airs, so it would be unjust to harshly criticize the film for [its] failings.... During one of those rhetorical speeches that seem written for Segal, he reveals that the moment Roger walked into his office, he assumed Roger was a junkie, or a street punk at best. Most whites who see the film will understand what Walter's saying, having done the same thing with the character."

Within this context, Cagin also offered one of the first positive reviews Denzel would receive: "In all fairness, neither Schultz nor Washington stereotypes Roger; they trust their audience to make that mistake. It's the most trenchant observation about racism in a film that's surprisingly full of them." On the other hand, the *Times*'s Maslin was very hard on the debuting Denzel: "Roger is simultaneously supposed to be exploiting and admiring his wealthy father, and Mr. Washington, while he is personable, can't make this believable." Graham, after downing the film, insisted that moviegoers "check out Denzel's performance and watch the beginning of what promises to be the debut of a rising star in other major films—hopefully."

Though Denzel was, in 1980, an untried film actor who considered himself lucky to be working in a major motion picture, he nonetheless managed to make his debut in a movie that addressed itself to what would be three of his most important concerns, in life as well as in the films he chose to do: (1) his absolute belief in individuality and the need for each of us to discover himself as a unique human being; (2) his mixed emotions about assimilation of minorities into the mainstream as a worthy ideal that unfortunately remains out of reach for so many of ethnic origin; and (3) his total abhorrence of stereotyping, racial or otherwise. In 1988, Denzel added an element of self-criticism to his reflections on that first effort: "I felt bad about my performance, because I didn't know enough about comedy or filmmaking. One thing I did know: I liked the feel of performing before a camera."

2

A Soldier's Story

1984

A COLUMBIA PICTURES RELEASE

CAST: Howard E. Rollins Jr. (*Captain Davenport*); Adolph Caesar (*M. Sgt. Vernon Waters*); Art Evans (*Private Wilkie*); Denzel Washington (*Private First Class Peterson*); David Alan Grier (*Corporal Cobb*); David Harris (*Private Smalls*); Dennis Lipscomb (*Captain Taylor*); Larry Riley (*C. J. Memphis*); Robert Townsend (*Corporal Ellis*); William Allen Young (*Private Henson*); Patti LaBelle (*Big Mary*); Wings Hauser (*Lieutenant Byrd*).

CREDITS: Director, Norman Jewison; producers, Jewison, Ronald L. Schwary, and Patrick Palmer; screenplay, Charles Fuller, based on his stage play *A Soldier's Play*; cinematography, Russell Boyd; editors, Mark Warner and Caroline Biggerstaff; music, Herbie Hancock; production design, Walter Scott Herndon; set decorator, Tom Roysden; costumes, Tom Dawson; rating, PG; running time, 101 min.

St. Elsewhere gave me leave from their schedule to shoot the picture," Denzel said of his participation in *A Soldier's Story*. "There was some negotiation involved, but in the end they were good about it and let me go. I shot the first five episodes of the [1983–84 season of the] series, [then] was out for eight episodes. There was no problem having Dr. Chandler drop out of sight for a few weeks, since we had so many other characters to focus on."

13

Despite Denzel's continued insistence that he does not want to be burdened with the mantle of Sidney Poitier, the role of Peterson was awarded to Denzel by the very person who had directed Poitier in his most memorable role: Virgil Tibbs in *In the Heat of the Night.* Norman Jewison returned to the theme of race relations with *A Soldier's Story,* his film version of *A Soldier's Play,* the Pulitzer Prize–winning play by Charles Fuller. With a string of highly successful movies behind him (*The Thomas Crown Affair* [1968], *The Cincinnati Kid* [1965], *The Russians Are Coming! The Russians Are Coming!* [1966], *Fiddler on the Roof* [1971]), the Canadian-born (and, incidentally, gentile) Jewison—always on the lookout for intriguing material—caught Fuller's play in New York, where it was being performed at Theatre Four by the Negro Ensemble Company under the guidance of artistic director Douglas Turner Ward.

Jewison was immediately struck by similarities between this new work and his Oscar-winning Best Picture of 1967. Set in rural Louisiana during the final days of World War II, the play allowed an audience to easily accept its civil rights message by masking it in edge-of-your-seat entertainment. Present among the characters was a Tibbs-like figure. Capt. Richard Davenport, a northern black, investigates a murder, operating as a fish out of water in the Deep South, where the full spectrum of whites, ranging from illiterate rednecks through middle-class types to patronizing authority figures, deal with his aloof manner and obvious intellect.

Still, there were key differences between the two stories; if Jewison chose to film this one as well, he would not merely be repeating himself but offering a unique variation on a recurring theme. *A Soldier's Play* dealt primarily with racism within the black community; its isolated military situation added a new dimension. Davenport is both an officer and a lawyer, the first black man in those positions that any of the soldiers, white or black, have ever seen. Dispatched from Washington, D.C., his mission is to learn how and why a black sergeant was murdered on his way home from a drunken binge in the nearby town. Davenport is given a mere three days to complete his job. Upon arrival, Davenport finds his attempts thwarted by white officers, who assign him an entire barracks of his own rather than allow him to bunk with them. "The worst thing you can do in this part of the country," Captain Taylor (Dennis Lipscomb) tells Davenport, "is to pay too much attention to the death of a colored soldier under mysterious circumstances." Taylor simply assumes that the murder was perpetrated by white racists among the officer class or local Klansmen. Nonetheless, Davenport begins interviewing the men under the sergeant's command (their memories shown, in the film version, via flashbacks) in hopes that they might shed light on what happened.

But as he speaks with the strong-willed Peterson (Denzel Washington) and Sergeant Waters's flunkie Wilkie (Art Evans), among others, Davenport becomes aware of hostility on the part of these men toward Waters. This is due in part to Waters's constant humiliation of them plus his concentrated effort to destroy the ego of a well-liked country boy, C. J. Memphis (Larry Riley), which eventually leads to C.J.'s suicide. Davenport realizes that the black sergeant may have been killed owing to racial tensions within the black community, targeted by one or more of his own men due to his insistence that they ought to strive to be more white than the whites. The sergeant persecuted any member of his "team" who, in behavior and speech, reinforced negative prejudicial notions of black behavior held by whites: The theme this time was inverted racism.

Besides allowing him to mount a follow-up to *Heat* while simultaneously striking out in new directions, the director had another reason for being drawn to the material. At the very time when Fuller's story took place, Jewison, a teenager hitching through the South, had thumbed a ride past a similar military post. "I was eighteen," he vividly recalled years later, "and passed through the Missouri town where the last lynching had taken place." The rednecks who were giving Jewison a ride "told me I rode in the pickup truck that dragged the victim through the streets. This was said with a great deal of pride, which astounded me. I guess that was the seed of my desire to deal with the subject of race relations on film." Since he was already a civil rights liberal at eighteen and convinced he wanted to someday make movies, his essential subject matter was solidified at that moment.

So Jewison rushed backstage following the evening's performance and met Fuller, who was overwhelmed by the filmmaker's enthusiasm. One handshake was all it took to cement their decision to collaborate. Considering Jewison's impressive track record, one might assume he'd have little trouble getting such a prestige project off the ground. That was not the case; M-G-M and two other major studios turned *Soldier* down flat; though Warner Bros. initially agreed to finance the film, they, too, eventually reneged on the deal. The reason was simple enough: In the fifteen years since *In the Heat of the Night*, the economics of moviemaking—particularly projects involving blacks—had changed drastically. The "black-exploitation flicks" (*Shaft* [1971], *Coffy* [1972], et al.) had come into being, targeting ghetto-bound audiences, while alienating whites.

Films like *In the Heat of the Night*, made during the era of Dr. Martin Luther King, mirrored the civil rights leader's beliefs in integration of the races by offering drama that was equally appealing to white and black moviegoers. But King was now gone, as were such movies; in the wake of his assassination, his dream of a color-blind America appeared lost, both in everyday life and in the movies. Whites were attending films like *Superman* in suburban malls, while blacks were drawn to *Superfly* at decaying downtown movie houses. Jewison assumed responsibility to convince the studios that, in the early 1980s, the pendulum was ready to swing back again.

Fortunately, Jewison had recently signed a multipicture deal with Columbia, allowing him to produce or direct a quartet of projects as long as they were mutually acceptable to the filmmaker and the company. For his first, Jewison planned to create an important picture for such a low price tag that it would be impossible for the studio to lose money even if it were not a hit. Columbia did view *A Soldier's Story* as an offer they couldn't refuse. After reimbursing Warner Bros. for their efforts, Columbia upped the budget by $500,000, giving Jewison a total of $6.2 million, a respectable, though far from spectacular, sum. Bringing what would appear to be a large-scale film to fruition on what was essentially a B budget was a challenge to be relished rather than a cross to bear. Though Jewison had just been paid $1.5 million to direct Goldie Hawn and Burt Reynolds in the lightweight comedy *Best Friends* (1982), he readily agreed to work on *A Soldier's Story* for $80,000, the Directors Guild minimum at that time. Actually, Jewison would have done the film for nothing if membership in the guild had not precluded this. Jewison's coproducer and budget-control expert would be Ronald L.

Schwary, who had recently run the daily operations of *Tootsie* (1982).

Having just come off a star vehicle for Dustin Hoffman, Schwary was delighted to learn that 40 percent of the total budget for *A Soldier's Story* would be spent "below the line." Saving an incredible amount of money on director and actors (who all worked for scale) allowed him to spend every possible penny on costumes, set design, extras, etc. One luxury Schwary was able to provide for Jewison was a full week of rehearsal, on the actual sets, preceding the nine-week shooting schedule in Fort Chaffee, Arkansas—a rarity even on more expensive films.

Jerry Molen, the unit production manager who had assisted Schwary on *Tootsie*'s exhaustive New York City shoot, discovered Chaffee when he headed south, searching for a proper locale, hitting almost all of the bases in a nine-state, fourteen-military-base area. Many places, like Fort Benning, Georgia, were simply too large (with its seventy-five-thousand soldiers and civilians) to convey the intimate, isolated fort of Charles Fuller's imagination. Chaffee, built in 1940 and mostly inactive since the war, was made to order. The crew could arrive in September, shortly after National Guard trainees stationed there every summer departed, leaving the property virtually abandoned; the moviemakers could have it all to themselves.

That didn't mean production designer Walter Scott Herndon and set decorator Tom Roysden were going to have a vacation on this shoot. It was their job to make the post seem even smaller than it was, which they accomplished by, as Herndon later recalled, "concentrating mess hall, barracks, and motor pool close together," then "choosing angles carefully so that they're in view of each other whenever possible." In addition, the two built several wooden window screens of the type which would have been visible on all the buildings back in 1945. To save money, they did not make enough screens for all the buildings on view during the story. Instead, they checked each following day's location during filming, the night before any one building was to be used moving their limited number of screens from wherever they'd been the previous day to where they were needed for the next.

Herndon had been picked in part because of his familiarity with the South, having worked on a succession of Martin Ritt pictures about the area, including *Conrack* (1974), *Norma Rae* (1979), and *Cross*

Creek (1983). The most difficult task on this shoot was making the part of Arkansas which borders Oklahoma, and has a southwestern flavor not unlike New Mexico or Arizona, instead appear to be what audiences perceive as typically Deep South. To do that, Herndon traversed more than thirty-four hundred miles of back road until he finally found an isolated Louisiana-like bayou that was necessary for one scene as well as the town of Clarendon, located 190 miles from the fort. Clarendon could represent the film's nearby town, where the soldiers go when they want beer and jazz and where all the problems begin.

Jewison, meanwhile, had agreed to save money by working without a storyboard artist. He would also confer with his film editor, Mark Warner (who remained behind in Los Angeles), by phone rather than have him on the set. Russell Boyd, the well-regarded Australian cinematographer who had done the honors on *The Year of Living Dangerously* (1983) and *Gallipoli* (1981), had recently shot an acclaimed American movie, *Tender Mercies* (1983). Boyd's ability to visually convey the South's ever-oppressive heat convinced Jewison that he was the right person to create the mood for *A Soldier's Story*. Carefully planning everything out in advance, Jewison and Boyd would have come in right on time, within the planned fifty-four-day schedule of their shoot, were it not for a spell of bad weather, causing them to go over by one day.

One important production element was the hiring, whenever possible, of black artists, not only in the cast but also behind the scenes. Blacks were hired as department heads for transportation, hair, makeup, and electrical units. There were also black drivers, assistant directors, Director's Guild of America trainees, and dolly grips. They, along with the cast members, agreed to do the film by working on what in the business is called "European hours": Shooting takes place between nine and five, without a specified lunch break. Instead, actors and crew members visit a continuous buffet whenever they are not needed. That cast included three members of the original New York stage production: In addition to Denzel as Peterson, there were Adolph Caesar as the sergeant and Larry Riley as C. J. Memphis, a gentle, nonviolent blues artist driven to attack his own sergeant by the man's unrelenting hostility, much like Billy Budd and Claggart in Melville's classic tale. As in Melville, the innocent is then doomed, unable to understand what has happened to him or why.

Though minor overruns in postproduction and editing did bring the film's negative cost to $6.2 million, that was reduced somewhat when the company received a $50,174 check from the state of Arkansas. *A Soldier's Story* was the first film to receive a 5 percent rebate by the Arkansas Film Commission. Eager to bring Hollywood production to their state, the film commission offered the rebate to any company that spent more than a million dollars locally during a film shoot. At one point, the filmmakers feared that Arkansas was not going to come across with the promised amount, since book-keeping standards were extraordinarily strict. Every penny the company claimed they'd spent was checked and rechecked by Joe Glass of the state's film commission, who exhaustively pored over receipts and records. When Glass was satisfied that everything was in order, he reported back to the governor, and the check was cut. It arrived at Jewison's door with a note which read in part: "When I asked the Arkansas legislature to enact the Arkansas Motion Picture Incentive Act of 1983, I did so hoping to attract location filming to our state. When I asked Joe Glass to present your rebate check today, I did so hoping the presentation will indicate to the motion picture industry that Arkansas is serious about attracting location filming." The note was signed by the governor, a big film fan; his name: Bill Clinton.

Most reviews offered polite, restrained praise. Typical was Vincent Canby's, who, in the Sunday edition of the *New York Times*, called the film an "efficient, solid screen version of Charles Fuller's Pulitzer Prize–winning" play. It "is not great as cinema," Canby continued, "but it's a tightly constructed, socially conscious, enter-taining melodrama." One reason why Canby and others felt the need to praise this film, in some cases overlooking obvious weak-nesses, was the hope that the box-office success of *A Soldier's Story* might herald a comeback of serious films with black characters. At roughly the same time that *A Soldier's Story* reached theater screens, The *Cosby Show* debuted on NBC, immediately leaping to the number-one spot in the Nielsen ratings, proving that even white audiences could relate to a show about black characters if their personalities and situations were universal in appeal. *A Soldier's*

Story was perceived as something more than a movie: It could spearhead the type of film that might flourish during the eighties, if only the first such experiment made money.

A brain trust at Columbia's division of marketing was put to work; one strategy they devised was the creation of a ninety-second preview, which aired on the televised Emmy Awards show, thereby connecting the upcoming movie with high quality in mass entertainment in the public imagination. When the film received limited advance openings in the key cities Los Angeles, New York, and Toronto, print advertisements emphasized that this was the work of a "Pulitzer Prize–winning [author] and award-winning director." Ashley Boone, president of distribution and marketing for Columbia, commented: "You [have to] overcome any quick description of the movie that could be derogatory—e.g., 'a black movie.' That statement, which sounds virulently if unintentionally racist, comes from one of Hollywood's few top-ranking black executives.

"The first week," Boone continued, "people were saying to each other, 'There's a black movie playing.' The second week, they said, 'There's a good movie with a black cast.' And three weeks into the run, they said, 'Hey, there's a good movie.'" The ploy did pay off: Though never a blockbuster, *A Soldier's Story* rated as a solid hit, particularly profitable considering the low production costs. Columbia purposefully booked it into the Baronet, on Manhattan's East Side, which not only had a reputation for playing art films but also happened to be a small house, making the modest crowds that came to see *A Soldier's Story* appear larger than they actually were. "Long lines create a demand for a movie," Boone observed.

Aljean Harmetz of the *New York Times* noted that the strategy worked: On the opening weekend, she reported, "the film drew identical kinds of blacks and whites—upper-middle-class professionals over the age of 25," the very target audience the distributors (ignoring the issue of race) had set out to attract. The Baronet, which ordinarily has only a 10 percent black audience, boasted a 61 percent black audience for the run of the film, though blacks and whites left the theater feeling equally satisfied by a human drama about black characters that never threatened white sensibilities. As Donald Chase reported in New York's *Daily News* on the eve of the film's release: "In order for the new film to succeed, its story of the extreme, self-hating lengths to which a black man will go to assimilate, to participate in the American Dream, must have meaning for other groups in the national melting pot."

One major bone of contention was the ending, drastically changed from the play. There, Davenport steps to center stage, where he harshly informs the audience that as the late Sergeant Waters desired, the outfit did indeed move into combat, though ironically he was no longer around to gloat. A strange triumph, though, since every man in the outfit had been killed. The play thus suggested a sense of absurdity, even nihilism, as to the eventual outcome; the great "victory" Waters's men had at last earned was the dubious honor of being turned into the kind of cannon fodder that American whites had, for centuries, been reduced to. This distancing of the play itself from the fate of the men, a tone at once cynical and pessimistic, lent it an intellectualized antiwar sensibility.

Jewison's film, on the other hand, closes with an image of the sergeant's squad, along with every other black man on the base, marching off gloriously to war. There is no hint whatsoever that any, much less all, will be killed, while the soaring music is extremely patriotic. The ending then implies that the men have indeed won a great victory, the film taking at face value what the play seemed to sagely, even savagely, satirize.

When put on the spot about this, Jewison insisted: "Hundreds of movies have white soldiers marching off with joy and fervor. This is the first time in Hollywood history that anybody has seen black troops marching off to war at the end of a movie. These are black soldiers marching to war with a pride and a dignity never before seen on the screen." It's possible to consider that accomplishment a major victory, in that blacks have at last been integrated into the icons of movie mythology as well as into the army. The characters in the film are clearly experiencing "black pride," or perhaps more correctly, they are blacks who are experiencing "American pride." It's just as possible to argue that the movie has copped out on what was best about the play, an insistence that young black men are now merely being exploited in yet another way.

"Jewison deserves credit for struggling to get this script made," Jack Kroll argued in *Newsweek*, "but then why tack a Hollywood tag onto a writer's courageous vision?" In truth, though, Fuller—who wrote the screenplay, working in collaboration with Jewison—fully conspired in the thinning out and lightening up of his material. No wonder, then, that *Variety* more or less damned the film with faint praise, citing "the old-fashioned virtues of a good Hollywood production" in the service of "a liberal political message," making it sound as if Stanley Kramer had come out of retirement to create one of his 1950s message movies on the order of *The Defiant Ones* (1958), *On the Beach* (1959), or *Inherit the Wind* (1960). Like so many Kramer-directed film versions of fine stage plays, "Jewison's work is generally stagy in its pacing and emphasis," David Denby argued in *New York*, "and even the most ordinary lines are delivered with enough weight to sink a good-size freighter. Perhaps Jewison felt trapped by the successful stage production; he tries to compensate for the canned sound of the material with flashy cutting and overinsistent music, and as a result the movie seems merely worked up when it should be passionate."

Precisely the opposite approach was taken by Stanley Kauffmann in the *New Republic*, who in hindsight attacked the prize-winning play of two years earlier as "one more award for attempt rather than accomplishment," insisting that the Agatha Christie *Murder on the Orient Express* (1974) mystery plot diminished rather than enhanced the serious theme. "Fuller's dramaturgy had the effect of a series of rough-cut beads on a coarse string.... The mechanics creaked." Kauffmann believed that Jewison's added flashbacks worked, *Citizen Kane* (1941) style: "Now, though it's hardly deep, the work holds, and the themes are thus more pungently realized [by] Norman Jewison's directing skills."

Most critics, however, saw the film as an uncertain interpretation. Rex Reed brought up an important point when he noted that "the ending does not pay off—the identity of the killer is less a revelation than the true nature of the victim's character." Indeed, since Fuller hoped to convey his ideas through a whodunit approach, it's worth recalling that in any great genre piece the audience is astounded to learn the identity of the killer, then realizes it could not have been anyone else. But in *A Soldier's Story*, all the black squad members have equally acceptable motivations for killing Waters and an equal opportunity to do so. When we learn it was, in fact, Denzel Washington's Peterson, we experience no sense of epiphany; rather, that he was an entirely possible, if random, choice. Still, while Peterson's identity as the killer does not satisfy on the superficial level of murder mystery, it remains fascinating thematically.

One way to view the film is as a cinematic essay on the issue of assimilation, with Davenport, Waters, and Peterson perceived as a triad of symbols rather than mere characters. Waters is the tragic character because he stands midway between the other two and is torn apart by his inner conflicts. Waters represents the aging blacks of the past who were taught by parents and teachers that assimilation into white society was all-important in self-realization but who never managed to achieve that end. Davenport is the next generation to believe in the same thing and has clearly come a long way in terms of attaining such goals; he is the film's stand-in for Sidney Poitier. Peterson, on the other hand, is Davenport's doppelgänger, an equally handsome and strong-willed look-alike who takes the opposite attitude, demonstrating contemporary defiance by defending the supposedly "weak" black man.

Thus, when Peterson turns out to be the killer, it makes sense on a conceptual level: the radical young black killing off the ol' passé black voice, only to be arrested by another young black for doing so. Both Waters and Peterson hanker after "black pride," but the conflict between them erupts from their different definitions of that term. To Waters, it is pride in believing that blacks can be as good as whites at their own game; his aim is to show up whites, who will be stunned to realize the equality of blacks. To Peterson, it is pride in believing that blacks are essentially different from, and superior to, whites; thus, he refuses to play the white game at all. "What emerges is not just a whodunit," Tom O'Brien explained in *Commonweal*, "but competing visions of black history and future prospects."

Jewison had purposefully not cast Sidney Poitier as Davenport for fear of turning this unique project into an unofficial sequel, that is, *In the Heat of the Night II*. But did he blow it by not casting Denzel as Davenport? Many viewers felt that Rollins was stiff and aloof rather than cool but charming. On the other hand, Denzel had sterling notices, though some suggested he was wasted in too small a part. Donald Chase, in the Sunday edition of the *New York Daily News*, hailed Denzel's performance as "the strong-willed thorn in Waters' side." Pauline Kael, in the *New Yorker*, picked him out for special consideration, noting that as "Peterson, the best educated of the group, he never overacts, yet we always know what he's thinking, and he draws us into his detestation of the scummy sergeant." Rex Reed, of the *New York Post*, hailed the entire cast as "impeccable" but saved his special accolades for the performer who came across "most impressively...Denzel Washington as a proud private who feels his race has been insulted by the neurotic sergeant." Michael Grumley, of the *New York Native*, singled out "the handsome, unrelenting ferocity of Denzel Washington."

David Edelstein, in the *Village Voice*, had kind words for but one performer: "Only Denzel Washington's seething intellectual, Peterson—lean and dangerous and a ringer for Malcolm X—is a compelling figure." That Edelstein would note a Malcolm X quality nearly a decade before Washington played him in Spike Lee's film is significant. Though Denzel is the black star most accessible to general audiences since Poitier, there are marked differences.

In the film, there is an irony to the fact that his character is the one who kills Waters, as Peterson was one of the few squad members Waters admired. Peterson ("from Hollywood, California, by way of Alabama") is both educated and intellectual and will not bow and scrape before the white man. If he did not take a stand against Waters, then Waters would have wanted to serve as a mentor to Peterson, the nearest thing to Waters's ideal image of black manhood among his charges. But Peterson does take that stand, for while he is the proudest of all these black men, he rejects the essence of Waters's interpretation of black pride. Peterson knows that there is a difference between assimilating into mainstream America by divesting oneself of ethnic culture, history, and pride and doing so while maintaining those elements. Peterson not only likes C.J. as a person but enjoys C.J.'s dedication to black musical styles; he defends not only C.J. but African-American culture when he agrees to fistfight with Waters, a contest he would win if Waters did not cheat.

Indeed, the final irony is that Peterson's killing of Waters is not very different from Waters's pushing C.J. to take his own life. "Some things need getting rid of," Peterson tells Davenport; that's precisely what Waters would have said about C.J. And Davenport's retort, as an assimilated black man, is equally important: "Who gave you the right to judge? To decide who is fit to be a Negro?" It's what

Davenport would have said to Waters if Waters were still alive. Waters represented the first generation of black Americans to win begrudging mainstream integration by taking a subservient job and turning his back on his own identity. Davenport is the next generation, winning equal pay for equal work on an executive level, though never being fully accepted; Peterson is the third generation, insisting on a balance between seeking higher education and maintaining his heritage. Peterson was a new and important kind of part, perfect for a brilliant young black actor. Had Denzel played Davenport, he would have had to assume the dreaded mantle of Sidney Poitier. Though Peterson is a supporting part, it was the right one for Denzel to play.

Denzel's own feelings about this project, along with the difficulty of doing a role in a film that you've previously played onstage, were articulated in a 1985 *Hollywood Drama-Logue:*

Norman Jewison brought a certain amount of reverence to the project, but he also wanted to open the story up more for the screen. When you do a role 200 or 300 performances, you develop your own ideas about the character. It's difficult to give up any of your ideas but I'm pleased with what we got on the screen. It's such a strong story. Charles Fuller told me it just flowed from his pen. He had done two or three other plays years before, which had some of the individual elements *A Soldier's Play* had. They just all came together in this one. It'll be interesting to see what he writes next. Whatever it is, I'll be in it. He's already asked me to be in his next play.

3

Power

1986
A 20TH CENTURY-FOX RELEASE

CAST: Richard Gere (*Pete St. John*); Julie Christie (*Ellen Freeman*); Gene Hackman (*Wilfred Buckley*); Kate Capshaw (*Sydney Betterman*); Denzel Washington (*Arnold Billings*); E. G. Marshall (*Sen. Sam Hastings*); Beatrice Straight (*Claire Hastings*); Fritz Weaver (*Wallace Furman*); Matt Salinger (*Liberal Senator*); J. T. Walsh (*Jerome Cade*).

CREDITS: Director, Sidney Lumet; producers, Renee Schisgal and Mark Tarlov; screenplay, David Himmelstein; cinematography, Andrzej Bartkowiak; editor, Andrew Mondshein; music, Cy Coleman; production design, Peter Larkin; costumes, Anna Hill Johnstone; rating, R; running time, 111 min.

To be honest," Denzel reflected on his role as Dr. Phillip Chandler on *St. Elsewhere*, "I didn't give a lot of input into my character, because I didn't want it to expand too much. I wanted to remain in the background so I could do movies." The show's producer-director, Mark Tinkler, noticed that Denzel often seemed "distracted," particularly during the first two seasons; at times, it was obvious that Denzel did not know his lines. John Masius, a writer on the show, recalls: "There were times when he was doing theater every night and trying to raise a family. He had a very full dance card." One of that card's slots was expansion into films. Many actors employed on TV hope to play leading roles during hiatus, often with parts similar to those they are already known for from the series but in second-rate projects. Denzel was, as always, as smart as he was talented. He'd rather play a supporting part in a more ambitious effort, particularly if he got to do something radically different from what he was already known for, thereby "educating" his audience as to the extent of his talent. So he passed up several stereotypical leads in nominal movies to appear in *Power*.

In 1982, while Denzel Washington was in the first year of what would become a six-year run playing Dr. Phillip Chandler on *St. Elsewhere*, Maine-based journalist David Himmelstein, a specialist in covering politics, was attending Harvard on a Neiman Fellowship. During the election process taking place that year, he and another student assembled a lengthy loop of film, composed entirely of TV spots featuring candidates from around the nation. Noting the election results, Himmelstein became fascinated, while screening his own "movie," by the fact that almost every winning candidate had the same hairstyle, the same basic vocabulary, and the same way of delivering lines to the camera; also, the same approach to making eye contact and the same way of obscuring testy issues in order to appear vaguely idealistic without committing to anything specific or of true substance.

"It occurred to me that the candidates were all basically inter-changeable," he recalled years later. "There was no way you could tell them apart by listening to them or watching them, and I realized the guys who had put together the [TV] spots were at least as significant, if not more significant, in the [election] process. Today, eighty percent of a campaign budget for statewide office goes to media advertising—the guy who engineers that is hugely influential in any major race." With that in mind, Himmelstein began work on a film script intended to dramatize the situation; four years later, that movie would reach the screen, with Denzel Washington playing a significant supporting role.

Renee Schisgal, wife of writer Murray Schisgal (*Luv* [1967]; *Tootsie*) developed the script with Himmelstein shortly after leaving her position at Dustin Hoffman's Punch Productions. Taking an interest in the project, Madeline Warren—then a production vice president at Lorimar—convinced the company's president, Craig Baumgarten, that they ought to make this movie with a message.

Owing to his excellent realization of Paddy Chayefsky's *Network* (1976) nearly a decade earlier, which had touched on similar media-related issues, Sidney Lumet appeared the logical choice to direct. The movie that emerged was, in the words of critic David T. Friendly, "about the dehumanization of the political process and the dangers that these glitzy middlemen could portend for the democratic process." Lumet became enthused about doing the film, owing to his own trepidations about then current political candidates and the negative impact such computer-era slickness could have on us all.

"This is a piece about the [sorry] fact that there is no more one-to-one contact," Lumet explained. "A candidate doesn't talk to us anymore. They talk to us through someone else. These people are not corrupt. It's much more frightening than that, because we are not talking about evil people, we are talking about a system that is slowly evolving." The old political positions—liberal or conservative—have become less important than glibly manufactured images, at least according to this scenario.

As the focus of their tale, Lumet and Himmelstein chose the fictional character Pete St. John, a cold, aloof, haughty young man who has become a superstar within the media-handling career world. During the course of the film, Pete zips off in his private jet to handle three different political campaigns in two countries, dealing with them more or less simultaneously. While working with any one candidate, such as a Midwest governor (Michael Learned) whose divorce has hurt her chances for reelection, Pete appears cool and calculated. But while traveling between any two points, he shuts himself off from the world at large, incessantly banging away with drumsticks while listening to tapes of Gene Krupa on his Walkman, displaying a nervous energy his clients never see. Such actions suggest a detachment not only between Pete and the world but also between the "real" Pete, an intense, if private, lover of music with great soul, and the soulless, career-driven Pete the world knows—or thinks it does.

At one point, Pete takes on the task of transforming Wallace Furman (Fritz Weaver), a bland, nondescript millionaire from Manhattan, into a possible contender for the governorship of New Mexico. Pete dictates the color of the shirts Furman will wear and the stance he will take on such issues as nuclear disarmament to make him acceptable to the viewers of this essentially conservative area. Pete suggests that his client ride a horse to win the cowboy vote, and when the poor sap immediately falls off, Pete manages to salvage everything in the editing room by freeze-framing the shot of the horse rearing up, making Furman look like John Wayne in the finale of *True Grit* (1969).

Furman intensely attempts to tell Pete all about his deep commitment to a tax issue, but Pete refuses to even listen, waving Furman away: "My job is to get you in. Once you do get in, what you do is up to your good conscience." Not such a problem with decent men of good conscience like Furman, perhaps, though a difficult situation when Pete helps less pleasant people assume power. These include the questionable South American socialist dictator, who is made to appear a victim of violent terrorists, though in fact they are leftist freedom fighters who are correct in opposing his regime.

"I'm like Mother Teresa," Pete brags. "My work is only for the truly needy." The contrast to Pete is provided by Wilfred Buckley (Gene Hackman), Pete's onetime mentor and, following that, partner, who likewise has a great talent for the game. Buckley, however, only takes on assignments he personally believes in, helping candidates get elected if their ideals are ones with which he concurs. Buckley's old-fashioned idealism is portrayed through every possible surface detail, from his white suits, which recall a southern gentleman of days gone by, to his propensity for knocking down bourbon on the rocks instead of sipping the white wine that the yuppieish Pete prefers. Buckley is a moral man, if an alcoholic one. Still, the big problem with Pete (based at least in part on his real-life counterpart, David Garth) is, as director Lumet indicated, not that he's immoral but *amoral*; Pete cares not a whit about his clients' values, only for making vast sums of money as a result of his own skillfulness at transforming virtual ciphers into acceptable public figures by eliminating from view any off-putting extremism (left or right wing) while aggrandizing precious small virtues.

Pete was not always so ruthless; early on in his career he had dedicated himself to helping candidates in whom he believed. But that was in the early 1970s, and this is the mid-eighties; his journey toward amorality is meant to suggest the nation's broader, though similar, movement in cynical directions, a gradual stepping away from the intensely moral values of that brief period of political idealism. It would be easy to believe that Pete worked for sincere liberal candidates like George McGovern during that time and, following McGovern's landslide loss in the presidential election of 1972, gave up on all ideals to instead follow the big buck.

One major problem with the film is that we are constantly told, but never actually shown, that Pete is "the best at what he does." On-screen, Pete comes up with clever tricks, like suggesting a deep, dark suntan for Furman (unconcerned that the man's family has a history of skin cancer) and some serious time on the Nautilus machine for another client. Yet other than such familiar advice (which a real-life media adviser for some mayoral candidate in any modern American small town might offer), screenwriter Himmel-stein fails to come up with the extra-special tricks of the trade, strokes of genius that the average media man would never think of but a top-of-the-heap type like Pete would brilliantly and consist-ently come up with. The film's audience keeps waiting for some moment that will justify Pete's lofty reputation, enviable lifestyle, and gigantic fees, but it simply is not there on-screen.

Nor, for that matter, do we ever see why his ex-wife, Ellen Freeman (Julie Christie), is considered such a genius-level reporter; we're asked to take this on trust, though she never, during the course of the film, visits a newspaper or magazine office to write a story, nor does she file one by computer modem from her home. Like Buckley, Freeman is meant to be seen as a symbol of Pete's bygone morality, which explains why he has left both of them behind despite the fact that he still likes (in many respects, loves) them very much. Pete cannot relate to either if he has lost the moral values they still cling to. Instead, he engages in shower conferences with his pretty assistant (Kate Capshaw), setting up his next appointments between bouts of impersonal sex.

Pete faces his moment of conflict when he agrees to apply his skills to the campaign of Jerome Cade (J. T. Walsh), a cryptic Ohio industrialist who would like to win the U.S. Senate seat currently held by elderly liberal Sam Hastings (E. G. Marshall). Sam, Pete's political idol in the late sixties and a friend ever since, has decided to vacate his position for ambiguous reasons. Instead of supporting a likely liberal successor, Pete—while still admiring and respecting the senator—is willing to help fill that spot with Cade, the pawn of Arnold Billings (Denzel Washington), Cade's adviser and a lobbyist for Arab oil interests.

At this point, we're supposed to believe that Pete's ex-wife proves her integrity by deciding *not* to print the significant story she finds herself sitting on: The old senator is resigning because his wife (Beatrice Straight) has unwisely, if unwittingly, allowed herself to become the victim of an investment scheme cooked up by Billings for the very purpose of ensnaring her, thereby depriving the likable senator of his seat and allowing Cade to run against and beat some unknown. Though Ellen's decision might be seen as a decent act by people outside the Fourth Estate, any self-respecting journalist would consider it a terrible breach of integrity; it is her responsibility, if she truly is dedicated, to get that story—the truth—out to the public, for better or worse.

Friendship be damned, the journalist in her should (and, if she truly were the great reporter that this film would have us believe, *would*) force her to print the facts and communicate reality to the public at any cost. There's an irony, apparently lost on *Power's* writer and director, to the fact that she is praised for doing the very thing they then savagely satirize Pete for doing: withholding the truth from the public.

All of which makes clear that Himmelstein and Lumet, however sincere their social concerns, did not properly think through their ideas. At the end, when Pete finally achieves redemption by telling the good liberal senator that he should throw away his prepared speech and speak from the heart, we notice that the candidate receives a triumphant reaction from everyone watching the show. If this were the case, if sincerity really did outshine Pete's brand of codified slickness, then all the other "sincere" slobs running for office without benefit of a media makeover would have defeated all those clients of Pete's they opposed, which was not the case. Moreover, the notion that the public is so easily manipulated by money poured into the advertising and media coffers of political campaigns turns out, in hindsight, to be dubious. If it were this easy to legally "buy" an election, then multimillionaire and virtual unknown Steve Forbes would have handily won the Republican primary season in 1996, owing to his effective and inordinate media buys.

The film ends with a lengthy pan during which the camera purposefully moves at a snail's pace over an endless array of ultramodern computers and all sorts of TV recording equipment; meanwhile, on the soundtrack, an old-fashioned band plays "Stars and Stripes Forever." The impact is obviously meant to be ironic in nature, with a counterpoint effect between the old-fashioned democratic values in that traditional song and evidence of the media, which, in our computer age, can supposedly predetermine the outcome and, within the context of legally allowed operations, more or less "fix" an election.

One major problem with the film, though, is that it announces the dubious theories of the filmmakers as though they were some new and frightful revelation, as if they were the perceptive first messengers to deliver important knowledge bravely. In fact, nothing could have been further from the truth. As Stanley Kauffmann wrote in the *New Republic*, this computer-age gimmickry and its dramatic incarnation herein were

> ...just the latest instance of the recurrent American theme, Selling Out, joining up or not, which has been on America's mind at least since *Walden*. *Power* treats it as it's been treated ever since *The Hucksters* [1947; a Hollywood classic on the same subject, starring Clark Gable] forty years ago: with hustle, glitz, sex, and inside jargon. Gere keeps saying that he doesn't care about the clients' views: he just wants to get the candidate elected, after which the official is on his/her own. I can't see that this policy is any different from or worse than what most campaign management has always been—except that now, instead of flattering the hometown folks who cluster around the back of a train, the speaker can 'sell' millions at a time.

Simply stated, the technology has grown more sophisticated, though the technique (despite the filmmakers' naive view that they have stumbled on to something big and fresh) is as old as politics itself. Lumet and Himmelstein might have nonetheless employed this all-too-real situation as the basis of a powerful drama were it not for the unfortunate choice of Pete as the main character. He is simply too facile and self-satisfied (partly as written, partly as the narcissistic Gere plays him) to interest an audience much, even though he's an entirely accurate depiction of the type. How much more satisfying was the script by former Eugene McCarthy speechwriter Jeremy Larner for *The Candidate* (1972), starring Robert Redford, which appeared fifteen years earlier (so much for the "newness" of *Power*'s theme!) and said much the same thing about media manipulation but did so considerably more effectively.

In that earlier film, the main character was much like the liberal senator played here by Matt Salinger; Redford's McKay, a decent nonpolitical intellectual, is asked to run for a vacant senate seat against a supposedly unbeatable conservative opponent. In *The Candidate*, media consultants—all very much like Pete in *Power*—are accurately portrayed, but glimpsed briefly, in supporting roles. That was wise, since such people are not of the stature to serve as worthy centerpieces in lofty drama. In *Power* it's difficult to care much about Pete, who has already been totally corrupted when we meet him. When Pete suddenly reverses his long-held cynical attitudes, telling his own McKay-like candidate to follow his heart, we don't believe that events in the story would have so transformed him to the point of opting for personal redemption. This seems more wish fulfillment on the part of the writers rather than logical dramatic progression of his character as a result of what he's experienced.

Another major mistake was having the story flit back and forth between three different campaigns, affording them equal weight. While Pete certainly would do this, the film might have been far more effective had Lumet and Himmelstein focused on one campaign, merely suggesting the others as incidental material and backdrop. Then they might have managed to interest intellectually and involve emotionally their audience with what was at stake, rather than achieving only an anecdotal effect, a glitzy celluloid mosaic of a soulless, upscale world and the people who inhabit it.

Understandably, then, Vincent Canby of the *New York Times* labeled the work "the kind of fiction that doesn't do justice to it's own concerns. . . . This is a legitimate subject for examination, but [Lumet and Himmelstein] have dramatized it by manipulating images no less superficial than those created by their fictitious media consultants." Canby pointed to various "signposts" that, assuming a liberal bias on the part of the audience, indicate too simplistically whether we're supposed to root for or against any certain character. The U.S. senator who is introduced by his stand in favor of solar energy naturally turns out to be a good guy in every possible respect, whereas another who favors real-estate development on previously untouched government lands, we are not surprised to learn, is a virtual all-around monster.

Often critics refer to films which are so transparent in their symbols as appearing to have been written by a computer, and there's certainly an irony in that here, since computerized media work is what the film is supposedly against. Indeed, *Power* was, in many respects, the first film of the computer age. Previously, a device used in its production known as the Montage picture processor had only been employed for TV commercials and industrial postproduction, along with some episodic television. This piece of equipment, manufactured by the Massachusetts-based Montage Corp., allowed the person cutting a film to study his movie in a succession of different editing arrangements, without physically assembling edited prints.

As Lumet pointed out, "the process is far less physically demanding. The director doesn't have to wait around for the splice. Basically, the entire day can be devoted to the editing process instead of the splicing process. It allows you to be more creative because you can try almost anything you want."

"The end result of a day's work," Dan Gilroy noted of the new process in *Variety*, "is a printout of the cutting list showing film code numbers of each cut and a computer disk holding the stored information." The Montage technique had previously been used to create the very kind of political advertising that the filmmakers apparently abhor; they appear to have been uniformly unaware of the irony that they were making a motion picture which employed precisely the same approach they were attempting to attack, justifying Vincent Canby's argument that the rather superficial and obvious images in the film were often made to appear dazzling, far more important than they were, through modern media manipulation in the editing room.

This criticism also extended to the advertising for *Power*. The one-minute trailer that preceded the film into theaters featured the stylishly dressed Gere moving toward the camera while a rich baritone offscreen voice spoke the words: "More seductive than sex.

More precious than gold. More addictive than any drug. Nothing else comes close. . . . " But close to what? Finally, the five huge letters appeared, in black, against a white screen: POWER! Though effective, to be sure, the trailer gave no indication that the film itself would deal with politics and the media, hardly sexy box-office subjects. Ashley Boone, who had earlier presided over the marketing of the last Denzel Washington film, *A Soldier's Story*, now served as president of marketing for Lorimar. In his words: "The subject of politics was a rough sale. Politics can be difficult stuff when it comes to films. This is entertainment, and if people are spending money for entertainment, you must sell it as entertainment."

Which is essentially what Pete does in *Power* with his own clients and what the filmmakers are, ironically, attacking. There is a strange paradox, then, between the attitudes expressed in the film about media manipulation being used to dishonestly "sell" a political product that the public didn't fully understand and the media manipulation employed to dishonestly "sell" the film to that same public. "Politics and moviemaking are closer cousins than they might first appear," David T. Friendly wrote in the *L.A. Calendar*. "Both expend massive energy attempting to appeal to the lowest common denominator—one in the hopes of winning the most possible votes, the other in hopes of selling the most possible tickets."

Boone insisted that for weeks before the movie opened in Manhattan, Lorimar should plaster the word "power" in bold letters everywhere they could: on roadside billboards and on the walls of subways. Boone was aware that TV shows like *Dynasty* and *Dallas* had hit home by dealing with the theme of power in glitzy, glamorous situations and that if the public could be convinced that *Power* was just such a work (as a didactic cautionary fable about politics, it certainly was *not*), then it might be a box-office success. Intriguingly enough, the public smelled a rat (the advertising campaign, if not necessarily the movie) and stayed away in droves, which to some degree disproves the theory at the very heart of the film: that the public can be manipulated into buying absolutely anything if it's presented to them in briefly effective sound bites.

"In effect," David T. Friendly continued, "Lorimar is selling at least as much sizzle as steak [the old marketing cliché] in promoting the title without dealing with the subject at hand. . . . In a way, that's

the same issue that confronts the Pete St. Johns of this world."
Though Lumet and Himmelstein may indeed have been naive in
their thinking and pedantic as dramatists, their sincerity was never
in doubt; on the other hand, Ashley Boone's words suggest that he
was the Pete St. John of the movie business.

"The whole political process has become dehumanized," Sidney
Lumet complained at the time of *Power*'s release. "Even movies look
as if they were put together by a polling organization." That may be
true, but as Mike McGrady noted in *Newsday*, "Ironically enough,
that last charge happens to apply to *Power*. If a polling organization
were out to assemble the ingredients for a movie, it might well have
come up with something along these lines. The entire movie is as
glossy and high-tech as its metal-glass-plastic settings.... It's all
glitzy, fast-paced, lacking in credibility." In *Newsweek*, Jack Kroll
insisted that "*Power* becomes as slick as the world it tries to expose."

Simply, the movie, which set out to expose the problem of the
media was exposed in the media as being part of the problem. So
how, and why, did Denzel get involved? TV fame led to numerous
offers for summer employment in films. Invariably, though, the roles
were designated for a black man, either a clone of the clean-cut Dr.
Chandler or the opposite extreme: pimps, drug dealers, and other
lowlife types—all designated for a black actor—that, regrettably,
reinforced such stereotypes. On the other hand, Arnold Billings had
been written as a middle-aged white man. This was the very sort of
challenge Denzel loved.

In addition, the character was the villain of the piece. It's worth
noting that in the mid-eighties political correctness was just beginning to make itself felt; chances are, if a white filmmaker cast an
African American as the bad guy in his latest piece—whether the
role was written for a black or generically nonspecific—he would
risk incurring the wrath of black critics, who would complain that
the film was racist, teaching the mainstream audience, through
drama, that blacks were evil. The end result of such criticism,
however, was to rule out many talented black actors for intriguing
parts they would have been happy to play. Hence, the "reform
movement" served to lessen, rather than increase, the number of
parts going to blacks. The fact is, the best thing that can happen to

black actors is to be cast in as many different types of roles as possible, including villains.

And Denzel Washington was a black actor desirous of playing every imaginable part. Several years later, when he performed the title role in *Richard III* for Joseph Papp's Shakespeare-in-the-Park production, *Time* magazine's William A. Henry III noted: "It takes a lot of nerve to present a villain who is black" these days. Critic Roger Ebert added that "black actors are in a bind in this country. . . . Everyone knows that villains are more interesting to play" than good guys, though white directors are fearful of casting gifted blacks in such parts. Lumet should, then, be congratulated for awarding the part to Denzel, though, as a person, he was a different age as well as color from the character Billings as conceived by Lumet.

Denzel gave the best reading of any hopeful performer, so Lumet hired him, then rethought the part for Denzel in terms of Billing's age. Importantly, though, the character remains racially nonspecific. Arnold Billings is an upscale man who is intelligent, sophisticated, and corrupt; that is his nature as an individual, and with a black actor playing such a person, Lumet and Denzel were together able to convey their commonly held belief that blacks are capable of existing as equals on every level of society, doing so in every conceivable kind of way, good or bad. As a lobbyist for evil interests, Billings may be a bad guy, but no one can deny he's the best bad guy–lobbyist around; he's a black man (though the film never verbalizes this) who demands equal opportunity, then proves himself to be superior to his competitors. Not superior *because* he is black but *regardless* of color: because, as an individual in this field (however "bad" a field), he *is* superior in intellect and talent to everyone else, just as the film's dubious "hero," Pete, happens to be in his media field.

That, in Lumet and Denzel's perception, was an implicit blow, dramatically delivered, for civil rights, even though the race card is never obviously played throughout *Power*. Or, as Denzel has said, "I think all films can speak to people *across* color lines. I don't think that's a new concept. Do you think that only Italians go see Scorsese's films, that only Britons go see Attenborough's films, that only Canadians go see Norman Jewison's films? You have to question that [line of thinking]. *I* think people go to *good movies*."

4

Cry Freedom

1987

A UNIVERSAL FILM

CAST: Denzel Washington (*Stephen Biko*); Kevin Kline (*Donald Woods*); Penelope Wilton (*Wendy Woods*); John Hargreaves (*Bruce*); Kevin McNally (*Ken*); Alec McCowen (*Acting High Commissioner*); Zakes Mokae (*Father Kan*); Ian Richardson (*State Prosecutor*); Juanita Waterman (*N. Biko*).

CREDITS: Director/producer, Sir Richard Attenborough; executive producer, Terence Clegg; screenplay, John Briley, from the books *Biko* and *Asking for Trouble,* by Donald Woods; cinematography, Ronnie Taylor; editor, Lesley Walker; music, George Fenton and Jonas Gwangwa; production design, Stuart Craig; costumes, John Mollo; rating, PG; running time, 157 min.

I feel I made a connection with Steve [Biko]," Denzel Washington claimed late in 1987, reflecting on his association with Richard Attenborough's film *Cry Freedom.* "I read the script, and I had problems with it, but I said out loud, 'Steve, is this what I should do? I don't want to embarrass you. I don't want to misrepresent you.' That's what was important to me." Denzel may have been the first person to wrestle with problems over *Cry Freedom,* but he would hardly be the last. Indeed, the tepid reviews and hesitant support this well-intentioned but halfhearted attempt to assault apartheid artistically would eventually receive supported Denzel's immediate reaction as well as his less than enthusiastic decision to join the project.

Cry Freedom tells two stories in succession. In its first half, the focus is on Steve Biko, South African civil rights activist. The movie details his involvement with the movement during the mid-seventies as well as the subsequent attempts by the government, through strong-arm tactics, to silence him, which eventually leads to Biko's death owing to physical abuse while in police custody in 1977. In the film, these incidents are related from the point of view of Donald Woods (played by Kevin Kline), an affluent white newspaper editor of the *East London Daily Dispatch*. At first, Woods—never questioning the status quo's basic position—regularly attacks Biko in print. Then a personal meeting is arranged between the two men; almost immediately, Woods is won over, experiencing an epiphany, under-going an abrupt transformation as he suddenly realizes the moral outrage of apartheid.

Overnight Woods changes from reactionary custodian of the Establishment to crusader for reform, defending Biko and his atti-tudes in print. Not surprisingly, Woods is perceived by many members of his race as what Henrik Ibsen called an Enemy of the People. When Biko dies, Woods realizes his own reason for exis-tence. Having already written several books, *Biko* and *Asking for Trouble*, Woods senses that he must bring his message to the entire world, informing everyone everywhere of his country's terrible situation. But Woods is now a political prisoner, a bird in the gilded cage of his stately home. The film's second half chronicles what happens next as Woods packs up his wife and five children, attempting a great escape.

Such a story structure elicited mixed emotions, particularly from those who wholeheartedly agreed with the antiapartheid theme. The early Biko segments are, in the final cut, dwarfed by what follows. The final hour of *Cry Freedom* bears a bizarre resemblance to the last moments of *The Sound of Music* (1965), only with South African greenery substituting for the frozen snowcaps of the Alps: What we see is one more mythic Hollywood adventure about white heroes trying to escape the villains. No wonder, then, that Peter Rainer of the *Los Angeles Herald-Examiner* eventually tagged *Cry Freedom* as "virtuous, plodding, uplifting."

After the movie had been completed, Denzel recalled the first thing Attenborough, fresh from his Oscar for *Ghandi,* said to him when pitching the project. Already fearful about how many people, including Denzel, might react to his approach, the famed British actor turned director explained, in Washington's own words: "Dick told me flat out, 'Denzel, I couldn't get 22 million to do the Stephen Biko story,'" presumably the film Attenborough might have wanted to make and obviously a project Denzel would have loved. Denzel recalls "Dickie" continuing, "'I think we have a good story here, and even more than that, I *don't* want to appeal to the people who are *already* sympathetic to the cause.'"

Denzel, on the eve of the film's release during the 1987 holiday movie season, considered what Attenborough had told him, then continued in his own voice: "Which might have been the case had we just done the Stephen Biko story, maybe not.... I had a problem with it. I said, 'Damn, man, it seems like they still gotta do a story about—'" Hesitating, Washington presumably thought about Biko and his still-untold life story. Then Denzel caught himself, stopped in mid-sentence, and the dark mood passed. Other African-American actors might have complained about the film's compromised vision. But Denzel is not any other African-American actor, or any other actor, *period.*

So he shifted tone and changed his position; as the momentary mood of disappointment passed, Denzel's eyes lit up with optimism. "I shouldn't say that," Denzel insisted, reneging on the hard-line black-activist approach he nearly took that Biko's suffering was more noble, his story more significant, than that of Wood's. To him it was not a matter of black or white but how much one has given to the antiapartheid cause: "Woods suffered a hell of a lot more than *I* ever have and more than most other [American] black people that are gonna complain about this film ever have."

Suddenly, Denzel the apologist for the Hollywood movie industry was talking. So if *Cry Freedom* was the best that could be hoped for in 1987, he was ready to subvert any qualms and insist it was better than no movie at all. Still, one can't quite forget Denzel's earlier words of barely suppressed anger that suggest another side of this man, usually dormant, though never far from the surface. While before the nation's press corps, the two sides of Denzel Washington momentarily wrestled with words, and it was clear which one dominated. "I think Dickie's heart is in the right place," Denzel concluded. "The important thing to me was [giving] people a chance to find out who [Biko] is. I think we've done that. If there's not enough of him, then that's good, because that will whet people's appetite, and hopefully they'll get off their butts and go read a book!"

An idealistic way of perceiving the limitations of one movie! In part, Denzel's approach derives from his own religiously based positivism; in part, he was infected by the optimism of his director. "I am an aging male Mary Poppins," Sir Richard Attenborough likes to say. "I believe passionately that the human spirit is indomitable and that right, in the end, will prevail." Short, plump, and buoyantly positive, Attenborough—sixty-four years old at the time he made *Cry Freedom*, though projecting the energy of someone half that age—comes across like a diminutive Santa Claus without the whiskers he would don when he played that part in 1994's *Miracle on 34th St.*

Attenborough developed a liberal's conscience and progressive approach early on, from an upbringing in a family that worried more about world politics than polite niceties. "I come from a radical background," Dickie likes to tell people, "and these matters were not things you only talked about on Sunday after church. There was always an atmosphere, in our house, that in order to justify the luxury of your own existence, you had to be conscious of others. And you had to *do something* about it." Such a change-the-world attitude underlies all his work.

The film that would eventually become *Cry Freedom* began taking shape long before Attenborough ever conceived of *Gandhi* (1982), even before he first dreamed of moving from actor to director. In 1957 the young actor-liberal became ever more aware, through newspaper stories and reports on the "telly," of apartheid. South Africa's system of legalized segregation had been enacted in 1948, the same year America belatedly began its slow but steady move toward integration. Dickie was horrified; he listened intently to expressions of criticism trickling out of South Africa, particularly the words of Nelson Mandela, founder of the African National Congress. Dickie was disgusted when Mandela was arrested and began serving a prison term.

"The suppression of people is a global problem," Attenborough reflected years later, "but in South Africa prejudice and racism are *legislated*. The *law* says you may not have a passport, and the *law* says you may not go into that part of town. Something had to be done. I mean, really, you cannot sup with apartheid" without selling your soul. Happily, another spokesperson took Mandela's place: Steve Biko, founder of the Black Conciousness Movement. Dickie, meanwhile, was dedicated to changing things through the only option open to him: the art of film. Already, he had begun to craft such pictures as *Gandhi* (1982), *Young Winston* (1972) and *Oh! What a Lovely War* (1969). There was no way he could blithely ignore the ignoble apartheid system, as so many other theater and film people were doing.

One by one, he optioned the film rights for various books on the subject, then used his own profits from acting jobs to hire screenwriters, who transformed them into scripts. The right muckraking movie might make all the difference, stirring the world's conscience. Yet he firmly believed that any political commentary must be couched in strong drama, necessary to lure the masses in for entertainment; then he could slip in his ideas beneath the surface. None of the screenplays measured up; today, with good-natured humor, Dickie recalls an ineffectual item called "God Is a Bad Policeman." Rather than make a second-rate film, Dickie chose to put the project on his back burner. Then, in 1982, Attenborough presided over a unit screening of his recently completed *Gandhi*. An invited friend showed up with a third party, journalist Donald Woods. Already familiar with Woods's books on Biko, Dickie sensed, during their conversation, that Woods's own story, coupled with Biko's, would provide Attenborough with "something that could stand on its own," a movie with the box-office possibilities of *The Great Escape*, which Attenborough had starred in back in 1963.

Not wanting to proceed without a go-ahead from Biko's surviving relatives, Attenborough headed for South Africa, where he secretly (to avoid arrest) arranged to visit Biko's mother and his widow. "We would like you to try and make your film," the two women told him, "because you've taken the trouble to come and see us and because Donald was one of Steve's very closest friends." That was all Attenborough needed. He immediately flew to America to try to interest one of the studios. Onboard the plane, Dickie noticed in a newspaper that Frank Price (who had overseen the *Gandhi* project while running Columbia, over protests of executives, who complained that no one would pay to see a movie about an Indian pacifist) had recently moved to Universal.

"You never tell anybody anything, do you?" Dickie laughingly complained into the phone after ringing Price up upon arrival in Los Angeles. "When do you start [at Universal]?"

"Monday morning," Price replied.

At nine o'clock that Monday morning, Attenborough was waiting at the door to the producer's new office when Price arrived at Universal's "Black Tower" for his first day's work. Price ushered in his old friend and collaborator, then asked about the real reason for the visit.

"I want to make a movie about apartheid," Attenborough said, fearful the subject might not sound enthralling.

"Marvelous," said Price. "Based on what?"

"I've optioned two books by Donald Woods."

"I know them. They were optioned for a time at Columbia. How much is it going to cost?"

Stunned that "the deal" was apparently all set in a matter of seconds, Attenborough managed to mutter it could probably be completed for about $20 million.

"Get Jack Riley's script," Price said, referring to the initial stab at a screenplay at Columbia. In fact, that script would go through a dozen additional drafts as Attenborough and his growing coterie of collaborators labored to create a proper balance between Biko's tragic martyrdom and Woods's inspirational escape.

Shortly, *Cry Freedom* was in preproduction at Universal. Attenborough was thrilled when the project became ever more international. The government of Zimbabwe, where *Cry Freedom* would eventually be shot, invested $4 million of their own money on what is commonly called a *pari passu* basis for the facilities used to shoot in their country rather than merely collect profits from having a picture shot within their borders. Eventually, Zimbabwe would enjoy the distinction of hosting the international premiere (i.e., outside the United States) in their country. Though Frank Price eventually left Universal, which could have resulted in a newly ensconsed studio exec pulling the plug on projects initiated by the previous regime, Universal remained loyal to Attenborough and his project.

Casting, of course, was a serious issue. Attenborough said of the Biko role: "We had to have a man of charm, of erudition, of intellect, of perception, who was humorous, relaxed, yet confident." Initially, Dickie thought it might be best to cast a South African actor as Biko. He pursued this approach, going so far as to smuggle a number of that country's finest actors to read for the role over the border into Zimbabwe, where Attenborough was by this time headquartered. None had quite the charisma that was required; just as he had cast Ben Kingsley—the best possible actor available, though not Indian— as Gandhi, so, too, did Dickie decide to again go with the finest possible performer.

"So I made an appointment to see Denzel Washington," Attenborough recalls. "I had liked him in *A Soldier's Story,* but I didn't know if he could handle the role. He arrived early, and he said, 'I know almost nothing about this man.' I gave him a picture book with lots of shots of Biko, and I started to tell him about Biko's life and South Africa. As he listened, leaning against the mantelpiece, he began to talk to me—not with direct questions but with observations that had queries built into them. I saw then that he had elements in his own personality that led exactly to the quality of irresistible force that people felt in Biko. When Denzel talked, you *had* to give him the information he wanted. That was Biko!" When the film was completed and Denzel was asked whether it seemed strange, as an American, to be playing an African, he responded: "Look, I didn't come over on the *Mayflower.* I *am* an African, only a little removed," sounding more like Malcolm X as working actor rather than social activist, less like the usual racially unconscious American, Denzel Washington.

Principal photography began on July 14, 1986. Zimbabwe (Rhodesia until 1980) had been chosen as the site of the main exteriors. Denzel flew over on a plane that left London and stopped in Harare, capital of Zimbabwe (where Denzel disembarked), afterward proceeding on to Durban in South Africa, so several South Africans were on the plane with him between London and Harare. While boarding, they were stunned to see a black man in first-class. "One guy just looked right at me," Denzel later recalled. "He just couldn't believe it. I'm from New York, and I don't care. I looked him right in the face and said, 'You got a problem?'"

Denzel suffered from a certain arrogance. "I went over there with all my American anger and energy. I thought, What's wrong with all those crazy white South Africans? I'm going to get all the brothers together, and we're going to go get them! That was Western ignorance. A lot of those people have been fighting for twenty years. They've lost fathers and sons and brothers and sisters. All they want is peace. I just felt a little small after meeting them."

Disembarking, Denzel's experience of walking on African ground was "like a homecoming." He would later add: "I'll never forget Africa! I really felt the desire, the longing, for my roots. Even though I don't know specifically where I'm from, I felt very comfortable there," comfortable enough to return, whenever possible, with his wife and children. Of Biko, Denzel would comment: "I learned so much from the role. Biko had a tremendous knowledge and intelligence, verbal skills and speaking skills that fascinated me. And he was a very gentle man, a loving type of person. He was a natural leader, yet he didn't have to be up front all the time. He could pull people together with his analytical abilities."

Production designer Stuart Craig had noticed, during his search for a site, that of all other African nations, parts of Zimbabwe bear a striking resemblance to South Africa's eastern Cape area. The all-black tract housing, those crude living developments where South Africa's blacks continued to reside, had largely been abandoned in Zimbabwe but remained in place. Interiors, as well as some additional exteriors for the night scenes, including those at Biko's house, were built on soundstages at Shepperton Studios in England.

Craig and other members of the crew, working from Attenborough's conception, sensed that precise reality was less important than symbolic reality. Whereas Donald Woods's actual home was extremely unique in appearance, the mock-up Craig created bore no resemblance to that abode at all, even though there were abundant photographs for source material. But Attenborough wanted his film's Donald Woods to be something more than the historical character: a symbol for the comfortable white audience watching the film and, as such, a character with whom each viewer could identify. Instead of unique then, the film's house is typical of its class.

A major problem was trying to convey the glorious perpetual sunlight of South Africa, since Zimbabwe happens to be extremely different, weatherwise, with its clear-cut rainy and dry seasons. Obviously, the rainy season wouldn't do, so Dickie, Denzel, and company had to shoot during the dry season, which meant constantly taking freshly cut green grass and spreading it all over scorched brown lawns that would have given the actual location away. Shooting on two continents was completed at a final cost of $20.25 million, a tad over the original $20 million tag Attenborough had bounced off Frank Price but still a nice slice under the $21.5 million allocated as the film's finalized budget.

Denzel was then able to return to Hollywood, where he was shortly back at work, fulfilling his ongoing commitment to his American TV series. The contrast was not lost on him. "It was culture shock," he later recalled, "to be working there on a Thursday, fly twenty-two hours, then work on the *St. Elsewhere* set on Friday. Everybody here seemed so selfish, thinking about money and their own little existences. Coming from the South African border, meeting people who had been in prison for twenty years and coming home and seeing how we don't seem to care... It felt very cold."

Yet from the moment *Cry Freedom* appeared, there was an ongoing controversy. As critic Charles Fleming noted: "Attenborough the man is hard on apartheid; Attenborough the director is less so. 'As a fundamental policy,' Attenborough the man says, 'it is ghastly, so ghastly that it must be removed. You can't just chip away at it.' Attenborough the director, though, *does* chip away at apartheid, and the partnering of Biko's story with Woods's represents a compromise." Apparently, Dickie anticipated this wave of attack before it even began, attempting to defend his approach as not only acceptable but, beyond that, the only proper one: "I don't want to preach to the converted. It would be pointless to make [a little-seen art house] film and merely have [a small clique of already enlightened] people say, 'Oh, what a lovely chap you are.' I had to find subject matter that would not turn off the unknowing or the indifferent. It had to be *not* overtly political or preaching but something which had its political content encased in a story that a vast majority of the people in the world could identify with" and enjoy as entertainment.

In Attenborough's defense, it's important to emphasize that an artist—filmmaker, novelist, painter, what have you—must reserve the right to tell the story or draw the picture that most appeals to him as an individual rather than merely surrender to some sort of groupthink, telling the story a politically correct committee has dictated. Making the Steve Biko story would have been all wrong for Attenborough, since it would necessarily end with the man's death, thereby qualifying as a dark, depressing film, worthwhile and honest but not right for *this* filmmaker and his ongoing outlook. "I didn't want to make a picture of despair," he recalled, "where the regime wins."

By having Biko's death occur in mid-movie, followed by Woods's successful flight to freedom and publication of books about Biko, Attenborough ended his film on his longed-for positive note. "That [Biko] should die for nothing is a terrible" thing to imagine, Attenborough says. But that Woods would give up everything he had to follow through on bringing Biko's vision to the world "is a triumph of the human spirit, and I believe in it, fundamentally." Attenborough is a white filmmaker; in telling the story of Donald Woods, a wealthy white man (not unlike Attenborough) gradually transformed into an antiapartheid liberal, Attenborough was able to tell his *own* story. Still, none of this reasoning entirely justifies *Cry Freedom*, as the movie remains fair game for any critic who believes that Attenborough failed to pull off the intended mix.

"I am *not* an auteur [an esoteric director, challenging viewers to understand his complex, perhaps inaccessible worldview]," Attenborough insisted. "I am an entertainer. I am asking people in the context of *this* entertainment to question their attitudes about apartheid." It's worth noting, then, that *Cry Freedom* was not a box-office success. To auteurs, such commercial considerations may be insignificant as long as they have expressed personal visions to their own satisfaction. But to a commercial craftsman, admittedly insisting that everyone be attracted to his entertainment so he can then educate them as well, a financial failure suggests that his work failed on the very level he hoped for.

Peter Rainer summed up the attitudes of many critics when he wrote: "*Cry Freedom* is admirable as far as it goes, but it plays on our revulsion for apartheid as a way of earning extra credit. It's big and high-minded and right-minded, but it's also a gloss." Just as *Gandhi* had glossed over its title character's complexity, ignoring his darker side and less pleasant traits to provide a saintlike portrait, so did *Cry Freedom* similarly allow its audience to believe that Bantu Stephen Biko was South Africa's Martin Luther King, pleading only for equality with whites.

In fact, the real Biko often tended to the radical, sometimes urging black separatism, achieved if necessary by violence. Such harsher comments are not included in this "gloss" of a film. Attenborough also simplistically sidestepped the nasty conflicts between various black groups opposing apartheid, providing instead the false vision of idealistic blacks tightly and warmly united against a common enemy. *Cry Freedom* contains a white-bashing element, often implying that Woods was the exception, the only decent white in Africa. In point of fact, Woods was only one of many South African whites who believed that apartheid was evil; had it not been for others prodding him to meet with Biko in the first place, Woods would have never converted.

Rather than changing after listening to Biko intelligently explain his position, the case in real life, the film's Woods is inspired by the saintlike aura Biko here projects ("Biko is photographed in a burst of light, a holy radiance," Rainer wrote) and becomes an apostle. *Cry Freedom* plays better as religious allegory than as docudrama, the problem being that most moviegoers hadn't, and wouldn't, read the books, with their more complex version, simply trusting that what they were seeing on-screen was the truth. For dramatic purpose, Attenborough even chose to close the film with the Soweto massacre, though in real life that incident took place before Woods's run for freedom. Like Oliver Stone's movies, *Cry Freedom*'s impact depends on an audience's assumption that they are seeing actuality re-created, though the film quietly takes the liberty of freely dramatizing events.

Ironically, the lengthy sequences involving the Woods family's escape appear to be what lost the vast white audience, which had been intrigued by Denzel as Biko in the first half of the film and craved more. Nonetheless, critic Leonard Maltin came down on the side of Attenborough and, some would say, the angels: "Attacked in some circles for its 'armchair liberalism,' [the] film nevertheless brings attention to a worthy subject in the context of a good drama," hailing it as "sweeping and compassionate." Nowhere were the twin debates over "armchair liberalism" and historical accuracy more pronounced than in South Africa, where *Cry Freedom* was initially okayed by the censors for public consumption but, in late July 1988, following several matinee showings, was abruptly closed when the government overrode their own censorship board, fearing that the movie might provoke riots.

In *Beeld* (a widely circulated, pro-government paper printed in the Afrikaans language), Schalk Schoombie wrote: "Where distortions of fact appear, this is surely the time to debate them." Willem Pretorius added: "Perhaps you can say it is propaganda, and that the [black] good guys are too good and the bad [white] guys are too bad." Nonetheless, the film's essential vision was "something you cannot close your eyes to. This is perhaps the greatest reason people ought to see the movie." While Brian Pottinger of the *Sunday Times* was enraged by the "Hitler-versus-the-Cosby-family simplicity" of the conflict as portrayed on film, Peter Feldman of the *Star* (South Africa) commented: "It has been cunningly created and lovingly fashioned to transmit images that will distress, enrage and upset. It leaves nobody unmoved—whatever their political viewpoint. *Cry Freedom* must certainly be viewed. But if one has to ignore the politics that governed its making and judge it purely on its merits *as a film*, I found it unworthy of its lofty pretensions."

Significantly, the controversy did not spill over to Denzel's performance. The star, lauded both in America and abroad, won an Oscar nomination for Best Supporting Actor. The only complaint any critic voiced was that Denzel hadn't been allowed to develop the role as fully as he might have in a Biko biography. "He has mastered the man's contradictions with his edgy, sensuous performance," *Rolling Stone* reported. "While keeping the slack-shouldered bearing of one who's been beaten down, he never loses the surly, resolute pride of the rebel; this Biko is incapable of surrender." The *Hollywood Reporter* added: "His portrayal of Biko was imbued with such dignity, authority and an almost zenlike tranquility that he appears transcendent to everyone around him."

Pushing himself to become a true actor rather than capitalizing on star charisma, Washington took the same approach Robert De Niro, one of the greatest movie actors of the past quarter century and a personal favorite of Denzel's, previously employed for such projects as *Raging Bull* (1980): putting on weight and transforming his own appearance, as well as vocal inflections, to literally *become* the real-life person rather than merely *playing* at being that person. Denzel added thirty pounds so as to make himself look more like the available photographs and file film on Biko. Denzel also had a cosmetically filled in gap between his two front teeth filed away so as to appear somewhat less glamorous but more believable. Then, along with co-star Kevin Kline, he carefully studied the cadences of South African accents until his own was absolutely flawless, even to the harshest critics on this matter: South Africans.

Reviewing the film for the *Star* (South Africa), Rina Minervini wrote: "You would never guess that either of the actors was American. Top marks to their accent coaches." Even someone as critical of the film as America's David Denby of *New York* magazine noted that Denzel "makes Biko a dazzlingly intelligent man with a special gift of temperament. . . . Washington has mastered a way of withdrawing the obvious emphasis from his words that only makes them more emphatic. The softness of his touch draws you into his meaning . . . he is memorable."

According to Denzel in 1987, the film's social value far outweighed any inherent compromises. "Someone did a survey," he told reporters, "and twelve percent of the people they surveyed knew what apartheid is. I think the people that are gonna see holes [in the movie] are those who know the subject [from reading books and keeping up with the newspapers]. And Dickie kept driving that home: 'You have to lay it out there for [the general audience].' You might get it, I might get it. But there aren't enough of us out there to make it a successful film [without pumping up the action a bit]. The bottom line is, they spent [almost] twenty-two million. They did not make this film just to educate. It's business as well." Apparently, though, the internal wrestling match between the two Denzels continued, and the other side eventually won out. Because several years later, he announced publicly: "*Cry Freedom* was disappointing to me because it was supposed to be about Steve Biko. It shouldn't have been compromised by making it Donald Woods's movie. A cop-out? Yeah. You cannot sell the public short. The public is more sophisticated than we give them credit for."

5

For Queen and Country
1988
AN ATLANTIC RELEASING CORPORATION/WORKING TITLE FILM

CAST: Denzel Washington (*Reuben James*); Dorian Healy (*Fish*); Amanda Redman (*Stacey*); George Baker (*Kilcoyne*); Bruce Payne (*Colin*); Sean Chapman (*Bob Harper*); Geff Francis (*Lynford*); Stella Gonet (*Debbie*); Craig Fairbrass (*Challoner*).

CREDITS: Director, Martin Stellman; producer, Tim Bevan; screenplay, Stellman and Trix Worrell; cinematography, Richard Greatrex; editor, Stephen Singleton; music, Michael Kamen, Geoff MacCormack, and Simon Goldenberg; production design, Andrew McAlpine; rating, R; running time, 108 min.

I t was a good script," Denzel remembers when talking about his initial reaction to *For Queen and Country*. "Better than anything I've been offered here" in Hollywood. Unhappy with the writing that was coming his way, he'd already begun seeking out worthwhile projects himself, including smaller ones from other countries.

"My [initial] instinct was to cast a British black actor," filmmaker Martin Stellman admits, "but Denzel had gotten hold of the script, and he made it known he was desperate to do just this project." What Denzel wants, Denzel gets; following some serious negotiation, he flew to London, where a new wave of Angry Young Man movies was just then flourishing as a reaction to the current political regime.

Sammy and Rosie Get Laid (1987), *My Beautiful Laundrette* (1985), and the ironically titled *High Hopes* (1988) were, among others, produced in England. As critic Matthew Flamm put it, their collective aim was "to pour acid on the optimism of Margaret Thatcher's England." For Stellman, who had written *Defense of the Realm* (1986) and would cowrite and direct *For Queen and Country*, "anger is a great creative impulse. You're not left alone in Britain, the government is constantly shoved in your face, and you have a group of creative people who are pouring their anger and frustration into their work rather than channeling it into the political arena." America, meanwhile, was awash in elaborately empty escapism: *Return of the Jedi* (1983), *Romancing the Stone* (1984), and seemingly endless *Superman* sequels. Denzel realized that if, during hiatus from *St. Elsewhere,* he was going to appear in a worthwhile movie, he would have to leave Los Angeles.

For Queen and Country was filmed on a meager $3.2 million budget by first-time director Stellman. The focal character is called Reuben James, an intriguing allusion to a balladic folk hero. This new, fictional Reuben James, a former paratrooper, is very much a man of his time. As a tough, trouble-bound teenager, Reuben was properly straightened out by the discipline he learned in the military. Still, it seemed time to leave; Reuben grew disgruntled when not promoted despite the quality of his accomplishments over ten years. There was little doubt in Reuben's mind that this failure to rise through the ranks was due to race; he naively believes things may be better outside the service and so has returned to England, only to realize the country he's defended on foreign shores is blind and deaf to his simple desire to find a decent job.

During the decade that Reuben was overseas, extreme changes have wracked England in general and Bristol, his old neighborhood, in particular. Thatcherism has destroyed the government-backed job base that for years allowed the urban rednecks of England, white and black alike, to at least survive, perhaps even hope that they might someday climb the social ladder and find some elusive "room at the top."

Now all such support systems are gone. The white blue-collar underclass, for the first time experiencing rampant joblessness as compared to the drudgery of working-class jobs, must focus a growing anger somewhere. The Thatcher regime is too remote and distanced, so the anger is redirected at a handy "enemy," the even more desperate blacks who have journeyed to London, hoping for any kind of work. Racial conflict is now rife. Making matters worse, as a means of drowning their problems, blacks and whites alike have taken to drugs. Reuben, as played by Denzel Washington, emerges as a tragic figure, always attempting to hang on to the decent values he was taught in pre-Thatcher England, constantly tempted to give into the *nada* of the current life around him by embracing the absurd sense of nothingness. As Kenneth Turan of the *New York Times* (Sunday) would later put it, "*Queen* is a corrosive political melodrama where hopelessness and venality seep out of every frame."

Producer Tim Bevan, who five years earlier had founded Working Title pictures and was a mere twenty-nine years old at the time of *For Queen and Country*'s release, insisted that the importance of this picture and its ilk was due to the fact that "there's really no comparable [filmmaking] movement in the United States," even though the Reagan government operated on a parallel plane with Thatcherism. "There's not been any vitriolic anti-Reagan films made there. I just don't think there's the guts in Hollywood to make that kind of picture." But there certainly was in England, and Bevan knew from the moment he read Stellman's script that this was a story which deserved to be told.

Stellman, forty years old when he made the movie, possessed social attitudes which grew out of his background. Born and raised in London, Stellman had tried to concentrate on getting a conventional college education. But while attending Bristol University, he had forsaken his studies after becoming a member of an avant-garde theater group, Principal Edwards Magic Theatre, which employed the highly popular medium of rock 'n' roll as a way of communicating radical ideas to a "great unwashed" public that would not sit still for pretentious theatrical fare. Suddenly dedicated to living a life in the theatre of ideas, Stellman dropped out of formal schooling for the time being, also leaving the Magic Theatre, owing to his belief that it was perceived as nothing more than a bunch of on-the-edge hippies who were interested only in doing their own thing. Stellman, rather, wanted to do something that would be immediately involved with, rather than removed from, everyday reality. "Art shouldn't be elitist," he has said—rather, it should be for, about, and by the common people.

Stellman had run a youth drama group in London's Deptford district as well as an alternative school for the kids living there. In this capacity, he worked as a street and community theater director. It was during this time that he first met Trix Worrell, a talented black teenage performer. Sensing the extent of the young man's intelligence and potential, Stellman had encouraged Worrell to believe in the system and work within it, heading out into the world to prove his equality through what he did and said. Essentially, Stellman inspired young Trix to believe that anything was possible, that old barriers, such as race, had gradually but permanently been broken down.

Thus, Worrell went off to join the service, while Stellman opted for a three-year stint at the National Film and Television School, during which time he developed his script for *Defense of the Realm*. Stellman later recalled: "I had this blinding realization that filmmaking was the supreme amalgam of all the things" that most interested him, a perfect means of incorporating popular culture and unpopular ideas into a single work. When he and Worrell met again, for a friendly drink at a neighborhood pub, Stellman was disturbed to learn of the racism his former student had encountered.

The youth, who had served as a front gunner in a tough parachute regiment, was now bitter and resentful. "His alienation was very, very apparent," Stellman recalled. "What gave the thing poignancy was the moral dilemma of somebody who thinks he knows where he belongs but doesn't. He was British and black at the same time; where *did* he belong? I thought that was an incredible subject for a movie." Circumstances had gradually forced Worrell back into the ghetto, causing Stellman to finally question his own earlier liberal-optimist beliefs in the essential fairness of the system. So it was that the man who had already cowritten *Quadrophenia* (1979) with Franc Roddam, with its Who-inspired vision of Mods versus Rockers, now had yet another serious subject.

Nonetheless, on the eve of *For Queen and Country*'s release, Stellman, in retrospect, bridled at the notion that his movie was, first and foremost, a didactic tract, out to expose existing evils and change the world. "There's always been a concern to make the work populist," he reflected, noting that while *For Queen and Country* did touch on issues that were close to blue-collar workers who either had lost, or were in fear of losing their jobs, his main desire had been to create a strong, convincing work of drama, though there was no denying the immediate impact of the situation in which the protagonist finds himself. If it was necessary for Stellman to acknowledge the strong point of view his movie assumed, then he was unwilling to let *For Queen and Country* be tagged as an item fit only for academics, who would screen it at campus movie houses and then discuss the work's themes over espresso. "I'm not interested in making films for intellectuals or for the converted."

In Stellman's mind, his movie was not a story about South East London's blue-collar workers that only the more enlightened arthouse viewers would appreciate but a politicized *Yojimbo* (1961) or *Fistful of Dollars* (1964) that could, if properly marketed, pull in the blue-collar audience, which gravitates toward action flicks but might learn something about themselves and their plight while watching this film. "I consider *Queen and Country* a western," Stellman added, in the sense that Denzel Washington's Reuben James is not unlike Gregory Peck as Jimmy Ringo in *The Gunfighter* (1950), a relatively young man grown old before his time. After proving himself in battle, he desires to hang up his guns and live peaceably, gradually realizing that this is not possible; he will be sucked back into violent action over and over, haunted by his bloody past.

Despite any such entertainment-oriented considerations, there was no mistaking that this was a film from Working Title, the independent company that had been founded by twenty-something Bevan for the express purpose of regularly pillorying the policies of Thatcher. On his first day back in gloomy, ever-gray Bristol, Reuben is accosted by urban rednecks who hurl racist epithets at him, then is mugged by street punks. Shortly thereafter, his apartment is robbed by destitute area children, and while pursuing them around his high-rise building, Reuben trips over adolescents openly doing drugs in the halls. Reuben visits his old army buddy Fish (Dorian Healy), who once saved Reuben's life while they were stationed in Northern Ireland; Following that, Fish lost his leg in battle. Now, though, queen and country fail to compensate Fish for his effort. He argues endlessly with his wife, drinks to forget his troubles, and gambles away the little money they have, which ought to be spent on food for their kids.

Owing to his basic decency, Reuben would like to make the world a better place, specifically by helping this family, which comes to symbolize the entire working-class world. What he learns is that there's nothing he can do to alleviate their misery; when that realization strikes him full force, Reuben is in danger of turning cynical. His only job offers are from a black friend who wants Reuben to join him in buying and selling stolen goods from a now-wealthy white acquaintance who will pay Reuben to act as his bodyguard during a drug deal. Though he holds out as long as he can, Reuben is under pressure to succumb; his temper grows short when he goes out on a tentative date with Stacey (Amanda Redman), the white mother of one of the local kids. While walking her home, he's derided by white policemen, who drive by, shouting racial epithets.

Ultimately, the drama is the testing of Reuben: Will he, can he (indeed, *should he!*), continue to hold out against illegal offers proferred him and continued to follow the straight and narrow path when the Thatcher government makes no accommodations for the downtrodden, not even those veterans who, like Reuben and Fish, gave everything for queen and country? If a Hollywood movie had been made about such a situation, more likely than not it would have culminated in a contrived happy ending; not so *For Queen and Country*, which ultimately sees Reuben as victim rather than hero, at the mercy of forces beyond his control rather than the true shaper of his own destiny.

The movie was, for the sake of authenticity, filmed almost entirely in a South London housing project: Keston House was infamous as the most bleak living complex in London as well as a center for drug running. For eight weeks the crew worked in what turned out to be hostile territory, a unique situation for Denzel, who previously had been crowded by fans begging for an autograph. Since modern "film noir" took place largely at night, there were dusk-to-dawn shoots. In the movie, obnoxious characters hurl racist epithets at Reuben and Stacey; in real life, things were just as bad, for Denzel and Amanda Redman were harassed by locals whenever the two appeared together. Firecrackers and broken bottles were hurled down at the two while they attempted to rehearse a scene. There were twenty-two distinct locations in London's worst slums, and the actors had to be surrounded by armed guards every single second. Making matters all the worse, Denzel was concerned about his wife, at home in California and pregnant.

An important theme here, and a recurring concern in the Denzel Washington canon, is the concept of divided loyalties. Other blacks in the housing project question Reuben, causing him to look inward, searching for a sense of self. He is the black man who believed in the white man's propaganda, the beautiful-sounding inclusionist myth that if he views himself as a person who happens to be black rather than as a black person, he will be judged on the basis of his merit. His performance on the field of battle in Ireland and the Falklands had qualified him as an Englishman of the first order; if the myth were reality, Reuben would have received a hero's welcome home. Indeed, he would never have left the service, for he would have been promoted as a result of his accomplishments.

But the promise has been broken. Once more living in the black community, Reuben has again been ostracized, this time by blacks who cannot forget or forgive his desertion. Reuben is literally a man without a country. The most telling moment in *For Queen and Country* occurs when Reuben and his potential girlfriend, Stacey, decide to visit Paris together for a much-needed weekend away from all the ugliness. But when Reuben applies for a passport, he is told that according to the British Nationality Act of 1981—the ultimate in institutionalized racism from the Thatcher regime—he cannot receive an automatic passport, since he is no longer legally considered a British citizen. Reuben was born in St. Lucia, a former British colony, no longer officially a part of the ever-shrinking "empire." To receive a passport, Reuben would have to pay two hundred pounds, more money than he has. At that point, Reuben snaps; this is the straw that breaks this human's back. The decent man walks out of the petty bureaucrat's office and back to his housing project, at which point he immediately turns to crime. Shortly, Reuben is involved in a violent riot taking place on the streets, though this approach will not reward him any more than his previous adherence to the system did.

"Obviously, the issue of loyalty and where you belong is [one] that is very close to home [for me]," Stellman commented after finishing the principal photography. Born into an Eastern European Jewish immigrant family, Stellman had observed his father's ongoing attempt to assimilate into England's working-class society; he had remained aware of his own "otherness" all his life. Stellman admitted that ever since he could remember, he had experienced "the outsider's fascination for trying to understand, to make sense of this country I have always felt I somehow didn't belong to."

He hoped that the movie would stretch beyond the narrow, if immediate, concern of blacks attempting to survive within a white society, expanding from the specific to a more general statement about anyone who feels alienated from the Establishment. Still, the immediate question of blackness and Britishness was never overlooked. "*Queen and Country* could easily be titled 'the Chickens Come Home to Roost,'" the *Amsterdam News* (New York) reported, "as centuries of colonial exploitation is now drowning England in her own colonial juices. Masses of 'British subjects' crowd their adopted home looking for a better life, or just a change. The White British underclass vies for crumbs from the economic table, exchanges cultural values and language with former crown subjects from Jamaica, St. Lucia, Pakistan, and elsewhere."

It's all-important that Reuben is not merely black but was born in St. Lucia, then brought to England as a child, barely remembering his own history (much less that of his ancestors) in the Caribbean. In a typically American situation, this theme would be raised in many Denzel Washington films. Reuben initially trusts in the Dr. King "We know nothing of Africa" attitude and embraces assimilation but is forced, through difficult experiences on the street, which harshly educate him, to embrace a Malcolm X view. Indeed, Reuben—as played by Denzel—experiences the same dramatic arc as does Malcolm himself in an upcoming Denzel vehicle. For American audiences, then, *For Queen and Country* might be perceived as a cautionary fable: Fix the problems here in the United States before they degenerate to the levels they've descended to in England.

The casting of Denzel in fact became a serious problem. Stellman admits discomfort with the idea of an American movie star playing the part. "American cultural imperialism" is the way Stellman initially described the possibility of casting an American star

As Dr. Philip Chandler, the role he played on *St. Elsewhere* during the entirety of the show's run on NBC, from 1982 to 1988. Though a far cry from an idealized "role model," the all-too-human Dr. Chandler offered a positive image for African-American viewers. (courtesy NBC-TV Publicity Dept.)

As Roger, Denzel confronts his biological father, Walter Whitney (George Segal). An attempt at "serious" social comedy, *Carbon Copy* studied the split between blacks and Jews, insisting the two groups would be wise to unite against common enemies. (courtesy Avco-Embassy Pictures/Hemdale Leisure Corp.-RKO Pictures)

Michael Schultz, one of the few African-American directors working in Hollywood at the time, confers with Segal *(left)* and Washington *(center)* while filming *Carbon Copy*. (courtesy Avco-Embassy Pictures/Hemdale Leisure Corp.-RKO Pictures)

Sergeant Waters (Adolph Caesar) and Private First Class Peterson (Denzel) square off for a fight in *A Soldier's Story* between the two individual characters. Their antagonism symbolized the conflict between old-fashioned "Negroes" and those more youthful blacks with an emerging vision of African-American pride. (courtesy Columbia Pictures)

A Soldier's Story: The late Larry Riley as C. J. Memphis, an easygoing soldier who finds a friend, and champion, in Peterson. Even this early in his career, Denzel was carefully choosing roles that could not be easily categorized as simply hero or villain. (courtesy Columbia Pictures)

Denzel as Arnold Billings, the slick, smart, amoral oil-conglomerate lobbyist in *Power*. While still a member of the *St. Elsewhere* ensemble, Denzel chose film roles that were as removed from Dr. Chandler as possible, stretching his skills while ensuring that he would avoid typecasting. (courtesy Lorimar Pictures/20th Century-Fox Distribution)

(Opposite) Cry Freedom: Biko's proud, tortured face is illuminated by the flashlight of a white policeman as he is arrested at a random South African roadblock. (courtesy Universal Pictures/Marble Arch Productions)

As chief of police Xavier Quinn, Denzel had the opportunity to sing during one of this film's lighter moments; though based on a book entitled *Finding Maubee,* the film was rechristened *The Mighty Quinn* to take advantage of the Bob Dylan song, here played in reggae fashion. (courtesy Metro-Goldwyn-Mayer Pictures; photo credit: Susan Gray)

As *The Mighty Quinn*: With close friend Robert Townsend. Hungry struggling actors only a few years earlier, the two played opposite one another. The dichotomy between an assimilated black and one who clings to his ethnic culture would underline many future Denzel Washington films. (courtesy Metro-Goldwyn-Mayer Pictures; photo credit: Susan Gray)

As "Trip," the role that won him an Academy Award for Best Supporting Actor. Numerous critics noted that of all the *Glory* characters, only his was "anachronistic," a modern black consciousness inserted into the Civil War setting. (courtesy Tri-Star Pictures)

Glory: Trip (*second from left*) joins comrades in arms for the suicidal attack that provides the film's highlight. Historians still argue whether the action was a noble sacrifice or a terrible waste. (courtesy Tri-Star Pictures)

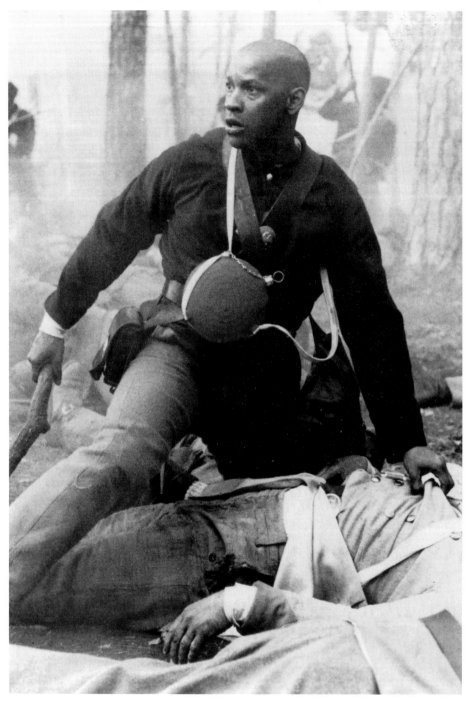

Denzel fought for this particular role, as it offered the largest "arc" of any character in Glory, Trip initially the most cynical about his white commander, though ultimately dying arm in arm with Colonel Shaw. (courtesy Tri-Star Pictures)

(however talented) in his film. After acquiescing, there were numerous complaints from Equity, the British actors union, that one of their own had not been awarded the role. Denzel openly admitted his own misgivings: "It just reflects the problems here and in the States. I don't want to have to take work from people here. The fact of the matter is, there wasn't anything for me to do back home. It's frustrating sometimes." Certainly, there were offers in Hollywood, but there wasn't anything *worthwhile* for him to do, a sorry statement about the American movie industry.

Still, Stellman wanted his movie to be commercial, and there is no black English movie star who could ensure that the picture would be booked into American mall theaters rather than the art-house circuit, where it would be preaching to the converted. Stellman rather saw himself as a missionary; he wanted to reach the uninitiated, win them over during the course of an exciting crime story. Denzel's name could draw in moviegoers. Moreover, production could not commence unless Atlantic Entertainment Group, an American distribution company, put up matching funds to come up with the relatively modest budget of 1.8 million pounds. Since there would be a first-time director at the helm (a situation that always gives investors the shakes), it became all the more necessary to appease them, so Stellman gave in to their desire for an appealing young American star.

As Sara Radclyffe, Tim Bevan's then thirty-six-year-old partner at Working Title, bluntly put it, "Without an actor of Denzel's stature, it would have been impossible to get the money." Denzel's personal advisers, however, were against his signing on. A career killer, they warned, though their definition of "career" was different from Denzel's vision of what he ought to be doing. "It's no big trick to make a lot of money," a character in Orson Welles's *Citizen Kane* said, "if all you want is a lot of money." Though Denzel, by his own admission, did indeed want to make a lot of money, such considerations had to be weighed against artistic satisfaction. Stellman, meanwhile, was worried that Denzel might not be able to master the character's unique accent: Having been born in the Caribbean, Reuben ought to have not only a touch of that background in his voice, but also the idiom of a particular London slum, in which he was later raised. Could Denzel get this special brand of Cockney precisely right, also spicing it with the Caribbean flavor? As Stellman put it: "I was struggling, I was really struggling," with this casting decision.

Stellman knew that for the piece to play properly, he had to have an actor "who could carry the movie on his shoulders, give me a performance of great weight and presence." Truth be told, the more than fifty black British actors he tested for the role were disappointing: "I wasn't sure of getting all that [I needed dramatically]. I'd be taking a risk."

Before making a final decision, Stellman screened *A Soldier's Story* and closely observed Denzel's performance. He was overwhelmed by the combination of conviction and depth, knowing that this actor would transform Reuben, as written on the page, into the kind of searing figure Stellman originally envisioned. "I thought, Why am I being so parochial? The prime considerations—power, presence, charisma—all of these things he had in great supply." Before filming commenced, Denzel moved in with a family in London's East End, remaining there for a week, studying their accents closely. Then he went to work with a speech coach to complete the illusion.

Denzel's reviews were nearly all positive. "In a terrifically subtle and powerful performance," Caryn James wrote in the *New York Times*, "Mr. Washington is true to the modest, struggling man he plays. His expression registers restrained anger and much confusion." *Variety* admired "a powerful central performance from Denzel Washington," who played Reuben James "with a convincing Cockney accent." Kathleen Carroll of the *New York Daily News* admired Denzel's "quiet strength" in the role, while Mike McGrady of *Newsday* pointed out that "Washington, Oscar-nominated for his role in *Cry Freedom*, continues to impress as he provides a clarity and definition along with, in this instance, a surprisingly effective Cockney accent." Peter Miller of *New York Native* concurred, noting that Washington delivered "his lines with an impeccable British accent."

Despite such glowing notices, Denzel, who has always bridled at comparisons with Sidney Poitier, could take umbrage at the fact that such comparisons were raised once more or take pleasure in the fact that he was in some instances acclaimed for doing the role differently than Poitier might have. In the *New York Post*, critic David Edelstein wrote: "Fortunately, the gifted American actor Denzel Washington doesn't fall into dignified, Sidney Poitier cadences. There's caginess in his silence, and his voice is a crafty purr. Washington's working-class English accent is good enough to be frequently unintelligible to Americans." That situation is in fact surprising, for representatives of the American distribution company were on hand to monitor the accents of Denzel and the other performers, owing to their concern that other British films had failed to do well in America largely because audiences were put off by the fact that the "English" was so difficult to understand the movie might just as well have employed subtitles.

Sometime later M. Pally, of *7 Days*, argued that Denzel slipped into the very sort of traditional Poitieresque performance that Edelstein insisted he so neatly avoided: "Of the many things Denzel Washington could become," Pally wrote, "I think Sidney Poitier should not be one of them." Denzel would of course agree with that but would be offended by what followed: "I'm afraid the typecasting is under way. Washington has played an upright black in *A Soldier's Story*, the saintlike Steve Biko in *Cry Freedom*, and a Dudley-Do-Right double in *The Mighty Quinn*, not to mention the righteous Dr. Chandler in the *St. Elsewhere* TV serial. . . . I thought this was his chance to break the mold and play a character with a bit more layering; but Washington's virtuous role in *For God (sic) and Country* undermines any complexity. . . . He plays the classic good guy." In Denzel's defense, the comparison seems forced; Denzel did *not* play the "upright black" Poitier-like character in *A Soldier's Story* but a murderer; in *Cry Freedom*, he fought against Attenborough's attempt to turn Biko into a black Gandhi and gave the character as much of an edge of anger as possible under the circumstances.

Georgia Brown of the *Village Voice* offered a rare negative review, insisting that "Washington is required only to change his expression from gloomy to grim," though even this remark suggests that the problem had more to do with the filmmakers and what they demanded from their actor than the actor himself. Indeed, critics were generally less kind to the movie itself than they were to Denzel, admiring the ambitions and integrity while insisting that *For Queen and Country* did not work as dramatic entertainment.

Newsday's McGrady dared attack the approach of a socially conscious filmmaker with the rough criticism many reviewers reserve for less ambitious artists: "This is a movie about issues rather than people. Symbolism runs riot; a brief romance is not merely with a woman, it's with a woman with a near pathological hatred of the gun Reuben is being asked to carry. There is a feeling that every role and every scene has been squeezed to fit a prearranged shape. Events happen but they happen on cue; they don't unfold naturally, and this takes some of the edge off *For Queen and Country*." For the *Post's* Edelstein, the film played "like a politically responsible *Rambo* [1985], and I only wish it were less contrived. . . . It's a thesis movie," hammering home a point at all costs, including the diminishment of the drama.

The question must be asked, why did Denzel decide to do this film? "What I found interesting about it is there haven't been any films made in the States that say anything about how blacks feel about war. Even *Platoon* (1986)—when I saw that film I thought, well, where am I in there?" Indeed, Denzel felt this way about Oliver Stone's movie long before he saw it; Denzel had rejected a role owing to Stone's stereotypical portrait of the black characters. *For Queen and Country* at least made an honest stab at dealing with such issues. The follow-up question: What did he think of the results? Reporter Diane K. Shah accompanied Denzel when, in June 1987, he returned to London, this time with his family. Following a busy day's activities, Denzel brought four-year-old John David to a cast and crew screening, while Pauletta remained at the hotel with daughter Katia, then one.

"I'm just going to make an appearance," he assured his wife, "watch a few minutes" of the film that had recently been hailed in *Variety's* review following the Cannes Film Festival screening. "I'll be back by seven."

At nine o'clock, Pauletta sat in the hotel lobby, nervously waiting. "I can't understand what happened to him," she said. "I mean, he's got John David. The child must be exhausted by now."

Just then, Denzel and John David appeared; Denzel, looking more drained than the child, dropped into the first empty chair he spotted.

"How did it go?" Pauletta asked.

"I don't know." he sighed. "It wasn't what I thought it would be. I think it needs to be recut. The music wasn't right, either."

"How was John David?"

"He fell asleep." Denzel rose and paced the floor. "Tomorrow I'm going to make a lot of notes; then I'm going to meet with the director. I think the movie needs a lot of work."

"It's probably better than you think," she said reassuringly.

Denzel shook his head. "John David had it right. After five minutes, he said, 'Daddy, let's go!'"

6

The Mighty Quinn

1989

AN M-G-M PRESENTATION

CAST: Denzel Washington (*Xavier Quinn*); Robert Townsend (*Maubee*); Mimi Rogers (*Hadley*); James Fox (*Elgin*); M. Emmet Walsh (*Miller*); Sheryl Lee Ralph (*Lola*); Art Evans (*Jump*); Esther Rolle (*Ubu Pearl*); Tyra Ferrell (*Isole*); Alex Colón (*Pastina*); Keye Luke (*Dr. Rej*); Maria McDonald (*Flirt*); Rita Marley (*Musician*).

CREDITS: Director, Carol Schenkel; producers, Sandy Lieberson, Marion Hunt, and Ed Elbert for A & M Films; screenplay, Hampton Fancher, from the novel *Finding Maubee* by A. H. Z. Carr; cinematography, Jacques Steyn; editor, John Jympson; production design, Rogert Murray-Leach; costumes, Dana Lyman; rating, R; running time, 100 min.

To get the girl," Denzel replied when questioned as to why he next agreed to do *The Mighty Quinn*, his first romantic lead. Though the film would be released by M-G-M, it had been developed by A & M Films as an independent production. Producers Marion Hunt and Ed Elbert had discovered A. H. Z. Carr's novel *Finding Maubee*, reading the book as part of their search for material worthy of developing as motion pictures. They found themselves falling under the spell of the West Indies texture, which allowed a relatively traditional meat-and-potatoes film of the police-detective genre to take on a fresh new flavor via literary Caribbean spice. They also liked the character of Xavier Quinn, who, within the crime tale, must face his inner self and consider his changing values in a way that most detective heroes do not.

"In its most elemental form," British-based producer Sandy Lieberson, who would join the team after the project's inception, said, "*The Mighty Quinn* is a murder mystery. But it is also about a man finding himself," a man who, by trying to better his lot in life, has become "alienated from his own culture."

Hunt and Elbert brought the property to A & M Films, moviemaking subdivision of the famed record company, which had already produced *Birdy* (1985), *The Breakfast Club* (1985), and *Bring on the Night* (1985). There, Gil Friesen and Dale Pollock—who made the decisions on which films would or would not be green-lighted—likewise were impressed enough with the concept to sign on as executive producers. One reason this project was so attractive to A & M was the potential for a spin-off, as a soundtrack album would be released by their music division in tandem with the finished film. In the entertainment industry, this is called "synergy": Fans of the movie would go out and buy the recording, while people who heard cuts played on the radio would seek out the film, or so everyone at A & M hoped.

"We could combine three styles of music—pop, R and B, and reggae and hopefully get a musical blend that would cut across a wide musical audience," Pollock explained, thereby rating as the crossover hit every record and CD distributor desires. Swiss-born Carl Schenkel, who had cut his teeth on European commercials, was hired to direct based on his art-house film *Out of Order* (1984), which concerned four characters trapped together in an elevator. Schenkel's ability to immerse audiences in the fate of such people, stuck in a claustrophobic situation, convinced the producing team that he could give their movie the proper suspense.

The moment casting began, almost every noted young actor of color contacted A & M in hopes of landing the part of Quinn, owing to its avoidance of stereotypes—pimps, drug dealers, and gangsters—then being offered. Denzel was always the first choice; his stunning work in *Cry Freedom* was all the producers needed to see before signing him in what, they hoped, might just be the first in a series of films about this memorable detective character. Denzel was attracted for many reasons, though one specific line of dialogue caught his attention. "Xavier's wife says to him, 'You're not one of them,' meaning the governor and the lawn parties," he later recalled. " 'And you're not yourself, either.'" Who are you? she wants to know. It's a question Quinn can't answer but one he will grapple with throughout the narrative. Perhaps it was a question which, on more than one occasion, the seemingly self-confident Denzel has asked himself.

"That's the essence of his dilemma," Denzel continued. "He's trying to fit in and be what he thinks he needs to be in order to excel. But, on the other hand, you've got this guy Maubee—what they would call him locally is a 'Roots Boy'—and he brings Xavier back to himself."

Once cast, Denzel suggested other performers he knew and admired. Singer-actress Sheryl Lee Ralph, who hadn't been offered a movie role in nine years, had become friends with Denzel when she volunteered to work in his annual Los Angeles Toy Drive, a charity he organized to deliver presents to underprivileged children at Christmastime. And, at last, Denzel had the opportunity to costar with old friend Robert Townsend, fresh from the success of his independent feature *Hollywood Shuffle*. Townsend said of his character: "I looked at Maubee as being the child everyone would like to remain. He's a Peter Pan and Robin Hood rolled into one. He's the lovable island boy. I think that Maubee has magic, and that's one of the reasons I wanted to do the part."

It was necessary for both actors to work on the unique West Indies accent, called "patois," so they would blend in with the native islanders who would play the film's supporting roles. Half the cast of forty, along with a quarter of the production crew, was composed of Jamaicans. Maxine Walters, born and raised in Kingston, had recently returned home after four years in Los Angeles. She was hired to work on the accents of the two young stars while the crew prepared to shoot. Walters recalls: "Denzel had done two pictures before this which required an accent: South African for *Cry Freedom* and Cockney blended with West Indies for *For Queen and Country*. The first thing we had to do when we got together was eliminate everything that came before. Denzel was very dedicated and didn't miss a session. We worked for six weeks before we started to film, and I literally saw him transform before my eyes. He did all his homework."

Producer Lieberson had chosen Jamaica over other possible Caribbean locales (the film's island nation is never specified), owing to the efforts of Prime Minister Edward P. G. Seaga, who was anxious to win back the kind of lucrative Hollywood deals Jamaica had known in the 1960s, when three or four movies (including James Bond films) were shot there every year. Filmmaking, like tourism, had fallen off sharply since the violent riots of the mid-seventies. Lieberson knew that Jamaica would be affordable when, upon mentioning that he'd need a helicopter for one shot, the government made one available from the country's small army. "We had to pay for fuel and the pilot's time," Lieberson recalled, "but there was no charge for the helicopter itself," though this would have been a major financial issue if one had to be privately rented.

Principal photography began on March 14, 1988, with most filming done in and near Port Antonio, a small city on Jamaica's northern coastline that the legendary Errol Flynn once called home. Before a funeral could be filmed in the hutlike village of Moortown, the locals requested that everyone involved in the filming participate in a voodoo ceremony called obeah, to put local undead souls to rest and not be haunted by them during production. Rum was poured on grave sites; then local *obeah* experts burned their ceremonial herb mixes while delivering the proper incantation. Apparently, it all worked; there were no delays owing to angry spirits during the shoot.

The luxurious Trident villas were used for the setting of right-wing opportunist Donald Pater's murder, the incident which sparks the problems encountered by Xavier Quinn. The villas also doubled for the home of Elgin, the mysterious white ruling-class figure who wants to pin the murder on Maubee and quickly hush everything up. Port Antonio's city hall became the office where black governor Chalk operates in toadyish conjunction with Elgin and other white power brokers. The filming was, in fact, not Denzel's first experience with Port Antonio; he, like Townsend and Art Evans (Denzel's *Soldier's Story* costar, here playing his loyal deputy), had previously vacationed in the area. Denzel and Pauletta spent some time at the resort Frenchman's Cove before he traveled to Zimbabwe to film *Cry Freedom.*

By refusing to name the actual island, the filmmakers allowed *The Mighty Quinn* to take on a universal quality, implying the generalized arrogance of American intrusion into Caribbean cultures. Pater has been decapitated, his mutilated body discovered in a Jacuzzi, the corpse literally swimming in its own juices. A wealthy but sleazy land developer, Pater was rumored to have ties to the CIA and, like them, was anxious to end any Communist insurgencies before they began. Solving Pater's murder is the first major case assigned to Xavier Quinn, recently returned from the States. There Xavier underwent a thorough training program, run by the FBI's ultramodern crime school. Quinn plans to impress everyone around him—particularly the white ruling class—by showing that his education wasn't for naught as he applies the latest state-of-the-art approaches to the case.

While the island whites may think highly of Quinn, the black locals have come to consider him something of a stuffed shirt. Even the nickname "the Mighty Quinn" combines elements of respect for the prestige he's achieved with an element of irony, suggesting he's begun to take himself *too* seriously. No one can deny that Quinn has climbed the social ladder, as his crisp *white* uniform suggests. The question for all the islanders is: Has Xavier lost touch with them emotionally and spiritually? Fear that he has causes his wife, Lola, to throw him out; though he protests he's merely trying to make a better life for them and their son, she wants to cling to traditional ways. That's as clear in her choice of careers as is Quinn's; Lola forms a reggae band and insists on preserving as much integrity in the music as possible.

A key early sequence throws the two boyhood friends together again. Xavier does not yet know about the murder; he's just been called to the scene of the crime. Speeding down a mountain slope in his official Jeep vehicle, he bumps into a motorcycle. The nonconformist Maubee, dreadlocks flying in the wind, drives wildly as he illegally speeds up that mountain from the opposite direction, clutching a suitcase, a pretty island girl, Isole, sits in his sidecar. The contrast between the two men is visually effective, implying the discrepancies that now exist between their lifestyles and mind-sets, one having gone Establishment, the other remaining a rebel. Quinn and Maubee are as fitting a contrast as, when back in the old Warner

Bros. crime films of the 1930s, Pat O'Brien and James Cagney played boyhood buddies who had grown up to be G-man and gangster, respectively. *The Mighty Quinn* offers a recycling of the plot from one of those beloved old potboilers.

Maubee would certainly seem to be the culprit. He's a hedonist, pure and simple: He smokes ganja, seduces numerous women (including whites visiting the island), and he has been known to pull off a couple of con jobs to get his hands on money. The decapitation was done with an ancient weapon that Elgin's wife, Hadley, insists was earlier stolen from their house by Maubee. However, Xavier knows, in his heart of hearts, that Maubee couldn't have done it. And he absolutely trusts the instincts of his estranged wife, who puts it simply: "Maubee's a lover, not a killer."

Nevertheless, Xavier has been ordered to pursue Maubee, and Maubee alone, for this crime. That isn't so easy, since Maubee has gone into hiding, thanks to an endless array of island friends who successively put him up for a day or a night. The black governor, fearful that a scandal might impact on needed tourist revenue, takes a "trickle-down" approach, letting Xavier know in no uncertain terms that his career as the island's leading police officer is on the line. Yet Maubee isn't arrested, partly because he's adept at alluding authorities, partly because, subconsciously, Xavier doesn't want to find Maubee too quickly, hoping that by delaying, he'll come across evidence pointing in other directions.

The Mighty Quinn contains a Hitchcock-like McGuffin: a suitcase filled with ten thousand dollars in U.S. bills, currency printed in the 1920s and 1950s, then recalled from general use and kept under lock and key in the Department of Treasury. What is such rare currency doing on the island? And why are two creepy characters, both of whom claim to be tourists, hanging around? The Ugly American "Mr. Miller" is an agent for the CIA, which has been secretly interfering with local affairs. Pastina, a mustachioed hit man, represents either organized crime or some Latin American terrorist group that seems to have been dispatched by organized crime. In fact, the money appeared as part of the American government's money-laundering scheme, involving counterrevolutionaries and an intrusion into Third-World affairs worthy of Oliver North and Contragate.

Xavier comes to realize how it all fits together while halfheartedly pursuing Maubee. He even meets and ostensibly arrests his old pal late one night, though they get drunk together in Maubee's latest stolen car and, in the morning, the suspect escapes once more. This sequence, incidentally, is the finest in the film, recalling the legendary late-night drunken confrontation between Burt Lancaster and Montgomery Clift in *From Here to Eternity* (1953). Also memorable is the meeting between Xavier and Elgin's slinky, available wife, Hadley (Mimi Rogers), who makes clear that she would like to have an affair with Quinn, hinting she's enjoyed such liaisons with other islanders, most recently Maubee.

As Hadley attempts to seduce Quinn, it becomes clear she's something more than merely an updating of the Lauren Bacall film-noir temptress. Additionally, Hadley is a symbol, the seductive upscale white woman who threatens to draw Xavier even further away from his estranged wife, to whom he must return if he is to reclaim what was always best within himself. The fact that, in the finished film, Quinn manages to resist this island Eve's temptations points to what *The Mighty Quinn* wants to imply about the need for black men to avoid being co-opted and corrupted.

Yet it's important to note that *The Mighty Quinn* originally included a shot in which Hadley takes Xavier in her arms and kisses him sensuously on the lips. M-G-M requested that the moment be cut. Though that may sound like overt racism, executive producer Dale Pollock insisted that it was, in fact, cut, owing to reverse racism: White audiences didn't mind the kiss, but black audiences were furious. "It got this really visceral reaction," he recalls. Apparently, by allowing Hadley to kiss him, Xavier was perceived as being a traitor to his wife, a woman of color and therefore a "sister." Black women in particular were offended. Eliminating the kiss drastically changed the thrust of the scene: Rather than be tempted and slip away, Xavier now appears strong-willed by rejecting her.

Nonetheless, Denzel—the same Denzel who would later walk away from *Love Field*, with its potential sexual encounter between himself and Michelle Pfeiffer—complained: "It's sad that it goes on in life but that it can't go on on-screen." He also insists that he never believed the kiss would ever be seen. "When they shot that scene, I said, 'You're wasting your film, this isn't going to be in there,' and they did cut it." In addition to an interracial love scene that the public didn't get to see, there was another first for the actor, who made his on-screen singing debut. At one point, Xavier—frustrated with his inability to find Maubee, disgusted by the white Establishment, upset by his wife's absence—leaves his police station, symbol of his new prestige, and returns to one of the reggae clubs where he and Maubee hung out together in happier days. Jiving at the piano and jamming with locals, Xavier's burst of song allowed Denzel to play and sing "Cakewalk into Town." Most everyone agreed his delivery was fine. He'd obviously learned something about musical performance, first from his mother, then from his wife.

Few critics were pleased with the film, which received lukewarm reviews. Jami Bernard found the plot "muddy" and the action "tedious," resulting in "some lackluster international intrigue." Indeed, the "whodunit" story becomes convoluted: It turns out that pretty Isole, pregnant by Pater, killed him on orders from her aunt Uba Pearl (Esther Rolle), the local voodoo queen, by slipping a poisonous fer-de-lance snake into his room. Maubee, coming across this, beheaded the body to draw attention away from Isole, who was his lover, and toward himself, then stole the luggage filled with laundered money. But whether he'd arrived at Pater's villa to rob (but not kill) the man or only stole to confound authorities into thinking this was all a robbery-murder perpetrated by himself is never made clear.

Vincent Canby of the *New York Times* was kind, labeling the film "a breezy semitopical whodunit... though the characters and the plotting are strictly paperback; [the film] doesn't demand that you leave your senses at the door." Roger Ebert proved kinder still, hailing *The Mighty Quinn* as "a spy thriller, a buddy movie, a musical, a comedy and a picture that is wise about human nature. And yet with all those qualities, it never seems to strain. This is a graceful, almost charmed entertainment." But Julie Salamon of the *Wall Street Journal* hit the nail pretty much on the head when she summed up the situation thusly: "*The Mighty Quinn* has pretty scenery, good music and a capable cast, yet it's a letdown. The picture promises moonbeams and delivers hack work, laid out in standard-issue detective style." Indeed, while the music and scenery are above average, the detective story line is actually *sub*standard once the unconvincingly, murky motivations for the murder are belatedly revealed.

Notably, this was the first time that Denzel received top billing in a motion picture made specifically for distribution in America. Critics considered it closely to see if he could carry a high-profile film; most came away satisfied that he'd passed the test. "This marks Washington's first solo role," Abiola Sinclair wrote in the *Amsterdam News* (New York), "and he's definitely a winner. You can't take your eyes off of him. He's sexy in a humane rather than an animal sort of way." Bill Kaufman of *Newsday* agreed: "Washington puts a good spin on his portrayal of Quinn." Roger Ebert raved: "Denzel Washington is at the heart of this movie, and what he accomplishes is a lesson in movie acting. He has the obligatory action scenes, yes, and confrontations that are more or less routine. He handles them easily. But [also] watch the way he and Mimi Rogers play their subtle romantic encounter....The film stars Washington in one of those roles that should make him a major movie star."

Ebert then drew precisely the kind of comparison Denzel most appreciates, to any great actor-star of the past other than Sidney Poitier: "In an effortless way that reminds me of Robert Mitchum, Michael Caine, or Sean Connery in the best of the Bond pictures, he is able to be tough and gentle at the same time, able to play a hero and yet not take himself too seriously." Other critics again raised the Sidney specter, some positively, some negatively. As to the latter, *Variety* complained that "Denzel Washington [is] trying too hard to become the '80's Sidney Poitier," while Canby praised Denzel, claiming: "Washington gives the kind of smooth, funny, laid-back performance that could help make him the first black matinee idol since Sidney Poitier."

Though critic Abiola Sinclair praised Denzel's presence, Denzel's accent proved another matter: "While his accent sounds more from Trinidad or Barbados than Jamaica, it was endearing." But the criticism does not ring true: Though the film was shot in Jamaica, it takes place in a mythical island country. Thus, for Denzel to add elements of other Caribbean nations suggests that he was in tune with the nature of the film's conception of a composite Caribbean country. A few critics did demur, mainly those who disliked the movie. Jami Bernard complained that "Washington, a fine actor, is stiff and unmotivated in his starchy good cop role," though her choice of the word "unmotivated" implies that the script itself was at fault.

Importantly, though, the role of Xavier Quinn allowed Denzel to express more of his own personality than had been possible with any previous project. Like Xavier, Denzel is married to a singer, though she had put her career aside to raise their child and is now trying to reclaim her professional life. Like Xavier, Denzel at the time had one son, whom he attempts to raise as well as possible, trying to be a good father despite the demands of his chosen profession. Also difficult for the actor, like the character, is that he's handsome enough to have endless women, white and black, throw themselves at him. He must reject their advances if he is to make his marriage work, but while he struggles to do so, he cannot deny the appeal of such attention. Xavier, like Denzel, is committed to upward mobility, employing his talents to rise on the social spectrum, desiring to always make things better for not only himself but for his family.

Ironically, this film—which glorifies blacks who refuse to assimilate into white society—had a hard time at the box office, grossing under $5 million, precisely because it was marketed for ethnic audiences rather than distributed as a mainstream release. M-G-M execs were not convinced that a movie which questions the notion of integration could play to an integrated audience. "I was angry when [M-G-M] didn't get behind the picture," Denzel later recalled. "They had a bigger film, *Leviathan,* and they were in trouble at the time. But they had said, 'If you come out and hit these numbers, we'll get behind it.' Well, we came out with better numbers, and they didn't get behind it. That [attitude, that the film could only appeal to black audiences] was *it.*"

7

Glory

1989

A TRI-STAR RELEASE

CAST: Matthew Broderick (*Robert Gould Shaw*); Denzel Washington (*Trip*); Cary Elwes (*Cabot Forbes*); Morgan Freeman (*Rawlins*); Jihmi Kennedy (*Sharts*); André Braugher (*Searles*); Jane Alexander (*Mrs. Shaw*); John Finn (*Mulcahy*); John David Cullum (*Morse*); Alan North (*Governor Andrew*); Bob Gunton (*General Harker*); Cliff De Young (*Colonel Montgomery*).

CREDITS: Producer, Freddie Fields; director, Edward Zwick; screenplay, Kevin Jarre and the books *Lay This Laurel* by Lincoln Kirstein and *One Gallant Rush* by Peter Burchard, as well as the published letters of Robert Gould Shaw and other historical sources; cinematographer, Freddie Francis; editor, Steven Rosenblum; music, James Horner; production design, Norman Garwood; rating, R; running time, 122 min.

F reedom was not given to us in some paternalistic way," Denzel Washington commented during a break on the set of *Glory* in Georgia during mid-February 1988. The actor found a moment to reflect on his latest movie's message: "It was something we had to claim with blood." Then, comparing *Glory*, with its sincere attempt at enlightened education, to the white-oriented history lessons he'd received years earlier, Denzel quietly but firmly stated: "Well, they never taught *me* that in school!"

Indeed, very few children—black or white—were in the past informed that members of all minority groups played significant roles in each and every area of our shared American history. But that was before recent, belated consciousness-raising. As to the Civil War per se, the movie's subject, there was scant evidence in either the earlier school textbooks or our popular films to indicate that 179,000 blacks served as soldiers, while another 30,000 African Americans were members of the navy; the death count–MIA for African Americans between 1863 and 1865 numbered 68,178, according to government records.

Many of those dead were members of the Fifty-fourth Massachusetts Volunteer Infantry, an outfit formed in February 1863 by a twenty-six-year-old white colonel born and raised in Beacon Hill. Robert Gould Shaw was a Boston Unitarian who had dropped out of Harvard during his junior year to join the army. While Shaw actively served in such battles as Antietam, where he was wounded, politicians busily debated the idea of establishing black regiments. It was deemed absolutely necessary; otherwise, the Union, in the wake of President Lincoln's announcement of the Emancipation Proclamation, would appear hypocritical. However, there was an abiding belief that black soldiers would turn and run at the first sound of gunfire.

Though Shaw, son of abolitionists who were strong believers in racial equality, dismissed such attitudes; in actuality, he initially did not want to assume command of a unit, black or white, considering himself too young and untried. But his strong-willed mother, Sarah, convinced him that it was his mission in life; so it was that Shaw became the enlightened colonel of the Fifty-fourth. In the film, Shaw's moment of indecision was eliminated for the sake of speeding the story along; that was one of several such decisions by the moviemakers that make this striking historical panorama less dramatic, on an intimate and personal level, than it might be. Indeed, it would be easy to imagine some screenwriter inventing the scene of Shaw's indecision in order to increase the dramatic potential.

Though Shaw and other union officers depicted in *Glory* are based on actual people, the black characters are, to a man, fictional: representational figures of various types of nineteenth-century blacks, ranging from intellectual freedmen to confused country youths to angry runaway slaves. This choice was made for various reasons, the most significant being that considerably less information exists about the black infantrymen, who to some degree walked faceless, if not exactly nameless, into history, as compared to white officers, whose stories are fully documented. Nonetheless, there are records of some of the regiment's black heroes, including Company C's William H. Carney, the first black soldier to ever receive America's highest commendation, the Congressional Medal of Honor. One avenue of criticism toward this generally well received film is that the producer-director-writer team (all of whom were white) might have stretched themselves further; several descendants of the Fifty-Fourth's soldiers did make it a point to introduce themselves to the moviemakers and offer to tell stories about their ancestors.

Be that as it may, Denzel Washington's role is of particular interest, considering the long list of wholesome heroes he'd played in the past and would again in the near future. Denzel did not chose to play the role that might have seemed a natural for him: Searles, the educated, elegant black who grew up as an equal with Shaw during their childhood at the Utopian experimental Brook Farm in the 1840s, only to awkwardly find himself serving in Shaw's command. That part went instead to André Braugher, who would later achieve full stardom and critical acclaim via TV's *Homicide*. Denzel instead chose the kind of part that, at that time, which might have seemed a natural for a tough-guy actor like Lou Gossett Jr.: Trip, a rugged runaway slave. Denzel described Trip as "raw and rough—a field Negro, not a house Negro, and he's a real survivor." The shift away from typecasting was an important career move but far from easy to pull off: "It was difficult to break myself down and become a primitive man; that was the challenge of this part."

Denzel's performances had heretofore been role models for black males in the audience, showing just what could be achieved, as well as moral lessons for whites, vividly illustrating that blacks could be their equals or superiors in every walk of modern, sophisticated life. Understandably, then, there was a certain amount of pain involved in portraying someone as "basic" as Trip. "He's a man who says words like 'onliest,'" Denzel recalled, touched by the plight of pre-Emancipation African Americans. " 'Onliest!'" Journalist Glenn Collins, a visitor to the set, noticed that it visibly pained Denzel to even mouth the kind of broken English that Trip speaks as a matter of course. Collins observed the actor as he shook his head sadly, in contemplation, then continued. "I've played a lot of the clean-cut roles, the intelligent parts." Then Denzel caught himself in error; education and intelligence are not one and the same. Trip's tragedy is not that he's unintelligent, although his lack of language skills might suggest that to the unwary. Rather, it's that he's been denied, as were most blacks of his time, the education that could have allowed Trip to blossom. "Not that Trip isn't intelligent! He's very cunning, a brilliant survivor. And then, one day, he finds himself in a place where he can make a difference."

That day, of course, is when Trip realizes that as a member of the Fifty-Fourth he can help prove, within the military microcosm, the equality of blacks in battle, hopefully suggesting to the greater macrocosm that blacks can, given the opportunity, prove their equality in all other fields as well, if given the opportunity. Trip is the most interesting among the film's black characters, the only one who "arcs" during the narrative's course. The others immediately appreciate, even idolize, Shaw as a rare, "righteous" white man, their nineteenth-century equivalent to Schindler and his Jews in *Schindler's List* (1993). Not so Trip, who, owing to ugly experiences in life, remains cynical and pessimistic to the last. "He's an instigator," Washington explained. "Wild, rebellious, angry. He's a product of racism who's *become* a racist. He hates all white people. Confederates most of all. But finally, in the end, when he sees the white officers make the maximum sacrifice, he [becomes] the most patriotic one of the bunch."

Importantly, *Glory* does not share Trip's initial antiwhite bias, instead presenting the character's bias as an understandable, if not necessarily legitimate, attitude for a black man who has never known righteous whites. The film is constructed so that we—black and white audiences alike—witness Trip's "moral education." He finally realizes that all whites are not alike and accepts the greater good that someone like Shaw wants to accomplish. The vision of the movie, then, is staunchly integrationist rather than black separatist, not surprisingly so, since it was made by white liberals—the contemporary equivalents of Shaw himself. "I love the Fifty-fourth!" Trip calls out around a nighttime campfire, announcing his character's change. During the final battle, it is Trip who seizes the fallen banner from a dead soldier and patriotically raises it on high.

No wonder, then, that in the final shot, Trip and Shaw are at last seen embracing, if only in death; they are the nineties version of Tony Curtis and Sidney Poitier in *The Defiant Ones* (1958), the white man and the black who experienced an at best difficult relationship but were eventually united, through shared experience, in the end embracing (by physically embracing each other) the fraternity of *all* men. Here, though, the vision is considerably darker than in *The Defiant Ones*. For the two men unite in death, not life. Nevertheless, the consistent final image of both films visually states the civil rights attitudes of the filmmakers.

So Denzel finally had the longed-for chance to stretch himself as an actor; one reason he won the Best Supporting Actor Oscar for this role, beyond his brilliant performance, was that he so effectively cut new ground. He also was able to address an issue he cared very much about; on the set, Denzel spoke fervently of the 1860s as a time "when black soldiers withstood an unbelievable amount of abuse. There was even a big debate about giving blacks guns." As historian Shelby Foote (*The Civil War: A Narrative*) explained, "Whites were afraid they'd be murdered in their beds." The film was made as much to expose this kind of hysterical fear, which existed even in the North, as it was to tell the specific story of the Fifty-fourth. This helps explain why the filmmakers took several liberties with the precise particulars of history in order to achieve their intended overview. Most members of the Fifty-fourth were educated Northerners, not an amalgam of such freedmen and former Southern slaves, as the movie suggests. But as Pulitzer Prize–winning historian James M. McPherson notes, this particular outfit was singled out to serve as a greater symbol for all of the 166 Negro regiments: "This is a film not simply about the 54th Massachusetts, but about blacks in the Civil War. Most of the black soldiers were slaves until a few months, even a few days, before they joined up. . . . That is the real story told by *Glory*. That is why most of the soldiers are depicted as former slaves."

To accomplish this, *Glory* follows the outfit through training and into various combat situations, culminating in the July 18, 1863, attack on Battery Wagner, a key fortification of Charleston, South

Carolina. To prove beyond anyone's doubt the courage of his men, Shaw volunteered the Fifty-fourth for what was known to be a suicide mission; some outfit had to launch a hopeless frontal attack on the fort, drawing away the attention of Confederate riflemen and artillery batteries, while other units slipped around behind. One-half of the Fifty-fourth's enlisted men were killed, total casualties reaching 1,515, including Shaw, dead early in the combat.

The moviemakers, working in a straight-faced and nonironic manner, apparently take such old-fashioned sacrifice at face value, while some contemporary viewers perceive this as a foolish waste. Pauline Kael went so far as to suggest, in the *New Yorker*, that "we in the audience, with our inescapably modern attitudes, can't help wondering if Shaw, in volunteering his regiment for the honor of being massacred, wasn't doing just what his racist superior officers hoped for"—creating a virtual genocide of young black men! Stanley Kauffmann of the *New Republic* offered an opposing interpretation of that scene: "Possibly the film's best achievement is in making credible this urgency to fight. If you have ever seen a modern audience, particularly of young people, at an older film in which men talk about wanting to fight in a war and being willing, if need be, to die, you will know how extraordinary it is that Zwick and colleagues make the soldiers' sentiments compelling."

Glory had a strange, long, fascinating genesis, beginning on the day when a little boy named Kevin, growing up in Michigan, was given a set of lead Civil War soldiers on his birthday, immediately developing a lifelong fascination for the Blue and the Gray. As luck would have it, the family moved to Wyoming, where Kevin rode his horse daily while his Hemingwayesque father alternated between working as a rugged rancher and fashion photographer. Kevin moved again, to California, when his mother broke with Kevin's father and remarried, this time to Hollywood actor Brian Kelly, star of TV's *Flipper*.

So Kevin was introduced to "the industry," first doing work as an extra, then playing bit parts on the series. He was soon convinced that he wanted to be an actor, an idea that changed after his mother remarried once more, this time to musical composer Maurice Jarre, who adopted Kevin. Now named Kevin Jarre, he was with his third father figure when Maurice scored *Ryan's Daughter* (1970) for director

David Lean. The legendary filmmaker befriended Kevin and asked the youth what he wanted to do with his life. When Kevin replied "act," Lean recoiled in disgust. If Kevin wanted to make his mark on movies, Lean offered, he ought to be either a writer or a director or both. Impressed, Kevin asked if he ought to attend film school. Lean shrugged and shook his head no, insisting that anyone could pick up what he needed to know technically by hanging around movie sets for six months.

What to do, then? *"Read!"* Lean commanded, and Kevin did, accepting Lean's list of classics that ought to be mastered. Before long, Jarre had written *Rambo: First Blood Part II*, hardly an artistic triumph but a start nevertheless. He was hoping to collaborate on a future project with another writer whose wife happened to be a dancer; so it was that they accompanied her to the resort town of Saratoga Springs, where she would perform with the New York City Ballet while they scribed away. Never forgetting his boyhood, Jarre found recreational time to slip away and do some horseback riding. The friend's wife snapped a photo of him in an equestrian pose; her boss noticed the picture when she showed around her summer snapshots at work.

The ballet entrepreneur was Lincoln Kirstein. As fate would have it, he'd grown up on Beacon Hill in Boston. Lincoln's jaw literally dropped when he saw the picture, which vividly reminded him of something that had strongly impressed him as a child, an 1897 statue of the Beacon Hill area's great hero, Colonel Shaw, on horseback, leading his men to "glory." When Jarre and Kirstein were introduced a few days later at Mother Goldsmith's restaurant, Kirstein inquired whether Jarre had ever heard of the hero. Kevin admitted that being something of a Civil War buff, he had, though Shaw was merely one of many officers he'd read about. Kirstein launched into a full-scale retelling of the Shaw story, which he'd researched after being impressed by that August Saint-Gaudens statuary tribute to the Fifty-fourth; later, Kirstein had written a monograph entitled *Lay This Laurel* (the title taken from a poem by Emily Dickinson) about the regiment's history.

Jarre was overwhelmed by the epic proportions of the tale as well as the devotion with which Kirstein related it. Soon Jarre was devouring the monograph, which convinced him that he'd found material for a great screenplay. He then sought out Shaw's own published letters, poring over them before going on to *The Journal of Charlotte Forten*, penned by the colonel's fiancée, a character who would, during the process of rewriting, be eliminated owing to the necessities of making a manageable-length movie. Jarre checked into room 421 of New York's Gramercy Park Hotel, then set to work writing the script, which was completed in four weeks. Then came the difficult job of trying to sell it. Jarre was fully aware that *The Birth of a Nation* (1915) and *Gone With the Wind* (1939) were exceptions that prove the rule. most Civil War films have done notoriously bad at the box office because, as compared to other war movies, there are no good guys or bad guys; all the combatants are Americans. This, coupled with the fact that Hollywood did not consider any black projects (other than crime or comedy exploitation flicks) to be profitable, made it unlikely that *Glory* would ever reach the screen. Writing it was an act of love at the outset.

Jarre's first stop was Merchant-Ivory productions, where such art-house films as *Howards End* (1992) and *A Room With a View* (1986) had been gently nurtured to realization. But the gorier elements of war, coupled with the necessarily substantial budget, ruled it out there. An agent-friend then let director Bruce Beresford see the script; he quickly committed, bringing Freddie Fields on board as producer. Fields was instrumental in setting the film up at Columbia Pictures. Everything seemed to have clicked miraculously; they were on their way!

Wrong. Executives at Columbia, fully aware that several important pictures about the black experience by white filmmakers (*The Color Purple* [1985] among them) had drawn sharp criticism from African-American scholars, wanted to be certain that such a situation would not occur with their project. So they invited an esteemed black historian at the University of Virginia to read the script. He was outraged, insisting it was blatantly racist. To the amazement of Jarre and Fields, their long-overdue tribute to great but forgotten black Americans was about to be derailed by an African American. Columbia now had doubts. At that moment, studio head David Puttnam exited, and when he did, Beresford disassociated himself with the project, moving on to *Driving Miss Daisy* (1989). *Glory* appeared dead in the water.

Fields, though, had been bitten by the bug; now he, like Jarre, wanted more than anything to get the movie made. Reaching into his own pocket, Fields continued to bankroll the preproduction with funds from his own independent production company. "Getting this movie made became a real passion for me," he later recalled. Fields brought the script over to Tri-Star. There Edward Zwick (the director of *About Last Night* [1986]) took an interest. The movie was eventually made for $18 million, a relatively small sum when set against the $50 million–plus budgets then being lavished on empty, escapist blockbusters.

Still, Jarre and Fields considered themselves lucky to get that much following four years of stagnancy, just as others who became associated with *Glory* felt privileged to be working on the project. "All of us are making a financial sacrifice to do this movie," Jane Alexander (who plays an uncredited role as Shaw's mother) admitted; she, like the other stars, agreed to be in *Glory* for a considerably smaller paycheck than might have been forthcoming for a more commercial project. That was true of all the movie's stars, including the only African-American "name," Denzel Washington. It's worth noting, though, that black talent—including a thousand African Americans hired as extras—was not only in front of the camera. More than 30 percent of the filming crew (which numbered 180) was African American; so was the stunt coordinator and thirty of the stunt men.

Considering the limited means with which they had to bring a film of such immense ambition to life, Fields and Zwick had to themselves haul cameras and carry the tripods across Pennsylvania's Gettysburg battlefield, enabling their crew to capture images of "reenactors" engaged in a restaging of Pickett's Charge. This footage would later be edited into the film, adding to its scope at no great cost. Jarre, meanwhile, saved the production some money by playing the small part of a Union soldier who first baits Trip, then cheers him on before the final charge: "Go, Fifty-fourth!"

Timing had also been instrumental in *Glory* "happening." The movie could not, and would not, have been made if it weren't for the work then taking place far from Hollywood, in academic centers all over the country, where scholars—many motivated by the political-correctness movement—were busy working on revisionist tracts which reevaluated history. Gradually, books and articles surfaced, the new ideas in time making their way into mainstream publications; likewise, college history teachers passed such information along to students, the ideas continuing to trickle into the general consciousness. No wonder, then, that the *New York Times* tagged *Glory* as "something of a highlight film of the new scholarship documenting the largely unrecognized role of black" Americans.

One of the film's most disturbing sequences details the real-life incident in which Colonel Shaw addresses his soldiers with horrible news: "You men enlisted in this regiment with the understanding that you would be paid the regular army wage of thirteen dollars a month. I have been notified that since you are a colored regiment, you will be paid ten dollars a month." Additionally, his men will not receive the three-dollar clothing money that white troops received, nor, for that matter, will they be issued shoes. As the black soldiers listen in stunned silence to this information, Shaw—visibly disgusted by the government's decision but, as an officer and a gentleman, determined to carry out his orders to the best of his abilities—then solemnly intones: "Regiment! Fall out to receive pay!"

As the other soldiers waver, Trip stands tall. The remarkable voice of Denzel Washington cuts through the stony silence like lightning: "Tear it up!" he calls out. As he does, Trip holds a pay waver in the air and repeats, "Tear it up!" As the philosophical Rawlins, Morgan Freeman agrees in word and deed, and now they are two; then, one by one, the others all join in.

"Tear it up!" the men chant in unison. "Tear it up!"

Then, they do; what appears to be a hail of confetti fills the air as the men rip their pay vouchers to shreds and fling them in the air, defiantly making clear that rather than inequal (or unequal) pay, they won't accept any money at all. Allowing himself the luxury of a slight smile of pleasure at the rightness of his men's actions, Colonel Shaw tears up his own officer's paycheck to make it clear that he is at one with them. Historically speaking, it was Shaw who suggested to his men that they engage in such a protest; the filmmakers, rewriting history to accommodate their modern audience, had Trip be the instigating figure, thereby assigning such positive action to one of the black characters. At any rate, the protest—and, above all, Shaw's angry letter-writing campaign to Washington, D.C.—did have the desired effect: In 1864, Congress finally approved a measure guaranteeing equal pay for the new black outfits, the Fifty-fourth included.

The question of offering what seemed to be an accurate depiction of history (thanks to the precise detail of such elements as uniforms and weaponry) while in fact presenting a 1990s politically-correct portrayal of events from the previous century became a major issue. There were those who claimed that Matthew Broderick, best known for roles in youth films like John Hughes's *Ferris Bueller's Day Off* (1986), had been cast not because he was right for the role but because of his vast audience appeal. Producer Fields scoffed at this notion, claiming: "He's not playing it safe in a Matthew Broderick role for a Matthew Broderick audience." True enough, Broderick stretched as an actor and performed commendably. On the other hand, Fields could hardly deny that dozens of less popular actors might have done just as well or that Fields wouldn't be pleased to learn that the already existing "Matthew Broderick audience" was lured into theaters where *Glory* played because of its star presence. Likewise, Zwick had to answer charges that he'd yuppified the material for his own generation: "I can't exactly remember who was the first to joke about *Glory* as being '1860-something,'" he laughingly admits, referring to his own hit TV series *thirtysomething*.

Jane Alexander consciously played Sarah Shaw not merely as a historical figure but, considering Sarah's women's rights attitude as well as her abolitionism, as a precursor of today's feminists. Is this true of Denzel's character, Trip, as well? Vincent Canby of the *New York Times* observed that "Denzel Washington, an actor clearly on his way to a major screen career, functions as the film's [probably necessary] late-20th-century black sensibility." Pauline Kael noted the early scenes in which Trip taunts the elegant, educated Searles as "a nigger who talks like a white man," nicknaming Searles "Snowflake":

> The putdown recalls the taunts in black exploitation pictures, and Trip's snarling manner recalls a whole raft of angry young men strutting their stuff. Trip's cynicism about white men has an inflammatory, rabble-rousing appeal for movie audiences. His style of defiance is *modern*; so is Washington's acting style. When

he's about to be whipped, he pulls open his shirt and flips his hands in the air in a gesture that spells out "Method Actor." He has a modern charge of ferocity; you're aware that it's anachronistic, yet it lifts you up. . . . You half expect Trip to proclaim himself a man of the Third World.

As to the whipping sequence, Denzel has admitted that he is hesitant about appearing in historical movies due to his reluctance to be involved with what he refers to as "slave films." The great fear is that they revive ugly images of past inequities, while reinforcing an old cliche from which African Americans want and need to remove themselves. On the other hand, Denzel notes: "The bottom line is that, as a black American, that's my history." So choice of material becomes essential. Avoiding anything on the order of *Mandingo* (1975)—those movies which superficially revive images of black men in bondage for exploitative, even pornographic, purposes—he feels compelled, however, to do such scenes when, as in *Glory*, they are presented for educational reasons within the context of a "serious" project. Considering the context, Denzel insisted to the press that he was proud, rather than embarrassed, of the scene in which Trip is whipped after leaving camp without first receiving official authority.

Civil War historians insist that an enlightened officer like Shaw would never have allowed one of his men to be whipped for a minor infraction. The filmmakers were aware of this, but once again decided to err on a minor historical point in order to be true to a larger historical issue: Such punishment did indeed exist, and they felt it necessary to remind their audience of this ugly fact. Denzel Washington wholeheartedly agreed with their decision: "Whipping—it's a very basic nightmare in American history." Ironically, he felt less pain than his costars: "It was tougher on the others than it was for me"; they were forced to observe but not interfere. "They realized that this is the way it was. It sickened them."

He bonded with the actor who had to wield the whip and who was having a hard time doing it, continually trying to ease up and make it as mild for Denzel as he could. "I had to tell him, 'Look like you're really doing it!'" In the scene, Trip manages to keep himself from ever crying out in pain, denying the officers the satisfaction of seeing this black man break; but when the punishment is finished, a single tear can be seen slipping down his cheek. The touch is memorable, but as Denzel admits, "That wasn't planned. It just happened. I was thinking, There is nothing else that they can do to me. These are tears of defiance, really."

But does that "defiance," as Kael claims, imply the intrusion of a modern African-American sensibility onto the past century when in fact things were different? Richard Bernstein, in the *New York Times*, insisted that "Denzel Washington seems at moments to be a somewhat backdated Black Panther," while John Simon of the *National Review* saw Trip as an anachronistically portrayed "streetwise, scornful ghetto black, and Washington plays him for full contemporary relevance." Denzel does not agree: "There were a lot of black soldiers like Trip. They were rowdy, they spoke out when they could, and some of them were killed. [When, like Trip, they first escaped from their slave origins], some went on to be loners. They lived in the woods, in caves, did whatever they could to stay away from the reach of their masters. Some of them later become scouts. The job was perfect for them. [So Trip] is *not* a twentieth-century invention."

Another key issue, one worthy of some debate, is the film's attitude toward war. A great deal of flag-waving, the final moment by Denzel himself, is on view here; the orchestral musical score, augmented by a boys' choir, is inspiring in an old-fashioned, patriotic kind of way. Zwick "wanted to show [the men] realistically but with a hint of reverence," Kauffmann explained. But he insisted that the overall tone was antiwar: "*Glory* contains no scenes of battle as glory; it is all brutal killing with gun and bayonet. The film isn't warmongering; it's the depiction of oppressed men with the means at hand to end oppression," that means being war. Not everyone agreed: In *Maclean's*, Brian D. Johnson described the movie's approach as "elegiac...The battle scenes are graphically brutal yet lyrical. In *Glory*, war is equal parts hell and heaven." Canby tagged the film's overall tone "celebratory," while Glenn Collins noted that "on one level, *Glory* is a lads-marching-off-to-war movie of the kind that Hollywood rarely makes these days" but which were highly popular during both World War I (*The Big Parade* [1925]) and World War II (*Back to Bataan* [1945]).

Though *Glory* does end on a grim, gory note, there is—as the title implies—an element of gloriousness to the film's vision of war. Bernstein noted:

> In many respects, *Glory* marks a return to an earlier conception of movie-making about war. It is a large-scale panorama with a cast of literally thousands depicting battle as the supreme test of manhood.... For several years now, as the movies have focused on the Vietnam War, combat has come to be portrayed as destructive not only of life and limb but also of personal values.... In *Glory* war is clearly hell. Nonetheless, the battlefield in *Glory* is presented as an arena wherein individual men come to have respect for one another. War is a place of ultimate questions and ultimate confrontations that forge brotherhood among men.

Is *Glory* simply a John Wayne–style, old-fashioned Hollywood rah-rah war film, *Top Gun* (1986) on the ground more than a hundred years earlier, only this time done with black actors playing the squad that used to be composed of white actors? "The film is honest in its depiction of the battles," Denzel says in the film's defense. "If that makes you want to go out and kill people, I guess that's up to you. It could just as easily cause revulsion. But you do have to remember that the only way we could get our freedom was with the sacrifice of blood."

The most significant issue, though, is the one already raised by *Cry Freedom*: dramatizing a story about the historical role of blacks by focusing on a white protagonist. All the officers are white; that is simply a matter of record, there being no black officers at all until after the Civil War, when Henry O. Flipper became the first African American to graduate from West Point, afterward serving in the frontier army. "After all," Denzel said, "the regiment's officers *were* white. That's historically correct, and you *have* to portray it that way." True enough; to have featured a black officer as a "role model" would be to sacrifice historical authenticity even further for the sake of political correctness; it's important that movies like *Glory* remind us of the way things were, however wrong they happened to be, so we can, as a sage once wrote, learn from history, then hopefully *not* be doomed to repeat it.

Denzel—still relatively fresh from the *Cry Freedom* experience—

admitted on the set: "I did express my concern to Ed and Freddie that the movie not be about whites, and I think the script reflects this." Veteran actor Morgan Freeman agreed with Denzel: "I think the movie has a good balance, focusing on both the story of Shaw, and the struggle of his men." To a degree that is true; *Glory* does alternate between the two. Yet to describe such a "balance" is to ironically imply an imbalance. Shaw, not the other white officers (seen in supporting roles), is set on one side of the scales of justice; the four key black characters (Trip, Rawlins, Sharts, and Searles), on the other. No one black character is given as much weight as Shaw.

Moreover, the movie *begins* with Shaw's creating the Fifty-fourth, then gradually introduces the black characters; they are perceived within the context of *his* story. As with *Cry Freedom*, a filmmaker certainly must have the right to tell the story he wants and chooses to tell; since the writer, producer, and director were all white, it's hardly a shock that they would gravitate (as Richard Attenborough had previously) to the story's benign white character. Besides, some might argue that the officer in charge of the outfit is the most logical person on whom to focus. That, however, is not necessarily true. For example, *The Battle of the Bulge* (1965), a movie about World War II's famous fighting in the Ardennes Forest, focused on the American commanding officer, played by Henry Fonda; yet another, and far superior film, *Battleground* (1949), barely even mentions the officers' names, focusing instead on the individual fighting men who glimpse their commander only at a distance.

A true "black film" about the Fifty-fourth would have offered precisely that, either with one African-American character (perhaps Denzel's) employed as the film's focus or from a standpoint shared by all four key black characters equally, ensemble style, as was the case with the aforementioned *Battleground* (which, of course, had concerned white soldiers). *Glory*, then, is not a black film, but a film about an enlightened white man who helped open the doors for black Americans. As that, it must be judged; it that, it happens to be extremely good. We are richer for it existing. That does not alleviate the problem, however. Ambitious films focusing on black characters are still few and far between.

Denzel, nevertheless, defended *Glory* from such charges, insisting that it was "not at all like *Cry Freedom*, where the last part of the movie was *only* about the white characters. The film is the story of a black regiment." When speaking to anyone arguing the other way, Denzel—ignoring any limitations, emphasizing the positive qualities—eyeballed the individual interviewer, insisting in a voice that allowed for no further discussion: "I think that the men of the Fifty-fourth would have liked the way we told their story."

8

Mo' Better Blues

1990

A UNIVERSAL RELEASE

CAST: Denzel Washington (*Bleek Gilliam*); Spike Lee (*Giant*); Wesley Snipes (*Shadow Henderson*); Giancarlo Esposito (*Left-Hand Lacey*); Robin Harris (*Butterbean Jones*); Joie Lee (*Indigo Downes*); Bill Nunn (*Bottom Hammer*); Cynda Williams (*Clarke Bentancourt*); John Turturro and Nicholas Turturro (*Flatbush Brothers*); Abbey Lincoln (*Lillian Gilliam*).

CREDITS: Director, producer, screenplay, Spike Lee; coproducer, Monty Ross; cinematography, Ernest Dickerson; editor, Sam Pollard; music, Bill Lee; production design, Wynn Thomas; costumes, Ruth E. Carter; rating, R; running time, 127 min.

Not in any way a nice guy—at all" is how, during the shooting of the Spike Lee film that would eventually come to be called *Mo' Better Blues*, Denzel described his character, the trumpet-playing bandleader Bleek Gilliam. Clearly, the career stretch that he had begun with *Glory* was now being taken further. Anyone hoping to drape a Poitier mantle over Denzel's shoulders would have to think again, as this young actor once again essayed a portrait of a fallible and imperfect man—the very kind of character that, a generation earlier, Super Sidney (as he came to be called) abandoned in order to provide the idealized role models Denzel knew would in time constrain a versatile actor's career.

As Lee worked on early drafts (originally called *Love Supreme* in homage to a noted John Coltrane composition), he formulated a story in which the charismatic Bleek keeps his quintet's jazz as pure as possible. Bleek steadfastly refuses to mainstream the music for the sake of commercial success. Bleek's foil is band member Shadow (Wesley Snipes), who ultimately sells out for easy stardom. But pure jazz means everything to Bleek. That's why he cannot commit to any one woman, bounding back and forth between schoolteacher Indigo (Joie Lee) and aspiring singer Clarke (Cynda Williams). Bleek is either professionally dedicated or pathetically self-absorbed, depending on one's point of view. His only real loyalty is to a boyhood pal, Giant (Spike Lee), the band's manager who gambles away their earnings. Ultimately, Giant proves to be the Achilles' heel that will destroy Bleek's career: Trying to rescue the diminutive loser from loan sharks, the trumpeter is so badly beaten on the face and lips that he can no longer play.

Though *Mo' Better Blues* was a work of fiction, Lee drew heavily on the jazz milieu he witnessed firsthand as a child. At the movie's end, Bleek turns his back on the ambitious diva to marry the schoolteacher; Lee's own mother, Jacquelyn Shelton Lee, supported the Lee family (there were five children) when bassist Bill Lee's own musical career faltered owing to his own similar insistence on integrity. During the 1970s, most jazz combos embraced the electric Fender bass, its big beat allowing for easy conversion to the then popular "fusion" sound. Bill Lee didn't care for rock or pop and was soon out of work. To suggest just such a situation, Lee wrote a scene in which Bleek turns down a chance to perform with the pop star Sade rather than tone down his absolute-jazz approach. Though the sequence didn't make it to the final draft, Lee's attitude permeates the finished film. (Such a noncompromising approach, it's worth noting, is precisely the opposite of Denzel's. Although he knew *Cry Freedom* would not be the Biko biography he wanted to do, he went ahead anyway, insisting compromise was necessary and what could be achieved would be better than nothing at all.)

Denzel believes that one must go on working, making the acceptable compromises necessary to continue; Lee argues that any compromise is, essentially, total corruption. Lee became embroiled in an ugly scene involving CBS Records, the company scheduled to distribute the soundtrack album for *Mo' Better Blues*. Executives there never expected the filmmaker to react strongly when they announced plans to release what the *New York Times* described as a "softened and sweetened version" of the song "Harlem Blues," which would have crossover appeal and be played on M.O.R. radio stations, thereby increasing consumer interest in both the soundtrack and the movie itself. Lee, recalling his father's battles of a generation earlier, balked at the idea; either people would experience Harlem jazz as it was meant to be heard or they would not experience it at all.

However, there was a practical side to Lee, who admitted: "An artist has to be a businessman today. Money means a lot. It equals power. If my films did not make the money they make, I couldn't make the demands that I make." One such demand was to employ the largely black cast and crew members he has formed, through the twin powers of will and talent, into an ongoing filmmaking family, on the order of those assembled by the Jewish Woody Allen and the Italian Martin Scorsese. Three of the key actors in *Mo' Better Blues*—Giancarlo Esposito, Bill Nunn, and Spike's sister Joie Lee—had been with Lee since his student filmmaker days, when mentor Martin Scorsese assured the young Lee that he did have the talent to make it; Lee met Scorsese when, after graduating from Atlanta's Morehouse College, he moved on to New York University, where Scorsese was teaching and producing his own early efforts. Wesley Snipes, who joined the stock company with *Mo' Better,* would shortly thereafter star in Lee's next film, *Jungle Fever* (1991).

Also essential to Lee's 40 Acres and a Mule production team were cinematographer Ernest Dickerson and production designer Wynn Thomas. They had long since proven their ability to collaborate on creating the unique Spike Lee look: a visual iconography which at first glance appears relatively realistic but, on closer examination, is heightened slightly in the direction of surrealism. Each element in every shot is given an extra edge that, taken together, conveys the sensation that we are looking at the world not as it objectively is but as it appears in the subjective perception of Lee, who, in successive films, shares his consistent, albeit developing, "take" with us. Lee's chosen subject, according to journalist

Samuel G. Freedman, is "the abundant black life that exists between the Cosby show and the crack house, the sort of life that rarely merits headlines, much less feature films"—that vast majority of black Americans who are neither rich nor poor.

No wonder, then, that the musician played by Denzel Washington would, despite his special profession, be depicted as living in a nice, normal middle-class development. Lee chose Beneath the Underdog as the name for the club that provides one of the film's settings, owing to jazz great Charles Mingus's insistence that jazz musicians were so far down on the social scale of things, they occupied that not-so-lofty place. Rather than shoot in some actual Manhattan club, Lee and his designer, Wynn Thomas, created their own symbolic place, concocting a composite of all the legendary clubs from years gone by. Beneath the Underdog is complete with a gold lamé fan spread across the length of the stage and a vivid 1930s-style silhouette of the New York skyline pointing upward toward twinkling lights in a dark night's sky.

Lee then worked closely with costume designer Ruth E. Carter to ensure that the agreed-upon look would be complemented by the clothing. Though the film is set in the present, suits worn by band members look to be out of the 1930s and 1940s, making visually clear that these performers belong to a classic tradition. One band member was even given a Thelonius Monk–type beret, another a Lester Young hat, suggesting that this is a crystallized portrait of classic jazz. The music, composed by Bill Lee and Branford Marsalis, meanwhile, aspired to the semblance of a jazz phantasmagoria. This mélange was complemented by the club's wall paintings, which evoked the Harlem Renaissance; the entire mis-en-scène causing critic Thulani Davis to coin the term "Afro-Deco" in response.

While his collaborators busily created the film's seductive demimonde, Spike continued to hone his central character. Bleek would emerge as a composite of varying jazz musicians from the past, sporting a haircut similar to John Coltrane's but delivering trumpet solos (performed by Terence Blanchard) in a performance style reminiscent of Miles Davis. Bleek, in Lee's conception, would emerge as a kind of jazz Everyman. "Musicians are low-priced slaves, whereas athletes and entertainers are high-priced slaves," Lee announced in his characteristically blunt manner. "It's their music, but it's not their nightclubs. A lot of money can be made off black artists, and a lot of what racism is about is financial gain."

Anti-Establishment, even anti-American, thinking underscores Lee's statement; he believes that racism and capitalism are fundamentally—perhaps, inextricably—tied together in our system. Transfer Lee's attitudes toward the realm of motion pictures and it isn't difficult to believe that his views on "nightclubs" spill over to the "studios" as well. Lee would probably agree with those black artists who endlessly dream of, and sometimes scheme to create, an all-black studio. Significantly, this is an approach Denzel has scoffed at. Spike's views appear almost antithetical to those of Denzel, who has never envisioned himself as a slave, low- or high-priced. As opposed to Lee, whose films are about the black community, Denzel has consistently expressed a view of himself as an artist whose color should not be considered.

So why did they collaborate? From early on in the planning stages, Lee had been consciously aware that this movie would mark a turning point in his career. The casting of Denzel was basic to his conception. "Of all the films I've written," he explained to visitors on the set, "this is the least ensemble style piece. It's Denzel's movie." Previous Spike Lee "joints"—She's Gotta Have It (1986), School Daze (1988), Do The Right Thing (1989)—focused on a wide spectrum of mostly black characters, played by lesser known, if not necessarily less talented, actors. The movies were then shot, either to maintain integrity or out of sheer financial necessity, on miniscule budgets. Nonetheless, those movies (and their relative box-office success) had established Lee as a force to be reckoned with by the powers-that-be. Though the $9.9 million Lee was allowed, by Universal, to lavish on this, his first true "studio" film, might not be comparable to the gargantuan amounts squandered on massive crowd pleasers, it allowed Lee his first shot at the big leagues.

Though Denzel, at this point, was not yet considered as bankable as, say, Kevin Costner, he was clearly on his way to achieving just such status. In only a few years Denzel would be commanding $10 million a movie, more than the entire budget for Mo' Better Blues. Following the Oscar for Glory, he enjoyed widespread critical acclaim as well as growing audience appeal. Such a star was precisely what the writer-director required. For the first time, he needed a headliner who was highly talented but also a verifiable matinee idol, able to cut across racial barriers and attract a wider audience. At the moment, there was only one such person.

"He's magnetic," Lee said of Denzel, for whom he specifically tailored the role of Bleek. "He's a great actor, and women love him." While in the process of casting the film, Lee made it a point to catch Denzel in *Checkmates* on Broadway. Though the show was not a hit, Denzel's charisma came through. "The minute he came [out] onstage," Lee recalls, "all the women started *oohing* and *aahing* and that kind of stuff. *Women love them some Denzel!*" However, Lee initially remained cautious, believing that Denzel had seriously compromised himself by going along with Attenborough's approach to *Cry Freedom*, then agreeing to appear in *Heart Condition*, an upcoming comedy that reduced the issue of racism to a vulgar joke.

Lee perceived his own films as alternatives to such stuff. "The more films I do—that [means all the] more options, more roles for black artists. They might not have to do those other type of roles. I think [exposure to my films by a large audience] has an impact because I think people aren't going to buy that bullshit as before. The more successful my films are, it lets Hollywood know that white audiences go to a film with a black lead in it, too." So while disparaging such movies as *Cry Freedom* and *Heart Condition*, Lee took a defensive attitude toward Denzel's decisions to go with those projects: "A black actor is not going to get the quality roles, quality scripts, offered to him that are offered to a De Niro or Jack Nicholson or anybody of that [acting] caliber [who doesn't happen to be black]. That's just reality."

A "reality," it's important to note, that Denzel would continue to demolish by competing with those actors for racially nonspecific parts. In blaming the situation on the system itself, Spike Lee took the opposite approach from the one Denzel has taken throughout his career. (In fact, with *The Pelican Brief, Philadelphia, Crimson Tide,* and *Courage Under Fire,* he would all but disprove Lee's thesis, showing that talent will win out over color.) Also important is that Lee's words about black actors are reminiscent of what he had to say about black musicians; though, as a movie star, Denzel was already relatively high priced. In Lee's view Denzel was an expensive slave, owned by the white Establishment. However vivid Lee's depiction of the jazz world may be, by implication *Mo' Better Blues* can be considered a movie about the movie industry, with the Shylockian club owners serving as satirized stand-ins for movie moguls Lew Wasserman and Sidney Sheinberg.

While the combination of Washington and Lee (the best black actor of his time at last working for the most talented black writer-director around) may have seemed a natural to some, the partnership represented an uneasy merger. With Denzel onboard, some sort of a compromise—dreaded word to Lee, positive one in Denzel's vocabulary—had to be reached. That compromise proved possible because of Denzel's respect for Lee's talent and what he hopes to achieve. "Well, have you written your own version?" Denzel has repeatedly told blacks who complain about the way they're treated in films made by whites. "The solution is to make your own. And that's the solution Spike Lee takes."

Lee's films strike out with artistic anger against antiblack bigotry, each successive joint offering some new variation on the same loudly proclaimed message; Spike's films are about characters who are black and the issues they must deal with as African Americans. Though Denzel may not actually employ the word "assimilation" when expressing his point of view, most of his movie roles and certainly his own lifestyle combat racism by illustrating the successful assimilation of blacks into the mainstream. Even the sleek, elegant way he dresses—wearing fashionably casual clothes no different from those of a white star of comparable status might choose—advances this notion. Lee, conversely, prefers to affect an ethnically funky appearance, decking himself out in a maroon zoot suit (while directing as well as when on-camera), capped by his trademark turned-about cap. Lee's movies call out for a preservation of the unique ghetto culture as a part of a black nationalism movement. One man is a symbol of Afrocentricity; the other, of integration.

Denzel and Spike, then, composed not a natural alliance of talents but rather a moviemaking odd couple. As Denzel put it, "I don't have as much of an agenda as Spike does. I'm not trying to move people in any area. It's just the movie business, you know." They communicated their respective philosophies, and their give-and-take turned up on-screen, to the detriment of the film. *Mo'*

Better Blues offers a strange, even confused message. In a bizarre, unsatisfying way, the film begins as Spike's vision of art in relationship to life, only to end as Denzel's statement on the same subject. Lee's concept was simple enough: To emerge as a true artist, a man must put his chosen medium above all else, including his woman and children. Both of Bleek's women complain that he gives them very little, though in its first act, *Mo' Better Blues* appears to be saying that for any genuine artist rather than the mere journeyman this is the way it is, should, and must be, however difficult or delicate the situation.

Even when enjoying sex, the true artist is, on some level, still thinking about his art, perhaps even how he will translate the joys of sex into a song. One early image depicts Bleek in bed with a lover, unconsciously moving his hand from her beautiful body to reach out and touch his nearby trumpet. As Samuel G. Freedman noted in the *New York Times:* "The camera lingers almost lecherously over the womanly curves of a trumpet and saxophone. As simple as the shot seems at that moment, over the course of the movie it becomes a powerful and shifting metaphor," the artistic instrument being Bleek's only great love object. Women come and women go, but jazz remains this man's mistress.

Denzel, on the other hand, has always put family first, career second. He insistently believes that with enough concentration and effort, he can and will balance the two, his human concerns always taking precedence over the artistic. He is at odds with the character he was called upon to play and, more importantly still, with the filmmaker for whom Bleek initially serves as mouthpiece. That helps explain why, toward the end, Bleek and the film do an astounding about-face. Instead of being tragically ruined by the beating that renders him unable to perform, Bleek embraces the situation, proposing to and marrying Indigo, opting for the straight-and-narrow, self-sacrificing life as opposed to the selfish world of the artist. He makes a living at a normal job, lovingly raises his kids, and appears happy, even relieved, that he can no longer play the trumpet. The film concludes with a ten-minute dissolve montage in which this family's perfect sense of domestic bliss is visually chronicled. Corny, sappy, and conventional in a Washington way, this completely contradicts the thrust of the film's Lee-dominated first half.

Despite their significant differences in attitude, it isn't difficult to understand why Denzel would have been attracted to certain elements in Spike's emerging script. The essential ambition was to show the jazz artist, black or white, as he had never before been presented on-screen. Lee was adamant that the numbers be performed in their entirety; in most jazz films, only musical fragments are presented, the filmmaker cutting away to atmospheric interludes. More significant still, Lee had recoiled in dismay at Clint Eastwood's *Bird* (1988) and Bertrand Tavernier's *Round Midnight* (1986), both films extending the myth that jazz musicians are dependent in nature and invariably hung up on drugs that ultimately destroy them. They are, according to such movies, doomed natural geniuses, managing to create moments of great music via sudden bursts of improvisational genius before expiring early. Though this may be true of some jazz artists, Lee considered them the exception rather than the norm.

Having observed his own father and his various colleagues over a period of years, Lee drew his own conclusion: Most jazzmen are self-sufficient, avoiding drug and alcohol addiction. They labor at length to master the necessary skills, practicing by the hour. In Lee's movie, his jazz musicians would be depicted as conscious craftsmen, achieving lofty reputations through hard work. This fit in well with Denzel's own ongoing comments about the need for concentrated effort on the part of actors, other artists, or anyone who wants to excel at whatever it is he does in life.

Moreover, Lee wanted to avoid another cliché he found offensive: the ongoing movie myth of the black male corrupted by his love for a seductively dangerous white woman. His jazzmen would experience good and bad relationships with women of color rather than relying on the "white bitch" notion that harkened back to 1970s black-exploitation flicks in which the good black hero is nearly corrupted by a white woman, only to find redemption in the arms of a "sister." This approach let Denzel off the hook, considering his difficulty with interracial love scenes in *The Mighty Quinn* and *Love Field*.

Nevertheless, the film's sex sequences—involving the two black women in Bleek's life—proved highly problematic. The great irony is that this first true romantic black idol of mainstream moviegoers has a terrible time performing love scenes, whatever the woman's color.

Denzel's mastering the trumpet so that the audience would believe he was actually playing could be accomplished through hours of diligent study with jazz great Miles Davis himself; slipping into bed with one or the other of his gorgeous leading ladies proved something of a nightmare. Also ironic: When initially asked what attracted him to Lee as a filmmaker, Denzel responded, "What I liked about Spike's first film was that it hit some points that hadn't been hit in movies, like black people kissing on film. I can recall feeling uncomfortable watching black people kiss in *She's Gotta Have It*. We're not used to seeing that." Apparently, watching is one thing, performing quite another. Responding to one (female) interviewer's questions about Denzel's upcoming romantic scenes, the ordinarily sophisticated, unflappable, articulate actor suddenly sounded like an awkward teenager: "Yeah, it's a departure, in dealing with two women in one movie, yes. A love story with black women. This is the most sexually charged film I've done, I guess you'd say. Or—we'll see."

When those sequences were finally completed, he and Lee admitted that this aspect of the work led to heated tensions. "It's too fleshy for my taste," Denzel reflected. "I don't like feeling the way I felt during those scenes. And [Spike] knew, 'cause we always had arguments on those days. Those were things I didn't want to shoot." Lee laughingly confided to interviewers that Denzel was so uncomfortable with sex scenes, he repeatedly refused to take his shirt off. In order to get through one particularly hot bedroom sequence, Denzel played it all in his undershirt.

There were other problems as well. While filming this intense movie, Denzel was constantly campaigning for the Best Supporting Oscar (he'd been nominated for *Glory*) by doing as much publicity as possible. This dual responsibility regularly forced him to rush away from the set, after completing a scene, to hype himself and further his chances of winning (he eventually did), heightening the already evident dichotomy between the two sides of Denzel: the serious actor attempting to give his all for a personalized project by an ambitious artist; and the Hollywood star, hoping to score the biggest and best of all pop-culture awards. It's to Denzel's credit that he managed to turn in a fine performance *and* win the Oscar without showing any sign of strain on the big screen when *Mo' Better Blues* finally appeared or on the small screen when he graciously accepted his statuette. Indeed, part of the magic of Denzel is his seemingly effortless ability to balance the two sides of his life, though doubtless it takes a major effort, one that he's too smart, too subtle, and too sophisticated to ever let us see.

Members of Lee's ongoing community of craftsmen did notice that while Denzel was working with them, he never really became one of them. Several Lee regulars openly commented on the fact that Denzel kept almost entirely to himself, in his dressing room, rather than fraternize with cast and crew between takes. When various people tried to engage him in polite small talk on those occasions when Denzel did emerge from his self-imposed isolation, he brushed past everybody—never rude, though polite in a reserved, slightly aloof way—making a beeline for the set, where he would film the next scene before heading back to the privacy of his room.

Once more, that Denzel dichotomy made itself felt. The "African American and damned proud of it!" side was aware of the warm sense of camaraderie on Lee's set, a feeling that hadn't existed on the white-dominated projects with which Denzel previously was associated. But the star felt alternately charmed by and concerned about such a situation. Because there was always the other side, the "my color is not important, but my craft is" side. If he hung out and became pals with everyone, he would carry pleasant feelings with him when he stepped in front of the camera. But the whole point about Bleek Gilliam is that he's a loner, alienated from everyone. As any "serious" actor will admit, *concentration* on characterization immediately before the shooting starts is necessary for a successful performance.

"It was more difficult to separate myself from the group and stay in my own head, to stay concentrated," Denzel admitted. "It was tough for me to keep up my wall of *concentration*. It's usually easier to do when there's only a few blacks." Ultimately, if Denzel had to face the choice between offending coworkers and creating what he was after, the rugged individualist would win over communal loyalty: "I learned early on, when you do a film and people go to see [it], they don't go, 'Whoa, he stunk, but I bet he was nice to everybody.' [So] I don't get around those other people. I learned how to shut the door. I heard some stuff on Spike's set, people saying, 'Oh, he's so Hollywood, you know.' 'Cause when I come out of the room, it's almost like a boxing match. I've got my head—I've psyched myself up to play the role, focusing on that to the exclusion of all else."

At some point, though, Denzel did have to acknowledge that, for the first time, he was not working for a competent craftsman like Norman Jewison and Richard Attenborough, who direct films as if they were stage productions being permanently preserved on celluloid. Spike Lee was a real, true auteur: a writer-director with a personal vision of the world that he realizes in ongoing works which together form an oeuvre of art, even if individual films fail, rather than simple dramatic or comic entertainments, however successful. If he played his cards right, Denzel might become to Spike Lee what Henry Fonda had once been to John Ford: the perfect actor-star to incarnate, through his performances, a world-class filmmaker's vision. As different as the contemporary, radical Spike Lee might seem from the classic, conservative Ford, the very existence of an ongoing stock company and family of crew members suggests that all great directors work in much the same manner.

Even Denzel's comments about Lee's style of direction are interchangeable with what others have noted about auteurs dating back to D. W. Griffith: "He was more quiet than most directors I've worked with. He didn't have a lot of things to say while we were shooting. We communicated, but there wasn't a theater-type directing going on. He's more on the technical side of it. He expects you to come in and hit it. But he'll leave the camera on to allow things to happen. We would set up shots sometimes where he'd just set the camera up and say, 'Okay, start talking,' leave the camera on and see [what happens]. In that regard, there was a lot more freedom to be spontaneous. Probably some of the most interesting and funny stuff comes out of those times. He's mischievous. He likes to stir things up."

What he stirred up this time, mainly, was controversy. When asked during an ABC-TV *Prime Time Live* broadcast whether there was any message he could not include in a film, Lee answered: "I couldn't make an anti-Semitic film" because Jews run Hollywood. Apparently, with *Mo' Better Blues* he set out to push the envelope by cruelly caricaturing the club owners. When no self-respecting Jewish actors were willing to take on the Shylockian roles of Moe and Josh Flatbush, Lee cast a pair of Italian actors, John and Nicholas Turturro. David Ansen complained in *Newsweek:* "Coming from a self-proclaimed enemy of ethnic stereotyping, this is inexcusable." Caryn James of the *New York Times* concurred that "the Flatbush brothers are loaded with despicable traits typically used to disparage Jews, their greed inseparable from their Jewish identity."

"All Jewish club owners are not like this, that's true," Lee said in his defense, "but these two are." Following that line of reasoning, however, Clint Eastwood and Bertrand Tavernier could insist that there were indeed some drug-addicted and codependent jazz musicians, so Lee should not have complained about their films. White filmmakers could, in that same vein, defend their use of black stereotypes (the pimp, the drug addict) by stating the same thing. The complaint of Lee, and others in the black community, is that such stereotypes are regularly shown without being offset by other, more positive images of blacks. That certainly is a fair complaint. Likewise, then, James noted that "because there are no other Jews to offset them, they become tokens of an entire ethnic group."

Lee retorted in print (his *Times* op-ed piece was titled "I Am Not an Anti-Semite") by insisting, "What I try to do with all my characters is offer what I feel are honest portraits of individuals with both faults and endearing characteristics." But the Flatbush brothers have absolutely no "endearing characteristics," in sharp contrast to the white pizza-parlor owner (played by Danny Aiello) in Lee's *Do the Right Thing*, a portrait of a fundamentally decent if flawed man. That character, however, was Italian, not Jewish. "There is a double standard at work," Lee complained, challenging anyone to tell him why he doesn't have the right to "portray two club owners who happen to be Jewish and who exploit the black jazz musicians who work for them." The double standard, however, was exercised by none other than Lee himself, who angrily dismisses any film by whites that exclusively shows negative images of blacks.

"If critics are telling me that to avoid charges of anti-Semitism, all Jewish characters I write have to be model citizens," Lee angrily admonished, "that's unrealistic and unfair." He is, of course, correct on that point. What he failed or refused to grasp, however, is that absolutely no one was telling him this. All anyone wanted was precisely what he claimed for his own work and what he demanded from others: that individual Jewish characters be balanced portraits of people who are partially good and partially bad or that Jewish characters who are bad be balanced by others who are not.

Surprisingly, the Anti-Defamation League of B'nai B'rith issued a statement condemning Lee for "dredging up an age-old and highly dangerous form of anti-Semitic stereotyping," particularly disappointing from Lee, who has angrily reacted to negative stereotypes of black characters in other people's films and here "employed the same kind of tactics that he supposedly deplores."

To be fair to Lee, it's important to note that he's also hard on blacks, too, in *Mo' Better Blues.* At one point, Bleek peers out at the audience in his nightclub and realizes that it's composed almost entirely of Japanese and German tourists, all fanatical supporters of black American jazz. "I'm sick and tired of playing for everybody but my own people," Bleek hisses. "They don't come out. We don't support our own." Then, at Lee's request, Denzel mouthed the dreaded "n" word he would later loudly object to in scripts by white filmmaker Quentin Tarantino. "If I had to rely on niggers to eat, I'd starve to death. Jazz is our music, but we don't support it. It's sad but true." These are the attitudes of the filmmaker, who witnessed such lack of support firsthand when his own father failed to appeal to black audiences that preferred Motown and, later, rap.

Lee has also been attacked for his simplistic and underdeveloped depiction of female characters both in this film and previous movies. Charges of anti-Semitism, then, ought to be viewed within the larger critical context that holds that Lee is a sexist and a harsh critic of his own community. Simply put, Lee is not a nice guy—in person or as a filmmaker—nor, to his credit, does he pretend to be. His cocky personal attitude in TV advertisements for products like Air Jordan (he is, like Salvador Dali and Alfred Hitchcock, one of those rare "serious" artists able to hype and commercialize his own immediately recognizable image without damaging his lofty reputation) is also evident in his writing. Lee is not out to make friends, and if he wants to influence people, it is by forcing them to acknowledge, if not necessarily accept, his harsh view of the world, including his less than pleasing observations about Jews, women, and blacks.

Critics who had encouraged Lee's early efforts, then hailed *Do the Right Thing* as a masterpiece, all but dismissed *Mo' Better Blues.* To

Denzel's credit, though, they mostly took time out from their panning of the film to praise his work. Terrence Rafferty of the *New Yorker* found the picture "dawdling...all notions and no shape," adding that "Washington really has to struggle to make sense of his character. It's great to see him in a role as large as his talent deserves, and his magnetism and his intelligence keep the movie watchable even during its most aimless stretches, but the script doesn't allow him to shape the performance." Richard Alleva of the *Nation* found it "full of dramatically fruitless ambiguities" but noted that Denzel offered "a fine performance." David Denby of *New York* magazine complained about the "rush of unconvincing, melodramatic plot followed by a sentimental ending that is a complete cheat" but also observed that "Washington is funny and charming."

In *Vogue*, Elvis Mitchell claimed that Denzel "manages to be both supple and brittle, with the muscle and weight to move into the leading-man power base, perhaps the first black man to be taken seriously as an earthy and sexual presence on-screen.

However flawed, even disappointing, Denzel might have considered the end result of their first collaboration, he sensed that Spike Lee was nonetheless a major artist who would in time find his voice and create an important epic. Denzel wanted to be there, and be a part of it, when that happened; the film would, of course, be *Malcolm X*. In the meantime, though, Denzel said: "I see myself doing other pictures with Spike over time. I would think because we're truly contemporaries, we ought to."

9

Heart Condition

1990

A NEW LINE CINEMA RELEASE

CAST: Bob Hoskins (*Jack Moony*); Denzel Washington (*Napoleon Stone*); Chloe Webb (*Crystal Gerrity*); Roger E. Mosley (*Captain Wendt*); Ja'net Dubois (*Mrs. Stone*); Alan Rachins (*Dr. Posner*); Ray Baker (*Harry Zara*); Jeffrey Meek (*Graham*); Kieran Mulroney (*Dilnick*); Robert Apisa (*Teller*).

CREDITS: Director, James D. Perriott; producer, Steve Tisch; executive producer, Robert Shaye; coproducers, Marie Cantin and Bernie Goldman; screenplay, Perriott; cinematographer, Arthur Albert; editor, David Finter; music, Patrick Leonard; production design, John Muto; costumes, Louise Frogley; rating, R; running time, 95 min.

A round my [fortieth] birthday," Denzel told *Movieline* in 1995, "I was listening to this motivational speaker, Les Brown, who made this analogy about ghosts around [your] bed. He was saying when you die, imagine you had these ghosts that represent your unfulfilled potential. Things that should have been done, should have been experienced. People can say about me, or anyone, 'Oh, you're great at this,' but you have to look at yourself and say, 'How do I feel about what I've done?' That's all that matters."

Denzel's attraction to this Les Brown theory may help explain why, five years earlier, he had agreed to appear in *Heart Condition,*

105

playing one such ghost himself. This fantasy featured another of those popular cop-and-reluctant-companion teams, an odd couple composed of Jack Moony (Bob Hoskins) and Napoleon Stone (Denzel Washington) in a plot one critic dismissed as "*The Defiant Ones* meets *Topper* [1937]."

Moony, a Los Angeles vice cop, is the Oscar Madison figure, a gross slob who also happens to be an outspoken bigot. Stone, the team's Felix Unger, is an elegant lawyer: clever, successful, and a meticulous dresser. Smooth and slick, Stone's personality borders on self-possession. Stone habitually takes on seemingly "impossible" cases, winning via his charismatic ability to manipulate any jury. On several occasions, Stone has, in this capacity, represented a high-class hooker, Crystal Gerrity (Chloe Webb), keeping her out of jail through legal technicalities.

Crystal serves as a key bridge between the two men: Following their legal liaison, Crystal became intimately involved with Stone, though previously she was Moony's lover. That contrived situation makes this a difficult-to-buy film: It's hard to believe that Crystal, as upscale as a prostitute can be, would stoop to the level of the disgusting Jack Moony; conversely, it's impossible to grasp why Napoleon Stone, who could seemingly have his choice of pretty women, would stoop to Crystal. Writer-director James D. Perriott apparently trusted that viewers would nonetheless accept the opening sequence: An important Republican senator, stripped down to his boxer shorts and dancing about with two high-class call girls, suffers a heart attack and dies, though not before one of the women—Crystal—photographs the sexual activities. Though a conservative politician might well enjoy such a private indiscretion, he would hardly allow it to be documented, as such pictures could easily destroy his career.

"Keep this in case something happens to me," Crystal later tells Moony, handing him the film. Of course, something immediately *does* happen to her: D.C. power brokers dispense agents to abduct her so that the sordid truth won't reach the public. We're then expected to believe that Moony would forget about the film (despite the insistence in Crystal's voice) until the beginning of act 3, when it is at last employed to save the day. The roll of film serves the function of what Hitchcock referred to as the McGuffin, the little object that causes all the wild running around. In this case, though, it's less than plausible.

Stone, rushing to the scene to legally represent Crystal, is pursued by Moony. When the mean-spirited cop spots his enemy, his anger takes over. Moony makes a dangerous U-turn in the middle of heavy traffic, rushing off after Stone, running him off the road, then berating him verbally, even attacking him physically. This makes little sense: Why would a cop with even half a brain (Moony may be nasty, but he isn't stupid) think for one moment that he can violently attack an upscale lawyer in full view of witnesses? It's easier to imagine Mark Fuhrman assaulting Johnnie Cochran or F. Lee Bailey on the streets during a lunch break while the Simpson trial was in progress.

Shortly, Stone is killed, in what appears to be an accident, but the murder has been carefully prearranged by political conspirators who are out to cover up the senator's activities. A measure of the movie's illogicality is that the professional villains are supposedly dumb enough to kill the well-known lawyer of the woman who took the pictures rather than go after the downscale woman herself. On that same night, in an unrelated situation, the out-of-shape Moony suffers a coronary, owing to his rage over being reprimanded and suspended for his rough treatment of Stone. Moony ends up in the hospital, where the only thing that can save him is a heart transplant. The timing is perfect: Napoleon Stone's body is brought in, his heart is available, so before long, Moony is up and around. Only this time, the heart of a black man beats inside the body of a bigot.

If this situation makes Moony mad, it makes Stone even angrier: "If I'd known my heart was gonna keep a piece of racist scum like you alive," the spirit of Stone later tells Moony, "I never would have donated it in the first place." This conversation occurs after Moony is removed from his position as a vice cop by his superior officer, the African-American captain Wendt (Roger E. Mosley), who previously refused to promote Moony, since Wendt is fully aware of the man's unpleasant bigotry. So Moony finds himself sitting at a desk and pushing pencils, growing more frustrated than ever. Until, that is, the ghost of Napoleon Stone approaches one month after the fatality and announces: "I didn't die. I was murdered."

What Stone wants is nothing less than that his old enemy become an unlikely ally, tracking down Stone's killers. Moony must also find Crystal, who has mysteriously disappeared. As is so often the case with films of this phantom-companion genre, Stone is visible only to his reluctant partner Moony. This results in some hackneyed scenes. The potbellied little loser constantly argues with the tall, handsome spirit that dispenses advice as to how Jack must stop smoking, drinking, and eating junk food if he is ever to take proper care of Crystal. Other characters wonder if Moony has gone absolutely crazy, because he appears to be arguing with himself. Shortly, Stone insists that Moony get himself manicured, barbered, and fitted for new clothes. Now Moony can pass himself off as a rich john and make contact with Crystal, at which point the heroes foil the villains amid much shooting and running around. During all the screaming and shouting, Crystal is shot full of heroin by one of the arch–bad guys, a rather brutal incident for a "lighthearted" thriller.

Before the film reaches its overobvious and unnecessarily gory conclusion, Jack comes to realize that Napoleon is a pretty good guy, who ought to be taken for his worth as an individual rather than typecast according to race. By the same token, Napoleon learns to respond emotionally (in particular to the child he has unknowingly fathered with Crystal) for the first time. Though most of what happens is far-fetched, it's worth noting that *Heart Condition* was inspired by an actual incident: The concept occurred to the film's director when his friend, actor John Erik Hexum, accidentally killed himself while clowning around on a movie set with a gun filled with blanks; posthumously, he became an organ donor.

Initially, Perriott—making what he hoped would be a long-awaited jump from episodic TV writing and directing such shows as *The Six Million Dollar Man* to feature films—scripted the Stone character as a stereotypical black junkie, flamboyant and over the top, virtually the opposite of the conservatively dressed, soft-spoken character we encounter. Such a reinforced-negative stereotype is the kind of role Denzel has always avoided, so if he were going to participate, Napoleon Stone would have to be rethought. Apparently, Denzel was not alone: "Everyone who read it said the film would be slaughtered by the critics," Perriott later recalled, "so I rewrote it to make the character a slick Beverly Hills lawyer instead." In a politically correct age, it was acceptable to play the blue-collar, white heterosexual character Moony as the embodiment of a urban-redneck stereotype. "I still think it would be a purer piece if it had two real stereotypes colliding," Perriott admitted after filming was completed, making clear he was never completely comfortable with the imposed changes.

"I don't know if it would have been better," Perriott concluded, "but it would have had harder edges." Indeed, Hollywood regularly takes on projects that are attractive because of such hard edges, then gradually softens the material for mass consumption until what was most exciting about the idea has been all but eliminated. Other elements were also changed. The sequence in which Moony is thrown out of an all-black eight-lane bowling alley in Glendale was first conceived as occurring in a ghetto church, then revised in the second draft to a black law firm. Clearly, Perriott was caught in a politically correct vise: Though he believed the response to a single bigoted white daring to enter an all-black establishment would be one of outright hostility, he also came to realize that, as a white filmmaker, he could be accused of racial stereotyping.

"The last thing I wanted was a cliché [black] bar," he admitted after making the change. "There's enough in this scene that borders on exploitation. This is the one scene that I'm the least comfortable with," even though it had to be included if he were going to stick to his guns about what, through the ostensible comedy, he wanted to say: All the civil rights gains of the late sixties and early seventies, a period when ebony and ivory momentarily did appear able to exist in relative harmony, were rapidly disintegrating in mutual distrust. If any kind of reconciliation were to be reached, people who had grown as remote as his characters would have to find ways to break through and again perceive each other's common humanity.

This was a risk-laden project from the start, open to charges of racism, however inadvertent, if its intended antiracist satire did not play successfully. No wonder, then, that the film was "modestly" budgeted. Producer Steve Tisch originally planned to make *Heart Condition* for between $7 and $8 million. Clearly attracted to pictures dealing with the serious issue of racism via a comedic approach, Tisch previously had made *Soul Man* (1986), in which a white college student dons black makeup, passing himself off as an African American to win a scholarship. *Soul Man* and *Heart Condition* provide comedic allegories of assimilation: One character, through his own design or by divine intervention, becomes an amalgam of the black and white races, proving that compatibility is still possible, if far from easy, in our time.

Heart Condition appeared at an auspicious moment in time for New Line Pictures, which had been in existence for twenty-one years. One of the few independents to survive that long, New Line did so in large part because several of their low-budget shockers, in particular the *Nightmare on Elm Street* (1985) series, were successful. By 1990, the company was ready to cautiously edge into higher-budgeted and more prestigious productions, which—if hits—would change the company's image from an American-International for the eighties to a viable competitor with Hollywood's "majors"; a social comedy with Bob Hoskins and Denzel Washington might do that in a way *976-EVIL* (1989) could not. If a $10 million film rated as a modest undertaking by big studio standards, it created a major risk for New Line. In addition to suffering what, for them, would be a financial disaster if the public didn't attend their upscale item, critic Stephen Farber noted that "the danger, the filmmakers recognize, is that *Heart Condition* could turn out to be no more than a gimmick picture exploiting and trivializing the trauma of racial conflict" due to the "lighthearted, whimsical approach" taken toward "a volatile subject."

New Line seemed the perfect place for Tisch and Perriott to bring their project, given Perriott's refusal to sell the script outright, which would have allowed a more experienced director to bring the story to the screen. He wanted to be a movie director; one way of doing so is to write a hot script and accept a considerably lesser sum for it while insisting on being allowed to direct. Major studios would have been more likely to balk at such an arrangement, though the independent New Line was vulnerable: They hungered for a prestige project.

While the $10 million price tag represented the biggest budget for any New Line film up to that point, they were still shooting on a virtual shoestring, Denzel and Hoskins both taking less money than they would have received if working on a major-studio film. Another way in which the independent New Line scrimped was by shooting with nonunion crews, the same approach by which they'd brought their profitable *Nightmare on Elm Street* movies in so economically. That must have created something of a crisis of conscience for Denzel when the local Teamsters Union picketed the film, causing delays and waving signs that read, What Nonunion Means to a Studio Executive: Three Mercedes Instead of Only Two. A hard pill to swallow for an actor-star who often played the downtrodden under-dog and was perceived as part of the Establishment now crossing a picket line to work.

Upon release, *Heart Condition* was almost universally trashed. Vincent Canby of the *New York Times* quickly dismissed it as "careless and clumsy," while the *London Observer* noted, in typically British fashion, that it was "a comedy-thriller with more padding than a winter duvet," adding that "this flaccid, sentimental movie has not the ghost of a chance, or the chance of *Ghost* [1990]," a snide reference to that superior box-office hit with a similar premise, released at roughly the same time. A few critics were kinder; *Variety* called *Heart Condition* "a most engrossing and rewarding tale.... From a fantasy premise, Perriott develops a clever, action-laden comedy about racism bred from insecurity and male competition in a script well worthy of this top-notch cast." Most observers, however, insisted that the film was misguided, managing to muff a chance to make a big, important statement about racism by inadvertently becoming the very thing that was supposedly being targeted. The *Los Angeles Times (Calendar)* noted that *Heart Condition* "clearly plays up—some would say *exploits*—black-white distrust and hostility."

That, of course, is a far cry from what Perriott had hoped to achieve. In his view, the heart transplant would be a happy symbol that advanced the cause of integration, here made visible via two characters who become one: "The story of the heart transplant is an obvious metaphor. What it says is that we're all in one body, one country, one world, and so we'd better learn to live with each other." Perriott hoped his film would "be healing rather than divisive," though he was operating out of old-fashioned liberal notions about integration, left over from the early 1960s. In the early nineties, the notion of multiculturalism—which supplanted, even reversed, many earlier "old liberal" concepts—validated for many the idea of minority cultures remaining separate from mainstream American culture in order to retain the purity of their ethnicity; Perriott's script served as a slap in the face to such thinking.

"A gimmick masquerading as a story," David Ansen said in *Newsweek*. Critic Gary Giddins of the *Village Voice* spoke for many when he wrote that

> *Heart Condition* is a self-proclaimed comedy thriller that is neither comical nor thrilling. But maladroitness is no crime. What makes *Heart Condition* loathsome is the pretense of making a statement on bigotry and corruptness. Its take on racism partakes of racism... jokes are made about the superior genitals, lovemaking techniques, and sartorial elegance of blacks; though, inevitably, an obese black bonehead is introduced for the easy laughs associated with obese black boneheads. Besides, Stone— the movie's only real charmer and constant threat to Moony's self-image and (we eventually learn) the father of Crystal's child—is dead. That's the point. Mistuh Stone, he dead. Mistuh Moony, he live—and gets Crystal as well as Stone's son.

If we read the film as comical allegory, the final effect was a perhaps unconscious implication that the key function of the black male, as good as dead to begin with, is to help a white man end up with everything he, the black, wants in life, ranging from the woman both men covet to the son the black man fathered.

Why did Denzel Washington want to become involved in a film of this sort? While the film was being shot, Denzel declined to grant many interviews, having already become gun-shy of journalists due to past misrepresentations and misquotes. He did, however, issue the following statement: "I did this movie for one reason. Bob Hoskins. When I knew he was involved, it made the movie a 'go' for me. There's a great deal to learn from that man. He sure has some kind of energy. It's almost magical. But he also has this extraordinary patience. You can only be helped by acting with him." Anyone willing to take that statement at face value can assume that the relative merits (or lack thereof) of the script had little to do with the final decision. However, Denzel shortly suggested other possibilities for saying yes to *Heart Condition*. At a key juncture in the film, Washington's Napoleon Stone turns to his unpleasant companion and states: "Personally, I believe that racism—and this refusal to acknowledge me—arises from [your] feelings of inadequacy."

However unsubtly, the project did allow Denzel to make statements that appear to come from the man playing the part as much as from the specific character he plays. Denzel's ongoing desire to overcome racism through mass-market entertainments becomes even more apparent considering that everybody on the *Heart Condition* set recalls Denzel's insistence on numerous changes. When speaking about the picture with the *Los Angeles Times*, Denzel played down any social activism on his part: "There were things I felt weren't right [in the script], so they were fixed. It was rewritten quite a bit, but that's all part of the process." In another context, he added: "I suggest changes on *all* my films, and I'm getting braver with every film." However, this time around, something other than mere plot mechanics had to be fixed: "There were other things in the script I thought were too much." Perriott affirmed this was the case, explaining the situation thusly: "I had some material [in the script] that was offensive to Denzel. He said I was going over the top. We've got two polemic characters—the idea is to take a poor, white-trash cop and put him against a slick black lawyer. Denzel felt he, as a screen presence, would not tolerate ethnic slurs being hurled at him. I'm not a black writer, and I looked to Denzel for advice."

Perriott did listen to Denzel, in part because the fledgling director knew he had a major movie star on his hands, in part because he was admittedly nervous about the controversy that could possibly erupt, even as it had when *Soul Man* hit theater screens in 1986. "My one great fear," Perriott admitted, "is that the [critics] will find that one mistake [I may have made in handling the racial material] and nail me for it. So I'm watching out for it, and Denzel is helping me. The last thing I want is to be called a racist for this film."

He learned, as Quentin Tarantino would later discover on the set of *Crimson Tide*, that Denzel does not take the "n" word lightly, even when used for the sake of street realism. "There have been some 'niggers' omitted that offended Denzel," Perriott admitted. "A reference to 'spade' was omitted. But mostly it's subtle stuff, direction on how the scene is going to be played." One method of solving this problem was to allow Denzel's Napoleon Stone to react strongly to any racial epithets remaining in the script and, through his character's on-screen response, shading the audience's own response. At one point, Moony casually refers to Stone as a "spook"; Stone, though a ghost, clobbers him.

Producer Tisch backed up Perriott's decision to follow Denzel's advice, insisting: "Denzel had a lot of input about his character and about him as a black actor playing Stone, how Stone would be perceived by an audience. From my point of view, all of his questions contributed to a richer character." However disappointing the film may be, that character did embody many of the elements Denzel consistently insists on. The audience got to see not the street-pimp stereotype of the black male but a successful white-collar African American who has won assimilation into the upper echelon of mainstream society. Yet he is a far cry from a perfect Poitier-style role model, Stone's self-importance qualifying him as a flawed, and therefore interesting, human being. Though he is involved with a white woman, his status as a ghost makes it unnecessary for Denzel to engage in any on-screen sex with the romantic lead. And, like Bleek in the far more ambitious *Mo' Better Blues*, he eventually comes to realize that family values in general, and fatherhood in particular, offer spiritual salvation that's more important than worldly success.

Speaking with one of the few reporters granted on-the-set access, Denzel made clear that in his mind the racial theme was actually subordinate to a larger and more all encompassing issue, lack of self-esteem: "I think the film deals with insecurity—and racial insecurity is [merely] a part of it." Washington's concept of the work was that Moony's insecurity—his unconscious, though essential, reason for striking out vehemently against Stone—derives from his knowledge that he's a blue-collar working stiff; always has been, always will be. Moony is offended that Stone, despite any social hurdles the color issue placed before him, managed to gain a prestigious position in life.

That makes Moony uneasy about his own relative worth while setting up Stone as a perfect target for Moony's misplaced anger. Importantly, though, Stone is equally incapacitated by hidden hang-ups, though his aura of casual self-confidence neatly hides the fact that he suffers from an ongoing fear of commitment. That explains why he dates so many attractive women; closeness is what scares him. This makes the final arc to his eventually embracing fatherhood more poignant. And ironic: Stone has become "attached" in the fullest sense (via the heart transplant) to another human being, the last person with whom he would ever choose to be connected. "It's really a love story," Denzel concluded at the time, about "two guys who didn't know how much they were in love with this woman. And they find out. And come to realize that combined as one person, they become a better person." By broader implication, opting for inclusion rather than insisting on diversity is our only hope as a people.

This approach appealed to costar Hoskins, who completely altered his notion of the project. "A lot of it I didn't understand until I talked with Denzel," Hoskins admits. "I thought I understood it until we started working." Hoskins explains that Denzel persuaded him to see the Jack Moony character as a policeman who, several years earlier, was forced to accept, as part of the definition of his job and the existing system, that he would regularly enforce laws designed for the specific purpose of discriminating against blacks. During the course of such a life, Moony had been programmed into becoming the detestable person we meet at the movie's opening. Somewhere deep inside, though, is a potentially decent person, at last unlocked, during the course of the story, as a result of the relationship with a black man.

"The black-white relationship seems to be so important in America," Hoskins says, making clear that this was not a part of the daily life he had known in Great Britain, even though he hastened to add: "Not that we don't have racial prejudice in England." Still, there was a key difference, as Hoskins notes: "But racial prejudice was *legal* here [in America] not so long ago," as it never had been in England. "It was part of your system. There's a two-hundred-year history with blacks as part of it. Not so long ago, this cop [Moony] had to enforce the black-white laws."

The film could only come to some semblance of life on-screen if Denzel was able to convince Hoskins that it would be disastrous to play Moony as he'd originally intended, either a total buffoon or stock villain: "He's a total pig," Hoskins admits, "but like all people, he has bad and good. And he has to find the good inside."

Ordinarily, that's the kind of advice a director offers an actor; here Denzel was moving from actor to auteur, shaping the project even as he performed in it.

There was still another reason why Denzel saw possibilities in the project. If an actor is to enjoy an ongoing career rather than a brief spurt of popularity, it's important to find showcases for his varied talents, including comedy as well as drama. At this point on his career path, Denzel needed a showcase that would make clear to everyone his range, particularly an ability to play funny roles as well as the heavier stuff with which he was already associated. "The script has humor, wit, zaniness," he explained to visitors in his trailer during the final days of shooting, remarking that "people haven't seen me in this light. This is different for me. My friends say I have a good sense of humor, and I'm finally able to show it. I'm having fun just being silly. It's great, and it came at exactly the right time. I needed it."

The general public didn't perceive Denzel as "needing" anything in 1990, the year when everyone was labeling him the hottest young star in America. However, his candor makes clear that he wasn't caught up in his success and did indeed recognize that he *needed* a comedy showcase. "The appeal of *Heart Condition*," he continued, "was to do something lighter than I'd been doing, to stretch a little. Also, I'd been on the road for two years, in Africa, Jamaica, London, and Georgia. This offered a chance to shoot at home and to have some fun. I hope the movie will open up a lot more opportunities for me." It was a comedy; even if it wasn't necessarily the best of comedies, he could still use it to his own purpose, as a means of showing what other things he could do.

Many critics appreciated his relatively subtle approach in comparison to the bug-eyed acting of Hoskins. Vincent Canby claimed that "Mr. Washington fares better than his co-star, if only because Stone's laid-back personality is much easier to take than the hysterical excesses of Mr. Hoskins's character." *Variety* noted that "Washington creates a most compelling character in Stone, finding the rhythm of the role with an assurance that never flags." Even Giddins of the *Voice*, who found next to nothing to like about *Heart Condition*, did begrudgingly admit that "Washington manages a couple of interesting line readings."

David Brooks of the *Wall Street Journal* went considerably further. One of the few critics to praise not only Washington's performance but the film itself, he wrote: "Mr. Washington steals this exciting and intelligent police thriller from his co-star Bob Hoskins, which is the rough equivalent of Magic Johnson slamming over Michael Jordan. ...Mr. Washington makes a transition here from critic's favorite to popular star. His role is juicier than Mr. Hoskins's, but nobody could have expected Mr. Washington to be so magnetic, so comic, so unaffectedly engaging."

If Denzel derived satisfaction that at least this time around critics (finally!) did not compare him to Poitier, he had to conversely deal with the fact that reviewers automatically perceived this part, and the person who played it, in comparison to the work of *another* black actor. "The obvious comparison," Brooks continued, "is with Eddie Murphy. Especially so because *Heart Condition*, like Mr. Murphy's *48 Hours* (1982), is a winning, *Odd Couple* (1968) kind of comedy trapped in the body of a police thriller, but Washington is better than Murphy. He is less mannered, less dependent on formulaic gestures and profanity, equally charismatic, and when the script calls for dramatic acting, Washington possesses skills Murphy does not."

Understandably, such comparisons continued. "Washington gives a magnetic performance," David Edenstein wrote in the *New York Post*. "The part seems conceived for Eddie Murphy, but Washington is like a Murphy with taste and intelligence. He glides through the role, gives it the soft sell: all is in proportion. He even finds some pathos in this dead playboy. The sign of a real movie star is when you're not sure where the character's depression ends and the performer's begins, and it doesn't much matter. There's integrity there, whatever the case." Even in lesser vehicles, Denzel Washington was clearly emerging as just what Edenstein hailed him as: true movie star.

The trick now was to avoid getting a swelled head, and remembering that careerwise, acting must always come first. "I didn't start acting to be a movie star," Denzel claimed. "I started in the theater, and my desire was to get better at my craft. It's still my desire. I'm just an entertainer, an actor who works hard. Whatever labels people give me, that's not really me or part of my process."

10

Ricochet

1991

A WARNER BROS. RELEASE

CAST: Denzel Washington (*Nick Styles*); John Lithgow (*Blake*); Ice T (*Odessa*); Kevin Pollak (*Larry*); Lindsay Wagner (*Brimleigh*); Victoria Dillard (*Alice*); John Cothran Jr. (*Farris*); Josh Evans (*Kim*); Linda Dona (*Wanda the Prostitute*).

CREDITS: Director, Russell Mulcahy; producers, Joel Silver and Michael Levy, in association with HBO and Cinema Plus presentations; screenplay, Steven E. de Souza, from a story by Fred Dekker and Menno Meyjes; cinematography, Peter Levy; editor, Peter Honess; music, Alan Silvestri; production design, Jaymes Hinkle; costumes, Marily Vance-Straker; art direction, Christian Wagner; rating: R; running time, 97 min.

B ecoming an artist," Denzel explained to *Interview* in 1990, "you can lose touch with what people really want. I'm intrigued by appealing to a mass number of people. Not in all my work, but at least to see if I can do that, too. I think about the movies I went to see as a teenager. I didn't care if they were Academy Award–winning. I went to see *Three the Hard Way* (1974). You want to have a good time. Movies like *Cry Freedom* are informative, but guys won't spend fifteen dollars on Friday night to take their girls to see that. Making movies like *Cry Freedom* might show we're committed to doing something about issues, but people can see issues on the news for free. Besides, we can't take ourselves too seriously, even if we are trying to effect change." That statement helps explain why, one year later, Denzel could be seen in the violent action flick *Ricochet*, a clear departure from the serious stuff that had come before.

On Oscar night, 1990, Denzel—suddenly the proud owner of an Academy Award as Best Supporting Actor for *Glory*—was invited to Swifty Lazar's annual prestige party at Spago's. Denzel's agent introduced him to Joel Silver, the producer responsible for some highly successful films of the sort Washington previously expressed admiration for: Big, unsubtle, sandblaster action films, including the *Lethal Weapon* franchise. Denzel had admired Danny Glover's performance as a normal suburbanite, an imperfect but decent person and cop-hero who was black.

Silver cornered Denzel at this exciting but vulnerable point in his career, offering "the winner" a leading role in any of the eight films Silver was then planning. To Silver's surprise, Denzel agreed. Though he was perceived by the public as the star of serious art-house items, Denzel had accepted many of those parts because roles in big blockbusters had not been offered to him. Denzel knew that if an acclaimed actor wanted to pick and choose among the best projects being passed around in Hollywood, it was necessary to first become a superstar. That status, via the Joel Silver route, had given Glover, Mel Gibson, and Bruce Willis their current clout.

"My agent told me on Oscar night, 'Now, you've got to make a movie for this man,'" Denzel recalled during breaks while filming *Ricochet*. "And here I am, one year later, bleeding and hanging off of a seventy-five-foot tower." Needless to say, things did not turn out the way they were supposed to; *Ricochet* failed to hit big at the box office, nor was it marketed as a major summer or Christmas release, instead distributed as a minor autumn-doldrums "filler."

Ricochet's story line is a rip-off of a dozen film-noir plots from the 1940s, including Raoul Walsh's *White Heat* (1949), a sequence from that classic being included in *Ricochet* and making the movie appear even more disappointing by comparison. Such material was updated in terms of increased rough language, sexuality, and violence as well as in one other area, the most interesting element of the film: The upscale hero, played by Denzel, is a suave black man working successfully within the white man's system. Nick Styles is a self-important, in some ways superficial yuppie who eventually questions his own glib take on life when his career, family, and mental stability are threatened. The plot is a bottom-drawer variation on the timeworn tale of a decent assistant district attorney hounded by a bad man he once put away: *Cape Fear* redux, only without exotic Carolina backwaters. Escaped madman Earl Talbot Blake (John Lithgow) walks the streets again, vowing vengeance on Nick. Like other villains of his order, Blake is not content to finish Nick off swiftly. The obsessive Blake wants to destroy his adversary, piece by piece, taking sadistic glee as Nick, framed for crimes he didn't commit, falls from grace.

As with all films of this type, any interest in what happens stems directly from how clever, creative, complex, but, above all, *original* and *believable* the villain's Machiavellian master plot for vengeance appears. In *Ricochet*, it's often original, but never believably so. At one point, Blake kidnaps Nick, ties him up in an abandoned building, then has a beautiful blond prostitute force Nick to have sex with her. Though he resists, Nick can't keep from responding, eventually returning home to his wife infected with venereal disease. Additionally, Blake finds ways to seemingly connect Nick with child pornography and money laundering, causing Nick's fellow (white) lawyers to turn against him. The problem is, the villain's plot succeeds without a hitch until the hero finally turns the tables, at which point his own counterrevenge plan likewise goes all too well to be believed. In real life—and in superior movies of this genre, including *Silence of the Lambs* (1991)—there are always unexpected glitches that cause villain and hero to improvise in interesting ways. Not here; everyone is suckered in at every turn, even by the most preposterous pieces of planted evidence.

One of Blake's tricks is particularly transparent. In the opening sequence (designed as an audience "teaser" in more ways than one), Nick, while still a street cop, captures the crazed Blake at a downtown Los Angeles street fair. Nick does this by insisting to the armed villain that he himself is unarmed, suddenly segueing into a striptease to prove that there's no place where he could conceal a weapon. Then, nearly naked except for his shorts, Nick whips a hidden gun out of his jockstrap and shoots Blake in the leg. This allowed Silver to begin his film with a bang, in more ways than one.

It's an ostensibly "clever" variation on the *Dirty Harry* (1971) opening, plus Denzel's physique is amply displayed for his horde of female fans.

Later, Denzel's body is likewise shown off, soft-core porn style, when his boss (played by Lindsay Wagner) pushes herself into the police locker room where he and others are dressing, an act that is totally out of character for her. Both bits—as well as several later nude scenes—come as a surprise from an actor who claims embarrassment at performing nude on-screen. Why would he agree to appear nearly nude (as well as do an interracial sex scene) in the exploitative context of a crime caper, after balking at doing nudity and sex in such ambitious movies as *Mo' Better Blues* and *The Mighty Quinn?*

One element links *Ricochet* to other, superior Denzel films. When his Establishment cronies desert him, Nick has nowhere to go but back to those very streets from whence he came. In his former neighborhood, Nick rediscovers onetime best pal Odessa (Ice T), now a major-league drug dealer. Odessa instinctually realizes (Nick's white "friends" do not) that Nick is incapable of what he's been accused of and therefore must have been framed. As Henry Louis Gates Jr. noted in the *New York Times*: "Whereas the black exploitation movies (of the 1970s) romanticized ghetto culture and identified 'true' black culture as lower-class, the new guiltsploitation genre offers the fantasy of saving the black race, the 'soul,' with a rekindled brotherhood of color. This transcends paltry considerations of class, bridging the gap between the new black middle class and the lower classes left behind and ever growing."

Gates was not speaking specifically of *Ricochet* but of an entire genre of movies that presented the emerging African-American morality play for the nineties. Still, *Ricochet* stands as a case in point. Odessa agrees to help turn the tables on Blake, which he and Nick then (rather implausibly) do. At this point in his career, Denzel was repeatedly drawn to projects that cast him as an upwardly mobile black man who believes in the ideal of equality and attempts assimilation, trying to live in the white man's world, only to be dumped by the Establishment that seemingly had absorbed him as one of their own, leaving the character no choice but to return to the "brothers."

Ricochet's hero also happens to be a dedicated family man. One way of understanding Denzel's willingness to appear in this project is to view *Ricochet* as a vivid realization of his own nightmare scenario: Everything that could possibly go wrong with his seemingly ordered life does. When Blake frames Nick with the whore, Nick's wife doubts him, and Nick is distraught; family is for *him*, like the actor playing him, the number-one priority. Every one of us occasionally has bad dreams in which our worst-case fears escape the subconscious and dance about darkly while we sleep. An actor has the unique opportunity to exorcise such demons by playing them out on-screen.

Certainly, the star won artistic input and "Denzelized" Nick, making it clear that this character is closer to him than any other he'd previously essayed. When we first see Nick, he's playing basketball in the old neighborhood, insisting to old friends that "I never really left," but the looks on their faces suggest an understanding that he's no longer one of them. The athletically inclined Denzel also encountered the mother of his ruined boyhood friend "Cutch." In the film, Nick warns Odessa away from drugs for his mother's sake.

Nick moves from street cop to detective to assistant D.A. through a combination of pluck and luck. He works hard, studying at law school and applying himself at every endeavor, though things would not have gone so well had he not been at the right place at the right time to arrest Blake, with the arrest captured on video by a bystander, allowing for TV news exposure that transforms Nick into a media celebrity. Nick, like Denzel, is an African-American variation on the traditional Horatio Alger hero from the early twentieth century, the optimistic young man who believes in the American Dream, living it out fully through his own determination and the blessings of destiny.

Nick's father is, significantly, a Pentecostal preacher, as was Denzel's. "Everything I am and might be I owe to my Mom," Nick says, echoing a phrase Denzel has repeatedly used himself. Nick is dedicated to Twin Towers, a charity that cares for children; Denzel lavishes his time and money working for his own similar favorite charity, the Boys and Girls Clubs of America. The actress playing Nick's wife was made up to look as much like Denzel's own wife as possible; Nick's intense insistence that the rumors of his unfaithfulness are untrue ("I didn't lie to you...but I didn't tell the whole truth!") must recall the discussions Denzel and Pauletta had when, in the early stages of their romance, the two briefly broke up owing to the attention he received from other women.

By the movie's end, Nick—who has reclaimed his upscale lifestyle—realizes that he must balance mainstream acceptance with a regular return to the streets. As Nick and his wife prepare to return to their lovely home, he reminds Odessa that they will resume playing basketball on Sunday afternoons. *Ricochet* is, its obvious flaws notwithstanding, the most personal statement Denzel has offered of his actual life and the fears that haunt him; let's not forget, this is a multimillionaire who hides away piles of pennies owing to fear that someday everything else will be gone and such loose change will be all he has left.

Why was Joel Silver so anxious to make *Ricochet*? "In most action films," he explains, "which revolve around the teaming of two men, you're introduced to two guys who hate each other, are forced to work together, and by the end of the film learn to like each other. What fascinated me about the premise of *Ricochet* was that you started with two guys who hated each other. They get separated, and when they come together again, they hate each other even more. Their hatred is as much of a bond between them as the friendship between the guys in other movies. You might call *Ricochet* an 'antibuddy' movie." You might also call it *Strangers on a Train* (1951) without the train or the magical Hitchcock touch.

Steven E. de Souza, who penned the screenplay from an idea by Fred Dekker and Menno Meyjes (Steven Spielberg's collaborator on *The Color Purple* [1985]), is an odd duck in the movie industry. For years he was associated with the grungiest B pictures (e.g., *Commando* [1986]), only to hit the "majors" with *48 Hours* (1982), essentially a B-movie script redeemed by A-list actors Nick Nolte and Eddie Murphy. Purportedly, Silver was hoping that lightning might strike twice, electrifying *Ricochet*, the film doing for Denzel what the earlier one had done for Murphy. "The script tries to reverse some of the elements of the genre," De Souza said of *Ricochet*. "We tried to make Styles a bit imperfect, giving him hubris. At the beginning, he's a bit *too* ambitious, very involved in office politics. As the film progresses, he loses his career and his status in the community as he gets driven to the edge. The question becomes 'Will that save or destroy him?'"

Denzel's acting ability was sorely tested on the first day of shooting. According to the arranged schedule, he had to film an early scene in which Nick is riding high, then move immediately to a later sequence in which everything he has achieved is suddenly gone. So Denzel first donned a sleek Italian suit, covered in part by a full-length Nino Cerruti raincoat, looking elegant as he confidently marched down the steps of city hall, with TV tape crews crowding around, begging for a word from this legal superstar. Once director Russell Mulcahy (*Highlander* [1986]) had several takes, Denzel was rushed back to his trailer, where makeup and costuming were quickly changed. After lunch, Denzel—now shabbily attired—sat like one of the homeless at the pillars of the same building, done in by Blake's scheme.

"From the top to the bottom in six hours," Denzel said, laughing, after filming the two disparate moments. "Nick goes through just about everything in the course of this film." Tough on Nick, and tougher still on the actor, who had to go through it all in a single day. The opening street-fare sequence, in which hero and villain face one another for the first time, was shot on Olivera Street in downtown L.A.'s historic El Pueblo district. Their final confrontation takes place atop the Twin Towers; though the sequence supposedly occurs during a short period of time, Denzel learned firsthand the rigors of action-oriented filmmaking. He spent seven nights atop the seventy-five-foot steel structures. Strong winds and occasional rain made the filming of the man-to-man battle all the more difficult to capture on celluloid. The towers had been constructed from thirty thousand pounds of steel, shackled together by a mile of welding rod, erected by a dozen-man work crew on an empty hillside lot at L.A.'s Boylston and Colton Streets.

Two cranes, a police helicopter complete with searchlight, and a pair of police cars were necessary for the complicated nighttime sequence. For Denzel, the most terrifying moment came when he was required to hang from a broken metal spire he tenuously grasps while seventy feet high. Denzel decided that if he was going to do an action film, he might as well go all the way. So he performed the dangerous stunt himself rather than turn it over to a stunt man, as the producers offered to let him do. "Was I scared?" he replied to an observer when the shot was successfully completed. "You bet I was."

Then he grinned devilishly, adding: "But you get up there, your adrenaline starts pumping, your male ego kicks in, and you just do it." Later, when the movie was in the can, Denzel commented: "Actually, I was more scared later on, when I thought about it. I woke up one night thinking about [what I'd done] and said to myself, You must have been crazy!"

The critics were unanimous in their assessment of *Ricochet*. The *Daily News*'s "Phantom of the Movies" called *Ricochet* "sleazy and thoroughly implausible." The *New Yorker* labeled it "shock schlock," adding: "Extremism can be fun, but not when it's as calculated, sadistic, and nonsensical as it is here." *Variety* complained about the film's "nasty streak. . . . Too many people die with their guts splattered or impaled on a spike, and the clanging, banging, over-miked action veers into degrading ugliness often enough to be numbing. It's a turnoff."

Denzel survived this mess relatively unscathed. *Newsday* spoke for the vast majority of reviewers: "Though hardly Academy Award material, Washington's performance is sufficiently interesting to make us wish his character's inner conflicts could be explored in a more intelligent film." That's apt, for Denzel played his part as if he were embroiled in a far more serious character study; he comes amazingly close to making us momentarily believe there must be more substance to this film than we realize. "Washington does much to elevate the material in a charismatic, highly energetic performance," Amy Dawes noted in *Variety*. "Washington is appealing enough to get away with anything," Janet Maslin commented in the *New York Times*.

The moment Denzel signed to portray an action hero, he began extensive work with a physical trainer while adhering to a strict diet. "It's great to be in shape," he said while filming. "I haven't had a thirty-inch waist since I was eighteen." Then he paused, considered, and—probably thinking of his wife and kids and how he couldn't wait to join them for some fun times soon—added: "But I'll be happy when the film is over and I can go back to eating ice cream."

In retrospect, how does Denzel feel about the experience?

"*Ricochet* was the last time I sat in a movie and I went, 'I can't—this is not for me. I can't do this kind of movie.' 'Cause this is mindless violence. I can't be a part of this." Then, always torn between his honest impulses and loyalty to the system he's now an important part of, Denzel adds: "I shouldn't say *Ricochet* was a mistake. It's not one of *my* favorite films. But I talk to people, and some go, 'Man, that was one of the best movies you ever made.' So who am I to say? 'Cause you couldn't tell me there was a greater film made than *Superfly* when I was eighteen."

11

Mississippi Masala

1992

A SAMUEL GOLDWYN COMPANY RELEASE

CAST: Denzel Washington (*Demetrius*); Sarita Choudhury (*Mina*); Roshan Seth (*Jay*); Sharmila Tagore (*Kinnou*); Charles S. Dutton (*Tyrone*); Joe Seneca (*Williben*); Ranjit Chowdhry (*Anil*); Tico Wells (*Dexter*); Natalie Oliver (*Alicia LeShay*).

CREDITS: Director, Mira Nair; producers, Nair and Michael Nozik; screenwriter, Soony Taraporevala; cinematography, Ed Lachman; editor, Robert Silvi; music, L. Subramaniam; production design, Mitch Epstein; costumes, Ellen Lutter; art director, Jefferson Sage; rating, R; running time, 118 min.

L et's talk about this new movie I'm doing, about Indians and Africans," an enthusiastic Denzel suggested to *Interview*'s Veronica Webb in 1990. "Indians from India [as opposed to American Indians]. Did you see *Salaam Bombay!* [1988]? The woman who directed that is doing a picture called *Mississippi Masala*. It's about interracial relationships...I play this little country boy who manages a carpet-cleaning company, and one of his biggest contracts is one of these motels [run by recent Indian immigrants]....It's a small film. I'm very excited about it." In fact, Denzel was so excited—literally falling in love with the script when filmmaker Mira Nair submitted it to his office in October 1989—that he readily agreed to perform for a mere quarter of his ordinary post-Oscar salary in order to participate within the tight limitations of the project's $6 million budget. He also continued his tendency to collaborate rather than merely perform as actor-for-hire; as Nair recalls, "Denzel was very instrumental in guiding us towards finding out more about the black world in this story."

By "us," Nair makes clear that *Mississippi Masala* was the unique product of two collaborators, herself and screenwriter Sooni Taraporevala, who met while both were students at Harvard University. While still at college, the two women, aspiring artists, quickly realized that their common culture and shared vision, coupled with their complementary talents as director and writer, would allow them to function perfectly as a team.

The daughter of a government administrator, Nair had been raised in a comfortable section of Bhubaneswar, a town 350 miles south of Calcutta. While at boarding school, she developed an interest in theater, then attended Delhi University before transferring to Harvard. She cut her filmmaking teeth while working in the documentary tradition that would later infuse all her feature work. The first such film was *Salaam Bombay!*, a study of slum children originally planned as a documentary but expanded, thanks to Sooni's imaginative skills at dramatizing such situations, into a realistic fictional film. Nonetheless, Nair insisted on employing nonactors for most of the roles to emphasize authenticity, in the tradition of neorealism.

Nair had been fifteen years old in 1972 when Idi Amin, as part of his fiercely nationalistic program, ordered the forceful expulsion of all people of Indian descent living in Uganda. These Indians had been brought to East Africa in the late 1800s by the English. The transplanted Indians were employed, on a poverty level, to build the country's railroads, then left to fend for themselves, which they did. But since many Indians gradually carved out their niches as moneylenders and businesspersons, the Machiavellian Amin could exploit widespread resentment against "outsiders" (who had inhabited the country for a hundred years) and their supposed stranglehold on Uganda's economic base. Amin legally legitimized long-standing but previously unreleased antagonism toward the Indians.

"Africa for Africans" meant, to Amin, not an expulsion of whites but people of color whose specific culture was different from his own. Nair, growing up in India, had in no way felt any impact as a result of Amin's decision, which resulted in eighty thousand Indians leaving. (Notably, a hardy five hundred remained, choosing to live with whatever consequences they incurred.) Nair could not even recall the event, a distant incident to the then teenager in India. But while at Harvard, she read the novel *A Bend in the River*, a story of expulsion, as well as a *New Yorker* article by Jane Kramer detailing the lives of an uprooted Indian family that awkwardly resettled in London.

The stories had a strong impact on Nair, who had become an international citizen. "When people asked where I live," she explained, "I'd say, 'On Air India.' But [in actuality], you carry your home within yourself. That's a nice-sounding concept, but the truth is, you're torn." She determined to make a movie about people suffering through *diaspora*: the search for self that occurs when one is thrust from a comfortable cultural frame of reference into another. Nair might well have gone to London to observe firsthand the family Kramer wrote about, but research revealed that many such families had migrated to America and settled in Mississippi.

In March 1989 she determined to drive down to that state herself and learn the truth about the Indian immigrants. What she discovered was a human social form of *masala*, the hindi word for a variety of uniquely pungent spices mixed together. In Mississippi the Indians lived in a precarious, if relatively peaceful, relationship with whites and blacks. The first thing Nair noticed was that most Indians entered the motel business under the auspices of relatives already residing nearby, who legally sponsored immigrant newcomers, then lent them money to buy properties which they could manage with little or no command of the English language.

But unlike, say, Korean grocers, these particular immigrants were ethnically confused even *before* their arrival. In the eventual film version, Jay—head of the family—calls out on the day he's forced to leave Uganda: "I was born here! I have always been Ugandan first, Indian second. I have been called a traitor and a bootlicker by my fellow Indians. Uganda is my home." To a degree, these were Indians who believed in the rich culture and Hindu religion of their dimly remembered forefathers. But they were also Africans; most of them felt homesick for Africa rather than India, having never encountered the latter in anything but their grand-parents' stories.

Like all other unique subcultures that migrate to America, the Indians were necessarily faced with the age-old problem of choosing between full assimilation into their new homeland or continued loyalty to a time-honored way of life they physically, though not necessarily psychologically, had left behind. An element of grotesque humor, not lost on Nair, was evident in the way Indian motel owners maintained a bizarre double standard. While at home, adults insisted that their children adhere to strict moral principles; at the office, rooms were rented by the hour to prostitutes and their johns. This was "the deal" that Ugandan Indians made with the devil to survive.

The Indians would soon discover that maintaining old standards was easier said than done. In time, their children would leave to attend school; while immersed in the real junk-culture world of southern-fried roadside life, the next generation became completely Americanized, from their chosen clothing to their favorite music as well as social and sexual values. Observing this strange, fascinating situation left Nair with what she would later refer to as a new appreciation on her part for "the inexplicability of life."

The Ugandan Indians turned reluctant Americans "inhabited this no man's land," she explained to the *Times*, "yet it was their oasis. Here they were, face-to-face with truck drivers or lovers having a tryst, with blacks and whites. And yet here are these Indian hymns and the smell of garlic" in the air. Nair returned to the Northeast and convinced screenwriter Sooni Taraporevala to accompany her on a second trip so that they might begin work on a scenario. Sooni did, making her own previous personal experiences the basis for the Romeo and Juliet type of tale that would serve as the dramatic basis for their joint undertaking.

As a child, Taraporevala had grown up in Bombay, where her father ran a money-exchange business. Unhappy with her decision to attend college in America, he allowed her to apply to Harvard only because he was convinced she would not earn the scholarships necessary to make the great journey affordable. When she surprised him by qualifying, he was stymied in his efforts to keep her at home and loyal to "the old ways." Exposed in the United States to different ways of thinking that drastically altered her outlook on such issues as race relations and the role of women, Sooni inadvertently offended her father during visits home.

"I should not have sent you to America," her father would angrily scold her. On one return trip, Sooni brought along her current American boyfriend. Though she recalls her parents being polite enough to him, she later learned that they secretly prayed for a breakup, which did eventually occur. "You think with your heart rather than your head," Taraporevala's father insisted. That line clearly stuck, since years later she would put precisely those words into the mouth of Jay, the father of the young Americanized Indian daughter Mina in *Mississippi Masala*. A staunch traditionalist, Sooni's own father firmly believed that, however nice and bright a young man the fellow from Chicago may have been, the cultural gap between his daughter and that boy was impossible to ever bridge; love, in a conservative's view, most assuredly does *not* conquer all.

Such a family-versus-romance situation was the basis for the script, allowing for a tale of star-crossed lovers the director and writer hoped would have box-office appeal while allowing them to slip in some social commentary along the way. They quickly decided on a nonactress, Sarita Choudhury, for Mina. Raised in Jamaica, Choudhury had been held spellbound by her own father's tales of life in India, which became a charmingly remote fairy-tale kingdom to her. A huge fan of Bob Marley's during those years, Choudhury suggested to Nair that Mina wear a Marley T-shirt, visually suggesting the wide range of pop-culture interests that frustrate her conservative parents.

Twenty-five when the film was shot, Choudhury said: "When you have a mixed heritage, you can't be patriotic to any one place. The strength of that is that you're much more open-minded, but the downfall is that you have no home." The easy approach would have been for director and writer to create a romance between Mina and some white boy, perhaps modeling him on Sooni's own former boyfriend. Fortunately, the filmmakers chose a less expected, more rewarding route by having the handsome young man be black. This allowed them to deal not with the obvious form of racism—a person of color attempting to survive in a predominantly white world—but a more subtle, though no less insidious, alternative form of ethnocentricity.

In the story, Mina's father, once a prosperous lawyer in East Africa, has never properly adjusted to life in America or his notable drop in status from white-collar class to day laborer at a cheesy motel. "Africa for Africa—*black* Africans!" his onetime best friend, a black man in Uganda, insisted on the day Jay and his family were forced to leave. Jay still writes letters to the current Ugandan government asking to be allowed to return to his once luxurious property, which had been confiscated by Amin's minions. Their lack of response over the years causes Jay to grow bitter, so he directs his anger at local blacks. The two camps are composed of Indians who have never been to India and continue to think of themselves as Africans and African Americans who have never been to Africa but insist it is the land of their roots.

Denzel was the first and only choice to play Demetrius, an upwardly mobile young black who owns a carpet-cleaning business. Demetrius prospers in large part because he's hired to clean carpets at motels owned by Indians. Problems arise, however, following a minor automobile accident, depicted as if it might have appeared in a 1930s romantic screwball comedy. Mina, carelessly driving a borrowed car, slams into the rear of Demetrius's van. When Demetrius and Mina exchange phone numbers for the sake of insurance reports, the two are immediately attracted to one another. They decide to date, doing so secretly so as not to enrage either her family or his. But when they slip off to a nearby town for a romantic weekend and are all but caught in the act, her father is furious, insisting that the relationship be broken off. Jay also ensures that Demetrius's business will suffer by convincing the other Indian motel owners to cancel their contracts with him.

"Your skin is just a few shades lighter than mine," Demetrius insists to Jay during their key confrontation as one righteous man stands up against bigotry. Angered by the way Indians look down on the local black underclass—just as, twenty years earlier, Jay looked down on poor blacks unable to pull themselves out of poverty in Uganda—Demetrius exclaims: "I've never left Mississippi, but I do know something about the world. I know that folks can come to this country and be as black as the ace of spades, but soon as they come here, they start to act white—treat us like their doormats."

As Leah Rosen put it in *People Weekly, Mississippi Masala* is "about finding one's home within oneself and with those you love rather than in a specific place." The film does not subscribe to that popular liberal notion "assuming the moral superiority of the underdog": the widespread fallacy of assuming that any group of downtrodden people are ethically superior to those in power. All too often, the downtrodden delight in finding a group even lower on the social scale, which they in turn can look down on and berate. Happily, the film refuses to take sides between the Indians and blacks, any more than Shakespeare did between his Capulets and Montagues. Those two families, equally noble in rank and reputation, were equally susceptible to petty prejudices that, if left to rage uncontrolled, could have led to an all-out feud. David Ansen rightly pointed out in *Newsweek* that "the movie's affectionate satirical spirit...tweaks the hypocrisies of *both* communities without creating any overt villains."

Several members of Demetrius's family perceive themselves as Africans who are stuck, by circumstances, in America; the irony is that they fear, mistrust, and treat as outsiders people of color whose families really did inhabit Africa for nearly a century rather than embracing them as "brothers." Such an attitude is as illogical as that of the Indians toward them. By the movie's end, Demetrius and Mina will have to step away from both their respective families, however much they love certain individuals within those communities. The couple will, by their actions, prove that writer Sooni Taraporevala's father was wrong: The combined wills of two individuals in love *is* enough to conquer all the little differences that an older generation on each side believes to be all important.

As David Denby aptly summed it up in *New York*, "Nair links the two communities, wounded outsiders of color. *Mississippi Masala* is about homelessness, defined not merely as distance from a cherished land but as a refusal to take control of one's life, wherever it is, and live it to the full." No wonder, then, that Denzel wanted to join with Taraporevala and Nair on the project, which communicates ideas he holds dear. At the end, Demetrius and Mina are together, and we have every reason to believe they will indeed live happily (if not necessarily *easily*) ever after.

As a foil for Demetrius, there is his brother, who constantly expresses his desire to move to Africa, where he feels he would be much happier; in the context of the film, this attitude is as unrealistic, even absurd, as Jay's self-destructive longings for the same place. The film insists that one must be a realist and make the most of one's present situation; in Denzel's words, "Get busy!" That's just what Demetrius does, explaining to us why he—not his brother—is the film's hero. Just as Demetrius has assimilated into the rural South by competing with whites as a businessman and Mina has defied her family by assimilating into the culture by preferring T-shirts and rock to saris and sitar, so will the two of them create a true Mississippi Masala, eventually having a child who'll combine the best of both cultures while being a part of an American region.

"Without particularity or persuasiveness," the *New Yorker* explained, "Nair peddles an up-to-date peace-and-love ideology. She's created a movie for the multiculture," one that closes on a positive note: The romantic characters overcome. This is a clear alternative to the negative note sounded by Spike Lee's then recent *Jungle Fever*. It's worth noting that, had he wanted to, Denzel might have rather starred in that film, also about an interracial romance, though with a resoundingly pessimistic conclusion. He chose to pass on that project, allowing the role of a young upscale New York black architect who begins dating his white secretary to go to Wesley Snipes, his *Mo' Better Blues* costar. Denzel's choice was something other than a decision to play one character rather than another; it was a philosophical and political decision, a choice between being part of a positive or negative statement on the race issue.

Lee's *Jungle Fever* employs a similar plot to Nair's, ultimately conveying precisely the opposite message: Lee's couple, both fine people, eventually realize that their relatives were right and go their separate ways. Lee does not condemn the whites, who display a mixture of good and bad personality traits, much like his black characters. But the conclusion he draws is that the legendary American melting pot is nothing but a myth. Instead, his film says, we are separate but equal, a collection of subcultures that, at best, exist in peaceful coexistence with one another; at worst, breaking out in violent hostility.

This is not a statement that Denzel, committed through his lifestyle and chosen film projects to the idea of full integration of minority cultures into the broader fabric of mainstream life, could comfortably support. Nair's vision was more in line with Denzel's values, her very title suggesting a happy mixture of varied ethnicities within the boundaries of American regionalism. "Instead of making a big statement," Peter Travers observed in *Rolling Stone*, "she offers an intimately involving look at a clash of two cultures that are [tragically] blind to what unites them." Or as Denby wrote in *New York* magazine, "Nair fights the good fight against the current rage for ethnic chauvinism and separation. She knows that America is the only place where the races have even a chance of living together peacefully. A brave idea," one shared by Denzel, though not, apparently, by Spike Lee.

Brian D. Johnson of *Maclean's* found the film to be "fresh and charming," while Jack Mathews of *New York Newsday* spoke for many critics, hailing *Mississippi Masala* as one of the special little films that "transport us to places we've never been, introduce us to cultures we've never known, to lives we've never imagined, and return us to our seats uplifted and enlightened." Vincent Canby of the *New York Times*, tagging the film "sweetly pungent," noted that while *Mississippi Masala* had "been produced on a modest budget, it is a big movie in terms of talent, geography, and concerns, full of odd characters who are not neatly explained. It is melancholy without tears."

Denzel's reviews were uniformly excellent. Rosen wrote: "Washington's performance will make a believer out of anyone who ever doubted that he is an A-list movie star and sex symbol. This man is debonair. And magnetic. And he has an innate sweetness like Henry Fonda's but with even more steel." In *America*, Richard Blake concurred: "Denzel Washington has become a major star, and his balance of easygoing charm and intensity makes Demetrius believable and likable." In the *Times*, Canby noted: "Mr. Washington has a screen heft that gives the film its dramatic point." Denby wrote that Denzel "plays this man Demetrius—very responsible, a bit square [and, as such, much like Denzel himself!]—with dignity and force."

Intriguingly, Demetrius's former girlfriend in the film is a singer, not unlike Denzel's real-life wife; apparently, Denzel was allowed to collaborate on the creation of his screen character, making Demetrius something of an alter ego for Denzel himself. Demetrius is an imagined portrait of what Denzel might have been had he not had the opportunity to attend college, then try his hand at acting; Demetrius is not merely a homeboy played by Denzel but an image of Denzel as homeboy.

What was the appeal of playing (in Denzel's own words) "a little country boy"? It had to do with the fact that, in his post-*Glory* glory days, Denzel—finally being treated as a star—wasn't completely comfortable with that situation. "Maybe people are more excited [after the Oscar] when I meet them, and that's good. They're my fans, you know. [But] I don't walk past the mirror any slower.... Now, I'm trying to be more regular than regular. I look at myself now, and I say, 'Damn! I used to dress better' [when I had *less* money, prestige, and power]. *I wanna play a homeboy*. So I'm doin' one in life," dressing down during everyday activities as part of a concerted and conscious effort *not* to let himself be negatively affected by success. Part of the appeal of Nair's film, then, was its allowing Denzel to get back in touch with his own previous, simpler presuccess self, playing a homeboy on-screen as well as off.

12

Malcolm X

1992

A WARNER BROS. RELEASE

CAST: Denzel Washington (*Malcolm [Little] X*); Angela Bassett (*Betty Shabazz*); Albert Hall (*Baines*); Al Freeman Jr. (*Elijah Muhammad*); Delroy Lindo (*West Indian Archie*); Spike Lee (*Shorty*); Theresa Randle (*Laura*); Kate Vernon (*Sophia*); Lonette McKee (*Louise Little*); James McDaniel (*Brother Earl*); Joe Seneca (*Toomer*); John Sayles (*FBI Agent*); Nick Turturro (*Boston Cop*); Nelson Mandela (*Teacher*).

CREDITS: Director, Spike Lee; producers, Lee and Marvin Worth; screenplay, Lee and Arnold Perl, based on the book *The Autobiography of Malcolm X*, as told to Alex Haley; cinematography, Ernest Dickerson; editor, Barry Alexander Brown; music, Terence Blanchard; production design, Wynn Thomas; costumes, Ruth Carter; rating, PG-13; running time, 201 min.

I had to serve the man and try to find handles to make me feel more like the person," Denzel told *Parade* magazine, reflecting on his experiences playing Malcolm X first on the New York stage, then in Spike Lee's epic film. Denzel admitted that, physically and psychologically, he was as different from Malcolm X as could be. Malcolm, considerably taller, was extremely light-skinned, while Denzel, standing just a tad under six feet, is dark-complexioned. Since Malcolm's hair was red, Denzel had to undergo endless and painful dyeing attempts to approximate the unique color that had

137

earned Malcolm the nickname "Red." Still, those were relatively minor considerations in light of the differences between the two as thinking people. Their shared color aside, the attitudes of Malcolm and Denzel, like the life histories of the two men, stood at opposite poles.

Having grown up in an integrated neighborhood, with the constant attention of strong parents, made Denzel a perpetual believer in assimilation as the answer to America's race problem. Witnessing, as a child, his own father's murder at the hands of racist whites, then watching as his mother had to be confined to a mental institution when she couldn't cope, steered Malcolm's ship of life on a very different route. To play someone so far removed from himself, Denzel focused on the murder of Malcolm's father not merely as a brutal act but as the removal of a family institution from Malcolm's life, leaving him to always search for some form of substitute in a succession of makeshift "families," ranging from a Harlem gang to the Black Muslims.

Denzel, on the other hand, *always* had the reality of family to fall back on, even after his parents' divorce. It allowed him an anchor Malcolm lacked. "People saw him as a racist leader," Denzel conceded, "and in some ways he was. But you have to see behind the scenes to try and figure out *why*." What if Denzel had not received so much support along the way, had never experienced the lucky breaks that allowed his talent to succeed? He might have become bitter; in that case, he might have chosen a road similar to Malcolm's. Denzel came to envision the unfolding film project thusly: "This is a story about the evolution of a man. It's a spiritual, philosophical, political evolution. My prayer is to illustrate that and have that be some kind of *healing* for people."

In the 1981 off-Broadway premiere of *When the Chickens Come Home to Roost*, Denzel had played Malcolm during a single evening near the end of the great leader's life, involved in a fictional confrontation with his former Black Muslim mentor, Elijah Muhammad. The movie, on the other hand, would be both epic and biographical in nature, beginning with Malcolm Little's birth in Omaha in 1925 and chronicling a harsh adolescence without benefit of parents. Malcolm would become a pimp in Boston's sporting set during World War II, then move on, running with gangsters and show-business types in postwar Harlem until his unsavory exploits landed him in Massachusetts jails for six and one half years. As a prisoner, Malcolm became a devout reader and learned of Islam from fellow prisoners. Upon release, he ceased trying to be like whites and learned to hate them, joining the Nation of Islam.

As a spokesman for black nationalism and total separatism, Malcolm spoke derisively of "blue-eyed white devils." He emerged, in the popular symbolism of the time, the polar opposite of Martin Luther King, an advocate of equality through peaceful integration. Eventually, though, Malcolm came to realize that Elijah Muhammad was a hypocrite, secretly violating strict Muslim doctrines, including the bans on sex and liquor. Then a 1964 pilgrimage to Mecca allowed the disillusioned Malcolm to see firsthand that black Muslims could indeed embrace white followers of the faith in perfect harmony. Malcolm was stunned to note that "they were of all complexions, the whole atmosphere was of warmth and friendliness. The feeling hit me that there really wasn't any color problem here. The effect was as though I had just stepped out of a prison." Not the physical prison he had once been incarcerated in; rather, the prison of his own reverse racism. Malcolm appeared ready to re-create himself once more, embracing a more amenable approach and conciliatory tone regarding race relations. Before he could do so, Malcolm was, in 1965, assassinated by three Black Muslims, for the organization had come to consider him a traitor possessing a dangerous insider's familiarity with their organization.

When Denzel agreed to appear in *When the Chickens Come Home to Roost*, his main objective was to earn a desperately needed $125 a week as an actor. Denzel knew next to nothing about Malcolm; his own parents had been supporters of Malcolm's polar opposite, Martin Luther King. Searching *The Autobiography of Malcolm X* for the role turned Denzel's head around; for the first time, this rather callow, oblivious (at the time) young man came into contact with volatile ideas that forced him to reconsider all his previous middlebrow attitudes.

Frank Rich, of the *New York Times*, praised Denzel for his "firm, likable performance" in the play, noting the actor's insistence on complexity, as this Malcolm was "honorable and altruistic without ever becoming a plaster saint." The show did not enjoy a long run, however, so the actor's appetite for the role was barely sated. Denzel still insists that he knew at the time, in his heart, a more epic version would in good time come to pass: "When I did that play, I said to myself, 'I'm going to do this movie one day. I *know* it.'"

Someone else, a young film student who saw the play one night, likewise dreamed of doing a movie about Malcolm X with Denzel as star: a then unknown, aspiring director named Spike Lee. In fact, Malcolm's autobiography had already been optioned by producer Marvin Worth, who had made the controversial *Lenny*. And for several years following the completion of *A Soldier's Story*, Norman Jewison and Denzel excitedly talked about working together again on a *Malcolm X* film. Actually, the Canadian-born director had hoped to film the story long before he and Denzel had met. Following the commercial and critical success of *In the Heat of the Night*, Jewison had, throughout the 1970s, tried without success to get a Malcolm biopic going, headlining Sidney Poitier, the star of Jewison's 1967's Best Picture of the Year Oscar winner. Nothing happened, partly because Malcolm's inflammatory statements were then still too current to be incorporated into a major motion picture by one of the mainstream studios. But with the passing of time, Malcolm's story—now safely softened in our memories—became a viable project. As Denzel's star rose, Warner Bros. decided to take whatever risk might be involved.

Soldier's Story playwright Charles Fuller was hired to develop the screenplay. Then, in 1985, Alice Walker's important novel about black life in the early-twentieth-century south, *The Color Purple*, was released by Warner Bros., directed by Steven Spielberg directing. Though the film was a commercial success and the nearly all-black cast was unanimously praised, numerous critics—particularly African-American critics—complained that a white director had been allowed to make such a movie. Skin color was not necessarily the key issue; the problem was that *The Color Purple* obviously looked, sounded, and played as if it had been made by a well-intentioned, though misinformed, white filmmaker—someone who knew everything there was to know about making movies but nothing at all about what it felt like to be black. *The Color Purple* played like a Hallmark Hall of Fame production, polite and pleasant rather than a true cinematic rendering of Walker's angry literary document.

At that point, Spike Lee came into the picture. In his characteristically abrasive way, Lee announced to the press that no white director, however talented, could ever bring the essence of Malcolm X to full life on-screen. Warner Bros. decided that discretion was indeed the better part of valor. Studio executives unofficially suggested to Jewison that he take a hike from the very film he had himself proposed to them. And who better to hire than the very man who challenged Jewison? For his starting point, Lee—scraping the Charles Fuller treatment entirely—dusted off a two-decades-old screenplay, *One Day, When I Was Lost,* by the acclaimed 1960s novelist and essayist James Baldwin (*The Fire Next Time*), who had collaborated with a white screenwriter, Arnold Perl. Spike, in the dozen or so subsequent drafts he wrote himself, then drastically altered Baldwin's vision to fit more in line with his own.

Among other things, Spike created a character for himself: Shorty, a composite of various lowlifes who had been Malcolm's companions during his early years, when such young studs conked their hair to approximate a white look and dressed to the hilt in zoot suits. Malcolm's criminal acts of a degrading nature, including pimping and pushing hard drugs, were entirely eliminated by Lee, leaving the impression that Malcolm's worst offense was numbers running. The various people who influenced Malcolm in prison were consolidated in the film into yet another composite, called Baines (Albert Hall). Though Malcolm's wife, Betty Shabazz, had left him on three occasions owing to his male-chauvinist views that kept her from working at a meaningful job, their marriage was depicted in the film as being the image of sitcom perfection. At the end, Spike turned the film into a black *Spartacus* (1960) by having none other than Nelson Mandela himself play a teacher, telling his Soweto students the story. One by one, the little boys rise from their seats, thrust fists into the air, and announce: "*I* am Malcolm!"

Such an approach enraged a number of prominent black artists and critics, who protested the movie while Spike and Denzel were still in preproduction. In particular, poet Amiri Baraka (who, a generation earlier, had been known as angry young playwright LeRoi Jones), representing an organization calling itself the United Front to Preserve the Legacy of Malcolm X, announced that the emerging film would do a terrible disservice to Malcolm's memory. In their view, Spike and Denzel had clearly been co-opted by the

Hollywood establishment. With Warner Bros. spending nearly $30 million to make the film, what emerged could not possibly be a radical work; it would be darkened pablum, typical mass entertainment that would soften Malcolm X's image so that the resultant film could play in suburban mall theaters. Baraka insisted that this would "trash" the truth, resulting in a typically bland cinematic epic not unlike *Cry Freedom*, one more film that would, in Baraka's words, serve only to "make middle-class Negroes sleep easier."

Lee, assuming a public aura of calm that he perhaps did not really feel, stated flatly: "This film is going to be *my* vision of Malcolm X." By admitting this, he chose not to deny that there was a certain element of truth in Baraka's attack. A multi-million-dollar movie is indeed just that, a huge Hollywood undertaking. The irony is that Lee and other aspiring filmmakers had appeared, to mainstream observers, to be radicals when, over the years, they complained that Hollywood didn't put such major resources behind black projects. Now Hollywood had gone out on a limb and done just that, only to be attacked—along with Lee, still a radical in the eyes of many middlebrows but firmly entrenched as Establishment in the minds of true radicals—for doing precisely what they had for years failed to do.

Lee knew it was impossible to make a movie that would satisfy everyone; the necessary inclusion of inflammatory speeches in his film would upset entrenched conservatives, while an honest depiction of infighting among black nationalists would not sit well with true believers, who wanted propaganda that would portray all blacks as brothers. The filmmaker also realized, to his horror, that Warner Bros. was planning to merchandise hats and T-shirts with the famous X logo, as if this were yet another *Batman*. If Spike could only remain true to his own vision of Malcolm, then even if he did not satisfy everyone, he could at least draw satisfaction from the knowledge that he'd created a Spike Lee joint on a scale larger than ever before, producing the movie—however compromised by the necessity of reducing a remarkable man's full life to three hours and twenty minutes—that he'd originally hoped to make.

While accompanying Spike on location for *Rolling Stone*, journalist Joe Wood (editor of the book *Malcolm X: In Our Own Image*) observed that Lee's resolve was always in danger of crumbling:

There were so many people to please. Spike's interpretation had to answer to the Nation's followers, who didn't want to see Elijah trashed; to "family values" of black folk, the majority, who wouldn't stand for an R-rated Malcolm, to activists like Baraka who didn't want their symbol of black pride challenged; to the Hollywood community, which had difficulty seeing Malcolm as a subject worthy of a treatment as lengthy and costly as Oliver Stone's *JFK*. The noise, left uncontained, would have made it impossible for almost anyone to think, much less create. The challenge Spike faced was to listen to all the voices, especially the quiet ones, then to make a Malcolm all his own, Malcolm as he understood him, not a colorized version of the dead leader's autobiography. [But] the auteur's vision was blurring with his [opposing] perspectives as community activist and marketer.

One of the quiet voices that calmed Lee and helped him refocus was Denzel's. Since the actor had preceded the director to the project, there was a noticeably different balance of power than on the *Mo' Better Blues* set. Back then, Denzel had been an actor for hire, brought in to help the artist realize his ambition for a highly personal work; now Lee was the director who had been allowed to join in on what had already been planned as a Denzel Washington vehicle. The two had argued, heatedly at the beginning, on *Mo' Better Blues*; this time around, Denzel and Spike decided at once to succeed by collaborating rather than survive in conflict. Spike even offered Denzel the opportunity to contribute to the writing, particularly those scenes when Malcolm speaks before gathered multitudes. As with *Mo' Better Blues*, the two strong-willed, in many ways diametrically opposed, artists realized that they had drastically different interpretations of what Malcolm's story meant and what the eventual film ought to convey to the public. Still, without a patina of agreement, Denzel and Spike could not proceed, at least with any hope of creating a cohesive film.

Fortunately, then, both believed—based on their separate readings—that Malcolm's story was basically about one man's search for a father figure. The racially motivated killing of Malcolm's biological father would figure prominently in the dramatization. Malcolm would then move on to a succession of father figures—from his gangster-era boss, West Indian Archie, to his jailhouse mentor, to Elijah—each of whom ultimately disappoints the protagonist. Lee drew a pessimistic conclusion from all this: Malcolm's story was a tragedy about a man ultimately "crushed" (Spike's own word) by his experience in life, death offering him a kind of sad release from the emotional pain and suffering. Denzel saw it quite differently. In the end, Malcolm discovered God; while it may have been Malcolm's Islamic vision rather than Denzel's Christian one, God is God: The ultimate Father. Denzel therefore took the story as an optimistic epic; however sad that Malcolm's life was cut short, at least he had "found truth" (Denzel's words) before his death.

Denzel remained acutely aware that he himself had been raised on a principle which, to paraphrase Sammy Davis Jr., came down to one phrase: Yes, you can. On the other hand, Malcolm had been informed by a counselor, while just a child, that he could not hope to become a lawyer. This "advice," according to Spike's script, caused the previously positive little boy to opt for a life of crime. Attacking such crippling negative influences on an impressionable individual rather than propagandizing the cause of black nationalism was always Denzel's ambition. Certainly, he re-creates some of Malcolm's separatist remarks: "Today you do not know your tribal language or what tribe you are from. You don't even know your family's real name. You are wearing a white man's name. The white slave master who *hates* you." (The adopted "X" was an attempt to obliterate Malcolm's "white" name, Little.)

However important such lines may have been to Spike's vision, for Denzel they existed in the film to clarify the historical record. The point Denzel hoped to drive home was: "Take it from Malcolm! If you're taught all your life you're never going to do anything, then you can never do anything." The alternative approach, when a person is allowed freedom to realize his potential, comes in the form of Denzel's own lifelong preoccupation, hard work. "Being angry is an easy choice. Knowing yourself takes a little more effort." The philosophy he wanted to convey was that railing about injustice can be counterproductive. "Racism is a given. The question becomes: How do you deal with it?" To Denzel, one's realization as a human being through individual achievement is the only answer: "Get *busy* with yourself."

Coming to understand, via the experience of watching the film, that everyone can assume control of his own destiny would provide the "healing" element Denzel spoke of, the hopeful theme that can be derived from a seemingly depressing story. This is the shared attitude that ultimately explains why, despite differences over many issues, Denzel and Spike were able to work together, often agreeing to disagree but arriving at a common core that allowed the film to coalesce rather than tear apart at its seams. "This is what I like about Spike. Yeah, he talks about racism, but he doesn't dwell on it. Spike's *busy*. And I like that! *Go do something.*" As with *Mo' Better Blues*, it appears that Spike's vision dominated the movie's first half; Denzel's, the second. From the opening sequence, there is no doubt that the movie is Spike Lee's as Shorty and Malcolm parade, as in an old Hollywood musical, through the town; Spike adores the 1940s African-American street culture, and his imagery comes dazzlingly alive when cinematographer Ernest Dickerson films it through filters that shroud everything in a golden glow.

Denzel's quieter, more conciliatory voice dominates the film's latter portions as Malcolm moves in a direction the actor could readily approve of. Actor Ossie Davis, a close friend of Malcolm's who appears briefly in the film, says: "No one who knew him before and after his trip to Mecca could doubt that he had completely abandoned racism, separatism, and hatred." Recreating himself one final time as El-Hajj Malik El-Shabazz, the great leader was becoming a kinder, gentler Malcolm. As he stepped away from his previous vision of whites as devils, Malcolm was killed by those within his own community who were desperate to silence the new voice of accommodation, a voice that was not so different from Martin Luther King's—or Denzel Washington's. The movie's final moments lack the Spike Lee excitement of the earlier nightclub-gangster sequences; the mellowness suggests the dominant presence of Lee's actor-star collaborator.

On the eve of the film's release, Denzel made his feelings about the role absolutely clear: "Everything I have done as an actor has been in preparation for this," he insisted to the interviewers he regularly avoids but greeted to publicize this particular picture. If one believes in destiny, Denzel was right about that. Lest we forget, Denzel had been ready to quit acting and accept a conventional day job before learning he would play Malcolm off Broadway. Playing Malcolm X had served as a germinal event in Denzel's career; there was a satisfying sense of closure, then, as Denzel at last returned the favor. Having emerged as a full-fledged film star, he used his considerable clout to bring Malcolm to the screen. That helps explain why Denzel passed on several multi-million-dollar offers to do more action-adventure flicks, signing on for a year-and-a-half stint, with his entire salary deferred, and accepting instead a percentage of the profits to keep the initial budget down.

With the role came an even lengthier period of preparation than usual for the diligent actor. Denzel traveled to New York for a period of preparation so as to immerse himself in the city Malcolm had chosen to inhabit. He read everything by and about Malcolm he could get his hands on so as to understand the man's thought processes. Over and over, Denzel watched every piece of film or videotape on Malcolm that was available, gaining a full sense of the man's every mannerism and gesture. Then he sought out and spoke with every relative, friend, even enemy of Malcolm's he could track down, gathering a wide spectrum of attitudes by those who had known him firsthand. Denzel gained access to the FBI files on Malcolm and pored over them, learning many things that distressed the actor about Malcolm's unsavory early life and (temporarily held) extremist views. He signed up for Fruit of Islam classes, agreeing to eat only one nonpork meal a day, marching with them in formation, studying their ultrastrict doctrine; whether or not he also subscribed to their insistence on abstinence from sex, the happily married performer has not chosen to reveal publicly. "I was doing so much work," Denzel later explained, "I just sort of blended into the man as best I could. That was my desire."

A seemingly unrelated event transpired that affected Denzel's performance. The actor had been preparing for only two days when word reached him that his father had passed away. Denzel was already drawing on the spirit of Malcolm X, just as he had pre-viously drawn on that of Steve Biko, to guide him through the performance, making it valid in the fullest sense possible. Now, though, Denzel found himself drawing on the spirit of his father as well. Like Malcolm X's father, Denzel's had been a minister. At last, the two very different men—Denzel and Malcolm X—had something in common: grief for a deceased minister-father. Denzel's Malcolm X is a vivid biographical portrait, but like a true method actor, Denzel drew on his own recent loss to bring Malcolm's loss to artistic life. Denzel's sister Lorice observed that during the scenes in which Malcolm must preach, "his hand gestures and the rhythms of his voice were Daddy's" rather than the historical Malcolm X.

The moment this parallel was drawn, others fell into place. Like Denzel, Malcolm had been a "celebrity" who remained private, even guarded, about his personal life. Like Denzel, Malcolm was a great performer in front of crowds, albeit one who always wanted to drive home a point. Denzel's emotional depth in the role has much to do with his personalizing the part rather than merely approaching it in a cool, analytic manner. What we see also serves as an autobiography of the life he himself never lived, one he—or any man—might well have known had he been consigned to walk a mile in the shoes Malcolm X had to wear his entire life.

If there was one final problem in bringing the role to full fruition, it was simply that Denzel's own experiences hadn't made him angry in the way Malcolm X had become because of endless hard knocks. Nonetheless, journalist Lena Williams noted: "Beneath his surface of restraint, like many black Americans of his generation, [Denzel] harbors an anger—and a disappointment—barely kept at bay." He had to find a way to unleash that anger—unknown to others and even, perhaps, to himself—if Malcolm's anger was to appear real rather than playacted. Luckily for Denzel, he happened to be in New York, where cabdrivers do not regularly stop for blacks. "After I couldn't get a cab all day, I finally punched the door of a cab that passed me by," he recalls. The experience of being ignored wasn't pleasant, but he used it to his own advantage, drawing on the memory of such anger and diverting it into the performance. As Denzel puts it, "You ask all the right questions of your character and relate it to the experiences you've had to find a formula that works."

Denzel's great hope was that if the spirit of Malcolm X were indeed looking down, he would be happy with what he saw. Though that may sound like sentimental hogwash to many, to a devoutly religious man like Denzel, it was important. The answer came to Denzel on the day he was to deliver the first of Malcolm's legendary speeches. Director Lee was distraught. Their outdoors winter set was being pummeled by freezing rain; the speech was supposed to take place in fair weather. Feeling the pinch of budgets, Lee informed the crew that they'd have to shoot, anyway. Lights were adjusted, cameras readied, and then Spike called for Denzel to begin. The moment Denzel stepped toward the podium, the rain— miraculously, some would say—stopped. Denzel delivered the speech and turned to leave; as he did, the rain commenced. "That," Denzel later recalled, "was when I knew we were going to be all right!"

In Rahway, New Jersey, Denzel experienced some initial tension with Muslims who were wary about the way in which their hero would be portrayed. But he made his peace with them. Eventually, Spike moved Denzel, along with the cast and his black crew, off to Africa, where he had received permission to film Malcolm's hajj, or pilgrimage, to Mecca on actual locations. Denzel's wife accompanied him. It was when production ended and everyone returned to America for postproduction that the real problems began. While Spike oversaw the editing and sound mixing, the project went over budget; to make his raw footage ready for distribution, Spike would eventually require between $5 million and $7 million above the $28 million ceiling Warner Bros. had allotted. Warner executives Terry Semel and Bob Daly refused to extend any more money, leaving the Completion Bond Company, which served as the film's "guarantor," a legal right to shut down production even at this late date, taking creative control away from Lee. The director responded in typical fashion, claiming that they were treating him this way because of his color. Warner Bros. defended themselves, explaining that while they had never before taken away creative control from a black director, they regularly did it with white directors; therefore, they were treating Lee as they would any other filmmaker—as an equal, regardless of race.

As *Ebony* magazine would later comment, "Rightly or wrongly, racism is an old song for Lee. He is known to sing it whenever he doesn't get what he wants." In a hurried attempt to hold on to the film, Spike contributed $2 million of his $3 million salary, hoping that it would cover expenses. The amount proved to be only a drop in the bucket. Spike then turned to Hollywood's upper-crust black community, requesting they back him to form a united front. Within forty-eight hours, money poured in from the likes of Bill Cosby, Oprah Winfrey, Michael Jordan, and Prince. "This is an important precedent," Lee gloatingly announced, while actor Ossie Davis—who had twenty-five years earlier delivered the eulogy at Malcolm X's funeral—noted: "Black people with resources offer them to Spike in copious quantities *not* as an investment, *not* as a loan, but as a way of affirming black solidarity."

A movie lover may imagine a scene not unlike the finale of Frank Capra's *It's a Wonderful Life*, only with an African-American cast. Even before those funds had arrived, however, a red-faced Warner Bros. began writing checks to cover expenses when Lee went public, announcing his revolutionary plan to the press. Still, the friction between Lee and the company continued. Upon viewing his cut, the executives suggested that Spike eliminate the opening newsreel footage of Rodney King's beating, fearing that this linking of a recent event to Malcolm's story might have an incendiary effect on black audiences. Lee balked; he was, after all, not telling a tale from the past merely for its own sake but to make clear that the things Malcolm spoke out against were still happening. Lee stuck to his guns, and Warner Bros. backed down.

As for the film's final effect, David Denby of *New York* magazine spoke for most critics when he wrote: "Is *Malcolm X* great? There are some evasions and a few empty, grandstanding passages, but most of it is rock solid—stirring, emotionally challenging, and even funny. . . . The representative quality [of Malcolm] is there, but it's the triumph of this movie that Malcolm always seems like a struggling *person* rather than a symbol." Of the star, Denby added: "Denzel plays Malcolm with tremendous concentration combined with an essential modesty that is very pleasing. As a teenage gangster, Washington has the moves, the look, a warming smile. Later, as Malcolm becomes a street preacher, Washington puts steel in his voice. . . . Washington consistently underplays, and his charm makes Malcolm less angular and abrupt as a personality."

Richard Alleva of *Commonweal* went even further in his praise:

> In his gangster tux and with a cigarette dangling from one corner of his mouth, Denzel Washington is Clark Gable come again. . . . In scenes such as the one in which Malcolm quells a

rebellion in his burglary ring by forcing a rival to play Russian roulette with him, Washington helps Lee achieve just the sort of glinting, moonlight-in-the-gutter poetry we get from classic gangster movies.... [as the later Malcolm], Washington continues to score as he conveys his character's rage with an amused iciness that seems to amplify the anger rather than mitigate it.

Up to this point in his career, Denzel was the only important star who had avoided becoming part of a merchandising strategy. So how did he feel about the T-shirts and hats piling up on store shelves in anticipation of the film release? Denzel pooh-poohed such stuff, insisting that if the work were of the quality he hoped for, all the hype would not, could not, damage what he and Spike had achieved: "The hat goes on the top of the head; we're trying to put something between the ears and in the heart."

13

Much Ado About Nothing
1993

A SAMUEL GOLDWYN COMPANY RELEASE

CAST: Denzel Washington (*Don Pedro*); Kenneth Branagh (*Benedick*); Emma Thompson (*Beatrice*); Michael Keaton (*Dogberry*); Robert Sean Leonard (*Claudio*); Keanu Reeves (*Don John*); Richard Briers (*Leonato*); Brian Blessed (*Antonio*); Kate Beckinsale (*Hero*); Imelda Staunton (*Margaret*); Phyllida Law (*Ursula*).

CREDITS: Director, Kenneth Branagh; producers, Branagh, David Parfitt, and Stephen Evans; screen adaptation, Branagh, from the play by William Shakespeare; cinematography, Andrew Marcus; music, Patrick Doyle; production design, Tim Harvey; costumes, Phyllis Dalton; rating, PG-13; running time, 111 min.

I thought it might be a kind of nice work-vacation, a month in the country," Denzel said of his decision to accept a supporting role in Kenneth Branagh's film version of William Shakespeare's romantic comedy *Much Ado About Nothing*. Denzel had just come off *Malcolm X*; the year and a half of intense concentration on such a huge, heavy undertaking had left him in a state of near exhaustion. On the other hand, Denzel, who has always relished work, was particularly fond of the classics in general and Shakespeare in particular. And, of course, he was fond of breaking the color barrier by winning roles that had not been written with a black actor in mind. So here was a perfect project for the moment:

151

generally lighthearted in tone, allowing him to remain mostly in the background as a presence while leaving the more serious acting and directing responsibilities to others, and a wonderful opportunity for him and his family to get away from Hollywood for a visit to gorgeous Tuscany. He would maintain his visibility via a prestige production, without expending much effort. How difficult could it be?

As it turned out, more difficult than anyone could have guessed. *Much Ado About Nothing* looks properly lyrical and lilting on-screen, allowing mesmerized viewers to believe that producer-director Branagh and his wonderful cast merely danced and pranced their way through the joyous romp. Actually, the film, which appears absolutely effortless on-screen (as comedy must if it is to succeed), required great effort by all involved, Denzel included. No sooner was the cast settled in Tuscany than a late-August heat wave struck them, making it almost impossible to move at all, much less communicate a sense of perpetual airiness. In particular, the extensive night shooting proved terribly troublesome. Branagh felt taxed in a way he had not been while filming his spectacular epic based on Shakespeare's *Henry V*, finally walking away from the *Much Ado About Nothing* set in utter frustration, terrified that the unthinkable could actually happen: that the half-finished film might be closed down.

"You get to the moment when you think you're going to crack," Branagh later recalled. "I sent everybody away and just sat in the garden. 'Nobody ask me for anything or *need* anything.'" Denzel, meanwhile, had accomplished what, as an actor, he always does: becoming one with his character, in this case the benign prince Don Pedro, always ready to give the other characters a helping hand. So it was that Denzel approached Branagh, sitting off on the sidelines in a dark funk. Denzel then did what his character would have done for a friend in the film, hugging Branagh when the director needed it the most. "What's up, boss?" Denzel said with a winning grin. "Listen, you're allowed to have these feelings. If you send all the crew away, people won't take you for granted!"

Within minutes, Branagh was reaffirmed and able to return to the set, where he, Denzel, and the others completed the day's work. "He's good company, Denzel," Branagh says of his onetime costar. "I've got a lot of time for him."

Branagh's film, like Shakespeare's tale, is set in Messina, Italy. The story unfolds as Don Pedro, accompanied (unbeknownst to the good, wise, but naive prince) by his evil half brother Don John (Keanu Reeves), and fellow warriors ride victoriously home from the wars. Their plan is to rest up at the villa of old Leonato, celebrating the recent victory by wooing all the attractive women gathered there. Shortly, the sharp-tongued Benedick (Branagh) is matched off with his equal in wit, the sexy but unapproachable "shrew" Beatrice (Emma Thompson). These two insist that they can't stand one another, though the others aren't so sure that's the case. Meanwhile, handsome young hunk Claudio (Robert Sean Leonard) is busily courting Hero (Kate Beckinsale), Leonato's pretty daughter.

As always, in Shakespeare, the course of true love does not run smooth, else *Much Ado About Nothing* would be a brief one-act play. The evil Don John and his cohorts plot to convince the none-too-bright Claudio that his virginal fiancée is actually a wanton wench engaged in a torrid sexual affair. They accomplish this by placing a maid on Hero's balcony, where this girl makes wild love to another man, even as Claudio and the prince—having been manipulated by Don John to a hiding place below—gaze on, stunned and disappointed by what they see. Meanwhile, the prince and his good-natured friends are involved in their own considerably more benign deception. They conspire to make Beatrice and Benedick believe that each is in love with the other, then sit back and enjoy the results as rueful scorn transforms into mature love, of the mind as well as of the heart.

At first glance, the role of the prince appears minor, someone noble who merely stands around in the background, offering occasional advice. In fact, it is one of the most difficult roles in the play and, symbolically, the most important. Don Pedro is a variation of Shakespeare's continuing theme of the absolute ruler, upon whose shoulders the rise or fall of the kingdom (however little that kingdom may be) rests. Like all Shakespeare's rulers, Don Pedro is a complicated man who does not take this responsibility lightly. His every desire is to do good for his citizens, making certain everybody is properly paired off with a fitting mate so as to continue the positive peopling of the world, as God or nature meant it. Unfortunately, this causes him to be so busy worrying about others that he's always in danger of forgetting to focus on a woman for himself. Moreover, in spite of decent intentions, the prince is fallible, striving to be a perfect ruler but limited by his very humanity. He cannot help making mistakes, such as falling prey to the deception that has him, like Claudio, believing Hero is unworthy.

Why Denzel Washington—a black American cast as an Italian prince who's been reimagined by Britain's greatest scribe? Branagh had, early on, decided to mix and match popular American stars with English actors, including his then wife, Emma Thompson. "I always liked the ballsiness of American film acting, the full-blooded abandon," Branagh insists. "This play just seemed to require it." His ambition had always been to create a film that would not be relegated to the art-house circuit; rather, one which would bring Shakespeare to the masses, allowing everyone to grasp the fact that his plays are for the common man. The bard's comedies are just plain fun, not the inaccessible works of "high culture" many ordinary folks mistakenly believe them to be. So it was that Michael Keaton, of *Batman* (1989) and *Beetlejuice* (1988), was signed to play Dogberry, low-comedy leader of "the watch" who ultimately unmasks the villainous Don John, though only after delivering endless malapropisms. Canadian-born Keanu Reeves, having become a film star via *Bill and Ted's Excellent Adventure* (1989), flew to London, where he convinced Branagh he could handle one of Shakespeare's Machiavellian villains, the bad guy who manipulates everyone's perceptions until he is finally caught red-handed.

For the part of the prince, Branagh knew he needed an actor able to radiate great dignity tempered with the flaws of humanity, the very qualities Denzel had projected in carefully chosen roles ever since *St. Elsewhere*. No wonder, then, that Branagh considered Denzel perfect: "He has intellectual weight, spiritual gravity, and a powerful sexual and romantic presence," the actor-director remarked. The character's being color nonspecific made Don Pedro an attractive acting plum for Denzel. Though as a youth Denzel had made his reputation with a college performance as Othello, Shakespeare's only black hero, Denzel had since skirted offers to play that part again. Instead, he pursued every other Shakespearean role, from the wicked villain-prince of *Richard III* (which he did on the New York stage) to the decent hero-prince of *Much Ado About*

A man and his horn: as Bleek Gilliam, who puts his music above all; *Mo' Better Blues* marked Denzel's first collaboration with Spike Lee. (courtesy Universal Pictures)

(Right) As *Heart Condition*'s upscale but shady lawyer Napoleon Stone. Though he refused any clichéd street-people parts, Denzel likewise preferred not to play simplistic heroes. (courtesy New Line Cinema)

Heart Condition: Napoleon becomes guardian angel to his worst enemy, the bigoted cop Jack Moony (Bob Hoskins). This marked the second time Denzel appeared in a comedy with serious undertones about racism. (courtesy New Line Cinema)

Denzel Washington as Nick Styles, a policeman who rises through the ranks, only to find his white "colleagues" turning against him. *Ricochet* provided a nightmare scenario for assimilated middle-class blacks. (courtesy Warner Bros.)

Ricochet: A duel to the death between Nick and arch-enemy Blake (John Lithgow). Denzel accepted the role because his son wanted to see Dad as an action hero. (courtesy Warner Bros.)

Demetrius (Denzel) introduces Mina (Sarita Choudhury) to his family. Though *Mississippi Marsala* deals with racism, it occurs between differing ethnic groups, with whites relegated to the sidelines. (courtesy Samuel Goldwyn Releasing)

Malcolm X allowed Denzel, under Spike Lee's guidance, to take a character from total innocent to embittered cynic to hopeful reconciler of races. (courtesy Warner Bros.)

As Malcolm X, doing what he did best: speaking articulately and eloquently. (courtesy Warner Bros.)

(Above) As Gray Grantham, investigative journalist. The actor, who once considered a career as a reporter, had the opportunity to live out "the road not taken" in *The Pelican Brief.* (courtesy Warner Bros.)

(Opposite top) Denzel *(far right)* as Shakespeare's prince Don Pedro, joined by others of Kenneth Branagh's *Much Ado* ensemble. Though the character as written was white, Branagh insisted on color-blind casting; Denzel has regularly pursued racially nonspecific parts. (courtesy Samuel Goldwyn Company)

(Opposite bottom) Much Ado About Nothing: The prince realizes that numskull Dogberry (Michael Keaton) may have discovered a nefarious plot. After the rigors of playing the lead in *Malcolm X,* Denzel was delighted to do a nondemanding supporting role as a kind of "working vacation." (courtesy Samuel Goldwyn Company)

The Pelican Brief: Gray and Darby Shaw (Julia Roberts) find themselves in a "you and me against the world" situation. Director Alan J. Pakula, while setting up shots like this one, was influence by the legendary Alfred Hitchcock's visual approach. (courtesy Warner Bros.)

Nothing, insisting that critics judge him not as a black actor but as an actor.

The critics were willing to meet that challenge, most arguing that his Richard III was a major disappointment; "surprisingly muted," Mel Gussow had said, making no reference whatsoever to the actor's color as a pro or con, instead insisting that Denzel played the part poorly. "I know I will fail occasionally," Denzel responded, perhaps disappointed at the reaction but buoyed by the fact that he had demanded and achieved parity with other Shakespearean actors who succeed or fail in specific productions.

For the most part, Denzel's prince in *Much Ado* was more positively received. Vincent Canby of the *New York Times* wrote:

> More or less presiding over these perilous revels is Don Pedro, who, in the majestic presence of Mr. Washington, is a benign, wise but lonely prince. Don Pedro is much taken with Beatrice, but though tempted to become a participant in the dance, he remains aloof. Benedick is his friend, and his subjects come first. Mr. Washington is amazingly good as an idealized Shakespearean monarch, the sort of character that sleeps on a page but comes to life when played by a charismatic actor.

Canby's comments have merit not only as an assessment of the performance but for what it reveals about the actor playing the role. In most Shakespearean comedies—*A Midsummer Night's Dream*, for instance—there are three couplings at the end, including one for the prince, who, like the other good characters, must marry to extend his line. Three has always been a kind of magical number, in ancient religions as in classical drama; lest we forget, classical drama derives from ancient religion. Simply, there is something undeniably "right" about seeing three such couples aligned for a triple marriage. *Much Ado About Nothing*, then, is—as Shakespeare penned it—strange, seeming incomplete in that the prince stands aside, appearing excluded from the happy ritual he has helped accomplish for his friends.

As Canby noted, the prince momentarily flirts with Beatrice, though—sensing she and his best friend Benedick are made for each other—he backs off. It would have been easy enough for Shakespeare to employ a deus ex machina, ushering in a princely woman for Don Pedro, just as the Amazon warrior Hippolyta weds and beds Theseus in *A Midsummer Night's Dream*. Instead, the prince is left all alone, though at one point, Benedick actually advises him to hurry and find a woman for himself. This interchange is particularly poignant in Branagh's film version, thanks to Denzel's reaction. Suddenly, the prince—who has been maintaining an aloof position, smiling with patronizing nobility at the romantic foibles of others— is speechless. He knows Benedick is right, but he has no comeback. There is nothing he can say or do, so he stands there, looking sad and sheepish.

Had Shakespeare allowed for a royal lady to arrive at the last moment and charm the prince, how would that have altered this modern film? If she were white, then Branagh would, however inadvertently, automatically add a theme of interracial love. That might have proven difficult for Denzel, who recoiled from just such screen relationships by declining to appear in *Love Field* and, later, a new screen adaptation of *Othello*. Had she been black, on the other hand, then the color issue—which the movie chooses to ignore— would have been automatically raised, owing to an audience's awareness that this was indeed a black couple, clearly juxtaposed against white couples.

As is, the prince seems unfairly excluded at the late-night masque. Some audiences, unfamiliar with Shakespeare's original and unaware that the role had been written with a white actor in mind, totally misinterpreted the scene, incorrectly believing that the prince, being black, was unable, owing to restrictions in effect in Italy during the period when the story unfolds, to pursue one of the available women. The irony, then, is that for such viewers color did indeed become an issue, however much Branagh and Denzel wanted to avoid it. As for Branagh, he has claimed, that being every bit as color-blind as Denzel when it comes to drama, he never even considered the issue of color while casting: "Honestly, it never occurred to me that I had a black actor and a white actor playing half-brothers" until someone else pointed it out.

Anthony Lane of the *New Yorker* offered an even more glowing assessment:

Don Pedro is not an easy part—the sophisticate who gets badly gulled, a Pandarus too dry to risk the follies of love for himself. But Washington holds so much back, and trades so quietly on his own sexiness, that Don Pedro is the one character in whom your interest brightens rather than fades. When he and Claudio learn of their dreadful mistake, we see [Robert Sean] Leonard wince and crumple like someone having trouble with a contact lens, but Washington keeps still and absorbs the pain. . . . Washington never douses the good humor, but he alone convinces us of the gravity that lies beneath it.

Not all critics agreed. Though David Denby of *New York* magazine hailed the film as "rousingly entertaining and touching," he harbored at best mixed emotions about "Denzel Washington . . . graceful but muffled as the benevolent Don Pedro." In the *New Republic*, Stanley Kauffmann, who tagged the film as "a gem," then held Denzel to the actor's own criteria: "I was advocating color-blind casting some thirty years ago, always with the proviso that a black actor in a white role should demonstrate by talent that the producer would have been misguided not to use him or her. That was in the theatre. The proviso, for obvious reasons, is even more pressing in film. Washington is barely adequate, with little of the princely bearing he showed in *Malcolm X.*" However Denzel may have felt about the sharp words, he could derive some modest pleasure in knowing that his larger ambition—color-blind criticism—had been achieved.

The collaboration of Ireland's Kenneth Branagh and America's Denzel Washington may, at first glance, seem an odd combination of world-class talents. Then again, on the surface, a working relationship between Denzel and Spike Lee must have appeared a natural. But Spike and Denzel—other than their obvious connection of color—came to moviemaking with opposing outlooks on life, causing their working relationship to be a strained, if ultimately successful, one. Surface differences aside, Denzel Washington and Kenneth Branagh shared a sensibility in terms of life values and their attitudes about what movies ought to do and be.

Though acclaimed in the late 1980s as the logical successor to Laurence Olivier and Orson Welles, those previous boy geniuses who successfully translated Shakespeare to the screen, Branagh's life history has far more in common with Denzel's. Like Denzel,

Branagh was the middle child among three kids. The very notion of "family" was a strong influence on young Branagh as well. Branagh hailed from a simple blue-collar family, cutting his dramatic teeth on popular films rather than high-culture plays, as did Denzel. Branagh made his way up the ladder of success in live theater before moving on to film despite a class system in England which put as many obstacles before an Irishman as an African American faces in the United States. Branagh was not able to attend Eton or Oxford (just as Denzel didn't attend either of his first choices), which he later insisted was the key to his popular success. When Branagh states, "I'm essentially somebody who believes in popular entertainment," he precisely echoes statements Denzel has made.

In his autobiography, Branagh would insist that as an Irishman living and working in England, he suffered from a feeling of "belonging nowhere," a key theme of Denzel's recent vehicle, *Mississippi Masala*. When, to succeed in England, Branagh was forced to unlearn his Irish accent, he suffered the pangs of "losing an identity" to successfully assimilate, doing so because he was determined to succeed, much like Denzel. Growing up, Branagh and Denzel, in their distinct demimondes, had both been "chronic underachievers," each projecting hints of brilliance that might be unleashed if the proper profession was only discovered. Both impressed their fellows with a supreme sense of self-confidence, real or affected; both considered careers in journalism before accidentally discovering the theater via invitations to appear in school productions. Branagh has said that while walking out onstage for the first time, "a door had been opened" into the domain he realized was precisely right for him, which is almost word for word what Denzel has said; just as Denzel had Robinson Stone for his mentor, Branagh had Derek Jacobi.

Branagh describes himself as "boringly normal," a phrase that seems equally right for Denzel (the ordinary person, not the exceptional actor), who, on a Saturday afternoon, plays softball with his kids while many other Hollywood stars are out snorting cocaine. Describing himself as "a driven, puritanical Celt," Branagh early on locked into a work ethic, pushing himself to the limit while scorning those who hoped for easy ways out, much as Denzel does. Dinitia Smith of *New York* magazine described Branagh as "affectionate about his family, yet [there is] a stunning display of hubris." One recalls Denzel's early statements concerning not becoming a millionaire via his talents quickly enough and his warm connection to family. When Branagh described his vision of *Much Ado About Nothing* as being the "healing power of love," insisting, "I wanted to somehow imply a mood of reconciliation, tolerance, and forgiveness," his words recall those of Denzel, who said much the same thing about his ambition (as opposed to Spike's) for *Malcolm X*. Clearly, Denzel and Branagh hope for the same things from film: A movie should be a positive experience; it should play directly to the public rather than above their heads, even—make that especially!— if it's Shakespeare.

Branagh first had his idea for a film of *Much Ado About Nothing* in 1988, several years before the young actor-director turned *Henry V* (1989) into a bloody-good post-Vietnam action epic for the masses. While appearing in a traditionalist English stage production of *Much Ado About Nothing* that Dame Judi Dench directed, Branagh allowed his imagination to run wild as to what a movie could—and, with himself as director, would—be like. The scene in which Don Pedro leads his men into Messina was a rather staid affair, what with several soldiers stepping out onstage. Branagh, a big movie buff—*popular* movies at that—pictured, in his mind, Yul Brynner leading the Magnificent Seven over a hill on horseback. Before their arrival, the onstage ladies moved about respectably, making ready; Branagh recalled some of his favorite R-rated films, wondering if it wouldn't be fun to have the bawdy wenches rushing about topless. When Dogberry and his "watch" step onstage, Branagh felt they should resemble the Three Stooges at their low-comedy best. The eavesdroppings ought to be played as the progenitors of the romantic-screwball comedies Howard Hawks perfected in the 1930s. Benedick, made weak by his sudden love for Beatrice, ought to resemble streetwise Tony Curtis trying his best to come off like sophisticated Cary Grant in *Some Like It Hot* (1959), while the sharp word play between these two obvious equals was the perfect precursor of all those wonderful Spencer Tracy–Katharine Hepburn battle-of-the-sexes farces. Even the song "Sigh No More, Ladies" could be shifted from the film's middle to an opening in which it would be employed as an antique silent-movie sing-along.

Then, with *Henry V* a success, Branagh turned away from history and toward comedy, once more avoiding the "incomprehensible booming and fruity-voiced declamation" he so despised, sensing that they were what turned the masses off to most Shakespeare productions. Instead, he concentrated on a "naturalness" that would make the play easily accessible to the general public "in the same way that they would respond to any movie." Branagh relished casting Americans like Washington, Reeves, and Keaton because "they were free of actory mannerisms and the baggage of strutting and bellowing that accompanies the least effective Shakespearean performances.... We wanted audiences to react to the story as if it were in the here and now and important to them. We did not want them to feel they were in some cultural church," but *at the movies*, watching three of their favorite movie stars in an enjoyable comedy, though one which was written by William Shakespeare.

To achieve the proper balance between respect for Shakespeare's remarkable words and modern realistic acting approach, Branagh had two assistants on hand during the lengthy rehearsal process. Russell Jackson, of the Shakespeare Institute in Stratford-on-Avon, took the responsibility of making all the cast members (but especially Denzel and the other Americans) consciously aware of when they were speaking prose as compared to poetry, emphasizing the different demands of each on an actor. To keep the production from slipping into any kind of high-culture pretentiousness, Hugh Cruttwell, former director of the Royal Academy of Dramatic Art in London, was on hand to assist each actor in developing a "back story," rounding out the characters into three-dimensional people who would come across as believably motivated and totally immediate rather than waxworks figures from an old play.

If the characters were meant to be absolutely real, the surrounding atmosphere and mis en scène were something else altogether. Taking his cue from Shakespeare's own Renaissance theater, where such elements as costumes, props, and settings were all anachronistic rather than specific, Branagh consciously avoided setting his story at any one exact moment in history. Rather, he went for a look that captured an indefinite, magical feeling for some indeterminate golden age in the past, much as one might visualize it while listening to a spellbinding storyteller relate a fairy tale from "once upon a time." The "period," if one can call it that, falls somewhere between Shakespeare's own 1600 and the year 1900, when the modern age began and such happy magic suddenly disappeared from the world. The women's clothing appears vaguely seventeenth century; the heroic men's tailored uniforms, eighteenth century; the black leather breeches the villains wear resemble nineteenth-century S & M garb.

Yet if the vision exists as a collage from past periods, there is something supremely modern about the playing. As the heroes and ladies lounge around in the midday sun, the interracial as well as international crowd of attractive young people appear to have stepped right out of a Ralph Lauren advertisement. While scouting locations, production designer Tim Harvey checked out Messina in Sicily but found nothing of what Branagh had envisioned for his adult fairy tale. Searching further, Harvey fell in love with the idyllic, pastoral quality of Italy's central region, in particular the lush, seductive landscapes surrounding the stately Villa Vignamaggio in Greve, where, in 1503, Lisa Gherardini Giaconda (the model for the Mona Lisa) lived. All these touches come together quite perfectly, resulting in one of the most satisfying Shakespearean films of all time.

When questioned as to why he had wanted to do *Much Ado About Nothing* after *Malcolm X*, Denzel responded: "Because of Kenneth, because it's Shakespeare, and because it's something that will test me as an actor. Kenneth is doing something unique: making Shakespeare accessible to everyone."

14

The Pelican Brief

1993

A WARNER BROS. RELEASE

CAST: Julia Roberts (*Darby Shaw*); Denzel Washington (*Gray Grantham*); Sam Shepard (*Thomas Callahan*); John Heard (*Gavin Verheek*); Tony Goldwyn (*Fletcher Coal*); James B. Sikking (*Denton Voyles*); William Atherton (*Bob Gminski*); Robert Culp (*President*); Stanley Tucci (*Khamel*); Hume Cronyn (*Justice Rosenberg*); John Lithgow (*Smith Keen*).

CREDITS: Director/writer, Alan J. Pakula; producers, Pakula and Peter Jan Brugge; screenplay, Pakula, from the novel by John Grisham; cinematographer, Stephen Goldblatt; editors, Tom Rolf and Trudy Ship; music, James Horner; production design, Philip Rosenberg; costumes, Albert Wolsky; art direction, Robert Guerra; rating, PG-13; running time, 141 min.

After being asked why he had graduated from Fordham with a dual degree in journalism and drama, Denzel explained: "Acting is like investigative reporting. [In both fields], you search out your character." Considering his background, it only stood to reason that sooner or later Denzel would play the part of a journalist, using the professional road he opted to take—the theater—as a means of commenting on the kind of person he might have been had he gone the other route. Denzel had that opportunity when he followed his taxing part as a lawyer in Jonathan Demme's

162

ambitious, "serious" film *Philadelphia* with a jaunty turn in the superficial thriller *The Pelican Brief.* The two films were eventually released within a week of one another during the 1993 winter holiday season.

Though all actors express nervousness about the tricky notion of "competing with oneself" for available viewers, Denzel had the good fortune to be in two quite different movies, each with the potential to attract large crowds that had Christmas money to spend at the movies. While *Philadelphia* offered substantial fare for viewers in search of serious drama with something to say, *The Pelican Brief* presented pure escapism. However, the films did not, in fact, compete with one another; they offered alternative types of entertainment to differently inclined audiences. It worked: Though everyone in America did not go to see both pictures, nearly everybody who goes to the movies went to see one or the other. Better still for Denzel's rising star, there was also considerable overlap, as people who opted for one type of film during the first week of Christmas vacation decided to try something altogether different one week later. In either case, they confronted the presence of Denzel Washington.

In fact, Denzel goes so far as to credit the emergence of *The Pelican Brief* and *Philadelphia* as a double-barreled cinematic shotgun blast of box-office hits with being largely responsible for finally putting him over the top as a mainstream movie "item": "I don't know if it was because of *Philadelphia* or *The Pelican Brief* or both, but I can see the difference in my career as a result of those two films. There's a lot of people who would never go see *Malcolm X* or *Cry Freedom* or *A Soldier's Story,* but they'll go see Julia Roberts and Tom Hanks. And they see me and say, 'Well, he's good, too.' Then, all of a sudden, you're there"—there being superstardom for the general audience.

As different as the two films are, in both Denzel projects that supreme sense of self-confidence which, happily, never spills over into outright arrogance. "A lot of actors need to prove something," his *Pelican* director Alan J. Pakula admiringly noted. "I don't feel that with Denzel. He doesn't have that torture, that self-doubt, you find in some actors. Maybe it's a sense of self-belief." Pakula had bought the film rights to John Grisham's book even before the manuscript was printed, based on the concept itself and Grisham's mushrooming popularity. Following a little prodding by top-billed Roberts, making her comeback after a self-imposed two-year absence from the screen, Pakula, over the loud objections of Grisham, eventually cast Denzel in a role which had been written with a white actor in mind.

Then the director who on one occasion had compared Denzel to Robert Redford (who a decade and a half earlier had played a journalist for Pakula in the classic *All the President's Men*) raised the Sidney specter. Pakula insisted that his latest movie would allow Denzel to cross over into mainstream recognition just as Sidney had a generation earlier: "Poitier did *To Sir, With Love* and came out of it a huge superstar. Denzel is just starting to break through as a box-office star in the way Poitier did."

In *Pelican*, Denzel plays Gray Grantham, a newspaper reporter trying to make some sense out of the fact that two Supreme Court justices, who stood at opposite ends of the political spectrum, are assassinated on the same night, within hours of each other. Something big is obviously going down, though he can initially find no common thread to the killings; however many leads he tries to follow, they all bring him down dead-end streets. Then he comes in contact with a Tulane University law student, a young woman in a state of panic over something she refers to as "the pelican brief." Shortly, Gray realizes that this amateur sleuth has managed, through her sharp powers of deduction, to put together the combination which has eluded him.

Darby Shaw has no immediate connection to the case at all. She is merely testing her acumen, trying to prove to her lover, Professor Thomas Callahan (Sam Shepard), that she is a true pro at research. So Darby picks this intriguing occurrence and investigates on her own, opening a few files that no one else seems to think are worth considering. In so doing, she manages to make a possible connection between the two deceased men, one of whom was actually killed in a gay porno theater. Because this connection is environmental in nature, she dubs it "pelican" and turns the brief over to her mentor. He, in turn, hands it to an FBI agent and close friend Gavin Verheek (John Heard). No sooner is the pelican brief out and around in Washington than people start dying off like flies. Thomas is killed when he starts up Darby's car; she is smart enough to realize that the bomb was intended for her.

Terrified and suddenly on the run, Darby has no one to turn to—no one, that is, except Gray, a man she does not know. But she senses, from his reports, that he is perhaps the only other person in the country honestly attempting to discover *what* happened. Gray will be delighted to meet with a girl who happens to know *why*. Shortly, they are together, darting about in a desperate attempt to avoid the assassin, Khamel (Stanley Tucci), who killed both justices and now has his eye on a third, Rosenberg (Hume Cronyn). Meanwhile, a sitting president (Robert Culp), who combines the worst qualities of Nixon (manipulativeness), Ford (bumbling), Reagan (obliviousness), and Bush (influence-owned), dispatches his favorite minion (Tony Goldwyn) to try to cover up any connection between the dirty deeds and the current resident of the White House.

Ironically, the film received its most notable preview in Washington, at the White House, where President Clinton—a film buff—requested an advance showing. A tad nervous considering the content of his film, Pakula told the forty guests seating themselves for a postdinner screening: "Clearly, Mr. President, this is a far different White House than the one in our movie." Pakula later admitted to the press: "I could never have shown the movie [there] without pointing that out." Apparently, the disclaimer worked: Bill and Hillary Clinton loudly applauded the film, which appeared to be attacking their political adversaries rather than themselves.

A week later, a large-scale L.A. event was held at an in-spot, the Bruin, with Denzel and wife Pauletta prominent members of the entourage. Clearly, it marked the beginning of something big, professionally speaking. Denzel received rave reviews for his role: In *Variety*, Brian Lowry wrote that "Washington impresses as Gray, whose personality remained vague in the novel, allowing the actor to put his own stamp on the part. With his concurrent role in *Philadelphia*, Washington's stock should be so high by January that the best advice would be to buy now." Anthony Lane, while dismissing the movie itself, wrote in the *New Yorker:*

> Yet another seductive performance from Denzel Washington. As an investigative reporter, he's impossibly slick at schmoozing with contacts over the phone, and he knows how to wear a suit,

but no actor can do much with lines like, "if this thing reaches as deep and goes as high as we think it does..." At one glorious moment, he tries to solve the mystery by writing down "Law Firm" and "White House" on a piece of paper, joined by a series of arrows. Bingo! This may be an accurate representation of the way John Grisham sits down to draft a novel, but moviegoers expect a little more.

In truth, *The Pelican Brief*—performances aside—is not a particularly distinguished film. The Washington, D.C., settings appear murky rather than menacing on-screen, the character relationships are never properly developed, and the pedestrian plot takes nearly two and a half hours to unfold, though in essence the narrative is not all that different from any run-of-the-mill TV-movie thriller. The problems derive mainly from the difficulty in adapting Grisham's novels. As in books by his contemporary Tom Clancy, Grisham concocts plots that are at once conventional and convoluted, hardly a happy combination. But both novelists make them work for readers by employing the story lines as the mere skeletons of their books. The meat on those bones contain incredible amounts of richly detailed insider information that's shared along the way; whether it is Clancy's knowledge of state-of-the-art international intrigue or Grisham's of law, politics, and the interrelationship between the two, the reader receives a virtual education on such material, coming away with a true sense of edification. While being entertained, we have learned something.

That's just fine for a lengthy novel, which can offer discursive material to a reader who is in a position to slip in a bookmark at any point, take a break, then return at regular intervals over a period of time. It cannot be done in a motion picture, or at least a Hollywood commercial movie, which must move forward like a shark or die. Still, strip away all that good detail to come up with the "through line" for a film and everything that was best about the book is gone. No wonder, then, that Roger Ebert wrote: "It is depressing to reflect that this shallow exercise in Washington conspiracy has been directed by the same man who made a great film, *All the President's Men* (1976), on the same subject."

Still, Ebert—like most other critics—had only praise for Denzel's performance, even offering the very kind of comparison Denzel most appreciates—one that is color-blind: "Denzel Washington shows again how credible he seems on the screen; like Spencer Tracy, he can make you believe in almost any character." Ebert also acknowledged the "chemistry" between between Denzel and Julia Roberts, going so far as to suspend his role as objective film critic and comment on the audience reaction as everyone left the theater: "After the movie was over, I heard people complaining that they were never 'allowed' to have a love affair."

Another critic, Tim Cogshell of *Entertainment Today*, offered a similar observation, following his assessment that the characters, as written, didn't particularly interest him: "What I *did* find interesting was that Darby and Gray don't have the standard bump and grind scene required in these films. Although I haven't read the book and don't know if Darby and Gray get it on between its pages, I *do* know that if the film had been cast with, say, Tom Cruise or Mel Gibson, there would have definitely been a wild-thing moment. Even in the film, the attraction is alluded to. I guess Hollywood, for all its liberal rhetoric, hasn't got there yet."

Of course, readers of the book know that Darby and Gray do indeed get it on between the pages, which has been the standard approach of the thriller ever since Alfred Hitchcock perfected the genre with movies like *The Lady Vanishes* (1938) in the 1930s. The very process of jointly solving the crime causes hero and heroine to fall in love; the love scene is indeed obligatory in films of this type. Would that one could say that Pakula and company dared to go against the grain and succeeded in artistically undermining expectations. They did not. Someone like Martin Scorsese, Francis Coppola, or Jonathan Demme—truly inventive filmmakers—can and do pull the rug out from under audiences by denying them the very scenes that supposedly must be included; defying conventions of story and style is part of what makes them the world-class directors that they are. Pakula is, at best, a conventional craftsman; his movies work when, like *Presumed Innocent* (1990), they follow the rules precisely and are exercises in traditionalist moviemaking at its most skillfully uninspired.

Which is why, in *The Pelican Brief*, the lack of a love affair constitutes a major problem. Denzel has remained relatively mute on this one, though from previous comments we know just how he feels about playing interracial romance on-screen. It may not be white Hollywood but rather the black star who, in Cogshell's words, "hasn't got there yet." Then again, Grisham's negative reaction to the casting of Denzel may have caused Pakula to excise the romance rather than push the envelope with the temperamental writer. Whatever the reasoning, or whoever made the final decision, the loss is ours: Denzel and Julia are two of the most attractive young stars of the nineties, and the lack of a love story severely undercuts the film's potential as popular entertainment.

Audiences around America reacted much like the one that accompanied Roger Ebert out of the theater. Owing to the mainstream appeal of this picture, they happened to be racially mixed audiences. That such people saw no reason why the two shouldn't "get together" suggests something positive, the hopeful notion that there are plenty of Americans out there who really don't care about skin color; movie stars are movie stars, and they ought to do what we expect them to do, which under the circumstances is to make love. The casting of a black actor in a role written for a white man can be considered a coup for civil rights, though the lack of a logically emotional screen kiss takes us two giant steps backward as opposed to the single one forward. America's supposedly unsophisticated audiences are apparently way ahead of Hollywood's writers, producers, and even stars if they leave a movie like this wondering when our entertainers are going to catch up.

Was this relatively obvious and easy role a conscious choice following the grueling work, emotionally as well as physically, Denzel had put in on the AIDS drama *Philadelphia*, shot first but released one week after *The Pelican Brief*? According to Denzel, that was precisely "why I wanted to do it. The film that I did after *Malcolm X* was *Much Ado About Nothing*, which was exactly [the kind of lighthearted and nondemanding fare] I needed at *that* time. After having done *Philadelphia*, I needed to be chased by some bad guys and run around and just... you know what I mean. I read the script in what felt like minutes because it was so fast-paced, and then I read the book and went, 'Hmmm.' Because a *lot* had been changed from the book. Actually, I liked the script better!"

15

Philadelphia

1993

A TRI-STAR RELEASE

CAST: Tom Hanks (*Andrew Beckett*); Denzel Washington (*Joe Miller*); Joanne Woodward (*Sarah Beckett*); Jason Robards (*Charles Wheeler*); Antonio Banderas (*Miguel*); Mary Steenburgen (*Belinda Conine*); Robert Castle (*Bud Beckett*); Ron Vawter (*Bob Seldman*).

CREDITS: Director, Jonathan Demme; producers, Demme and Edward Saxon; screenplay, Ron Nyswaner; cinematography, Tak Fujimoto; editor, Craig McKay; music, Howard Shore; production design, Kristi Zea; special makeup, Carl Fullerton; rating, PG-13; running time, 119 min.

One smart thing that Jonathan [Demme] told me early on," Denzel recalls of the *Philadelphia* shoot, "was 'This is not about Joe Miller changing 360 degrees so that he's leading the gay and lesbian parade by the end of the movie. That would let the Joe Millers of the world off the hook.' I can't say that I know exactly what it [all] means, but a lot of guys come up to me and say, 'Man, you know, I like that guy. I like what you were saying.' and I say, 'Well, which *part* are you talking about?' And they go, 'Hey, you *know* what I'm talking about.' You see, they're still not knocking on the door. [In their own lives], they're pulling up their trousers and walking away."

By "knocking on the door," Denzel refers to a key scene in

Philadelphia which critics acknowledged as a fine "little" moment in a movie that dared to bring the heretofore closeted issue of AIDS to the attention of mainstream moviegoers. A few art-house flicks had touched on the subject, but *Philadelphia*—with its heavyweight stars, Bruce Springsteen title song, and holiday release—was designed to appeal to the masses, those flocking to mall theaters during Christmas vacation. The "to knock or not to knock" scene stands as a moment of truth for Denzel's character: one more well-defined and unique man but (expanding, in Denzel's words, "from the specific to the general") an urban Everyman, the universal "average Joe." This man's flaws, attitudes, and ingrained prejudices are, we note, the same as those of most people.

The "knocking" scene occurs as Joe, a personal-injury lawyer who has agreed to represent AIDS victim Andrew Beckett (Tom Hanks) in court, steps close to Andrew's apartment door. He stands there, too self-conflicted to move. Joe wants to enter and speak with this suffering fellow human who has touched something deep inside him. And, like every relatively educated person, Joe mentally knows, as every doctor in America insists but most average Americans refuse to accept, that you can't contract AIDS from casual contact.

Joe almost knocks, but thinks better (or, if you prefer, worse) of it. Then, in a gesture which conveys the collective homophobia of the American masses everywhere, Joe hitches up his pants with his thumbs and strides away. Stephen Rebello of *Movieline* described the scene thusly: "Washington pulls a perfect take on shuffling, hyper-macho befuddlement." It was Denzel, the actor, who created this perfect bit of business to express the larger idea that his director was after.

Demme was, of course, correct in creating only a limited arc for Joe. The most obvious and crowd pleasing way to go would have been to play Joe as an alcoholic loser, on the order of Paul Newman's character in *The Verdict* (1982). Joe could have then been a raging homophobe from the outset. Upon learning that Andrew, a highly successful lawyer, has been fired from his firm for supposed "incompetence" after everyone around him realizes that he suffers from AIDS, Joe would then take on the case only because of his own desperate need for money. The movie could have then offered a predictable transformation process as step by step Joe becomes enlightened, ending the film as a heterosexual crusading for gay rights.

Instead, what we see is far more subtle and, as such, more satisfying. Joe, though a cynical ambulance chaser is (in the film, if not necessarily in the script) a member of a minority group. As such, we might expect Joe to be somewhat more sensitive to prejudice. To a degree, it *is* true that Joe—always out to make a buck but clearly *not* destitute—takes the case in part because he believes he can make money, though also because he feels this fellow has been shabbily treated.

However sensitive Joe may be about prejudice toward blacks, it doesn't have any expected, assumed, or hoped-for carryover effect, making Joe more sensitive to homosexuals than some white man might be. Joe avoids physical contact with Andrew. When, after being turned down by nine other lawyers, Andrew first enters Joe's office, the lawyer methodically reaches out to shake his hand. But the second Joe realizes the truth of Andrew's situation and the nature of his health problem, he recoils, wishing there were some way he could wipe his hand clean. By the movie's end, just before Andrew dies, Joe is at last able to reach out and touch Andrew without giving it a thought. Joe has changed in small—rather, big— ways, but such changes are often the most significant in life and the most rewarding in drama.

The casting of Denzel as Joe was as effective as, in a previous era, the casting of Henry Fonda might have been. There are certain stars who, owing to something special (quite apart from performance talent) in their nature, automatically serve as audience surrogates. Simply, such actors are always *us*, or more correctly, a collective representation of us. Therefore, their emotional on-screen "journeys" move the audience in a way that a talented actor, creating the "specific" but unable to suggest the "general," cannot. Denzel, like Fonda, takes us along for the ride. Hopefully, then, the audience is able to learn from watching the character's mistakes as well as the correction of those mistakes, with the audience members emerging from the viewing experience as more decent people.

It's worth noting that Sidney Poitier, despite his considerable allure, never impacted on an audience, black or white, quite in this manner. He, like his characters, always seemed too perfect to serve as audience surrogate: An idealized role model for blacks, a figure admired by whites, Poitier was anything but an Everyman. Denzel, then, is the first black movie star to ever convey such a quality, doing so not only for black audiences (other black actors have indeed served as audience surrogates for narrow ethnic audiences) but virtually everyone. First in *Philadelphia*, later in such films as *Courage Under Fire*, Denzel literally broke the final color barrier by making it clear that a minority member can serve such a function for the general public. Denzel is not the Sidney Poitier of the nineties; he is a Henry Fonda for the multicultural millennium.

So the average Joe on the street, who knew he would probably have likewise not knocked but walked away, came away from the film at least a little less frightened of contact with an AIDS victim. It's also important to note, then, that this scene probably wouldn't have worked quite so beautifully with any actor other than Tom Hanks as Andrew. Casting a popular heterosexual actor in the role written as gay was as much a stroke of genius as casting a black actor in a role written as white. Beyond that, Hanks is a heterosexual actor who, like Denzel, was best known for playing the clean-cut boy next door. If Denzel is our Henry Fonda, Hanks is our James Stewart, a slightly goofier variation on the same essential all-American theme. Hanks's combination of affability and accessibility, quite apart from his excellent instincts as an actor, made it easier for an audience to accept Joe's final ability to embrace Andrew. Though on one level Denzel was embracing an AIDS victim, on another level entirely it was Tom Hanks, an actor audiences had emotionally "embraced" ever since *Splash* (1984). Having such a star play an AIDS victim changed the image of AIDS forever in the collective mind of the heterosexual majority, just as having a star like Denzel embrace an AIDS victim in some small way allowed that same majority to overcome their mental block about AIDS.

"I would have loved to have played the part Tom Hanks did in *Philadelphia*," Denzel once confided. Then he changed his mind: "Not to knock what he was doing, but I think it was much more difficult to play the part *I* played." Though there's a touch of hubris to Denzel's claim, he happens to be correct. It was Hanks who won the Oscar that year, just as, in 1989, Dustin Hoffman won for

Rainman. But anyone who truly understands acting knows that Tom Cruise had the more difficult role as the initially unsympathetic brother who gradually learns to love and respect his idiot savant sibling. The same is true with *Philadelphia*: Though Hanks's character physically deteriorates, his personality is locked in the first time we encounter him. Denzel, as Joe, had to carry the day, easing the audience along through one quietly traumatic confrontation with self after another.

Denzel insists—keeping consistently in character with his previous decision making about whether to do any movie—that he accepted the role not primarily because of the movie's message but because he was intrigued by his character, as written, as well as excited about working with the supertalented director Demme (fresh from an Oscar for *Silence of the Lambs*) and Hanks, an actor Denzel greatly admires. In truth, Denzel—who has recoiled from heterosexual lovemaking scenes—might have had a hard time playing the gay character, particularly the sequence in which Andrew kisses his lover Miguel (Antonio Banderas). There was actually a minor flap when word was leaked to the press that Will Smith, asked to perform just such an act in *Six Degrees of Separation* (1993), called Denzel for advice and was supposedly told, "Don't you go kissing no man in a film."

Apparently burned by the way that line looked in print, Denzel corrected himself, never denying he made the statement, though insisting it had been misinterpreted. What he actually meant, or so he claimed, was that if Smith was personally uncomfortable with what he'd been asked to do, then he should be true to himself— what he did or did not feel was right for *him*—and not do it. For Denzel, individuality is always the key to decision making.

Several of Denzel's female costars insist that he doesn't like to play erotic love scenes in front of a camera due to his basic family values: the fear that his children may see him seemingly being untrue to their mother, ironic considering stories in the press that insist he's been less than faithful in real life. Denzel would understandably have had trepidations about playing the gay character because of the embarrassment it might have caused his son among his macho (and now teenage) peers, hardly an enlightened way to make such decisions but Denzel's way nonetheless.

Once again, Denzel was playing a role that had not been written with a black actor in mind. As Jonathan Demme recalls about his casting coup: "Everyone has their little wish list. Denzel's extremely high on mine. Then I'm doing this white-bread *Philadelphia*. The next thing I know, I'm on the phone with Denzel. But this is not an African-American" role, Demme told the actor, apparently unaware of Denzel's perennial propensity for just such parts. "You've read the script," he said. "Do you think we'd have to make any adjustments in a character who is, in theory, written as a European person?"

"No," Denzel replied without hesitation. "Do you?"

"No, I don't," Demme said. Denzel had told Demme what he needed to hear: The character wouldn't be rewritten to bring Joe more in line with the actor's ethnicity. Meanwhile, Denzel had said precisely what Demme hoped he would: This was one actor who not only didn't want such accommodation but would refuse it if offered.

"Then I got excited," Demme recalls. "It never wore off."

The casting complete, Denzel and Tom set out to learn everything they could about the all-too-real lifestyles of their fictive characters. Hanks would have to lose more than thirty pounds for the part, doing so gradually, his timing dictated by a computer so that his own diminishing physique would suggest the actual weight loss of an AIDS victim. The trick was to physically appear weakened to the point of being unable to move about while maintaining the high energy necessary for him to complete the difficult shoot. Hanks read extensively on the subject of AIDS and met with many AIDS patients, while makeup artist Carl Fullerton and hair designer Alan D'Angerio headed for Los Angeles's various medical libraries and AIDS clinics to become more knowledgeable about the disease and make Hanks appear realistic for each individual stage in his deterioration.

For Denzel, it was necessary to mix with actual ambulance chasers. "I worked with some personal-injury lawyers, went to trials, learned how they think," he later explained. "It was harder for me to get [in touch with] the kind of homophobic attitude Joe has in the beginning... by the end, he understands this is another human being who's hurting and what he's labeled as shouldn't have anything to do with their relationship."

Early in the film, Joe howls: "I just don't want anyone in bed who has more hair on his chest than I do!" All the while, the snacking suburbanite waves a turkey leg in the air, as he might a sword. "We American males of *all* colors wear our prejudices with such pride," Demme smilingly said of Denzel's acting improvisation. "I *love* Denzel strutting around the kitchen, jabbing his turkey leg." It's important to note that it was Denzel who contributed Joe's line, as well as the accompanying bit of physical business, to underscore the patent absurdity of his character. "That's very real," Denzel later reflected. "I made that line up on the spot," probably having heard it said before. But was it Denzel psyching out his character, providing the missing material and bringing his character vividly alive? Or was it Denzel expressing his own inner fears through the medium of his character?

The key to the complexity of such a moment is manyfold. First, the character, written as an Anglo, represents every middle-class macho male in the audience, so Joe's attitudes are widespread and typical. Second, having the character played by an actor who is black enriches the situation. It implies the larger truth that there is indeed a black middle class made up not of perfect people but flawed, fallible (if fundamentally decent) human beings. This suggests to blacks who see the film that assimilation can be accomplished, though it won't solve all their problems, any more than it does Joe Miller's. Also, the casting implies an attack on the politically correct misconception that people of color are fundamentally more moral and pure than whites: before his transformation, Joe Miller suffers from the same stereotypical attitudes as whites, his color in no way making him more sensitive to the plight of other minorities.

Brendan Lemon, speaking with the actor for *Interview* magazine, wondered if perhaps "because you're black and Tom's white, people are inevitably going to think about racial discrimination as well as AIDS." Denzel replied: "There were a couple of scenes we shot that got at the parallels even more. There was this speech I give to some of my coworkers about discrimination [that was cut from the final print]. But I imagine that it was too on the [money], you know?"

The *New Republic* had their "Washington Diarist," correspondent Andrew Sullivan, report on the film from this very perspective. "This movie about AIDS was directed at black America. From its black costar to its hype in the black press, to a number of critical black-on-black scenes, it was an aggressively black, middle-class film. In downtown Washington, it was [even] shown at the theater usually reserved for blaxploitation movies. Moreover, it didn't talk of the disease as a heterosexual issue, as Magic Johnson and virtually every other black leader has done. It brazenly took a black, straight movie icon and made him grapple with a gay man. Denzel Washington's role for this reason took far more social bravery than did Hanks's. Homosexuality is more stigmatized in black America than even in white America."

"It's a film that doesn't have time to be about a whole lot of things," Denzel explained. "For example, there was a whole little subplot with one of the jurors that was taken out." Were any of Denzel's own favorite moments excised? "There was a scene where Tom asked me about taking his case. He says, 'Well, you know, you're a Republican.' I say, 'Yeah, that's right.' He says, 'You're a member of the National Rifle Association.' And I say, 'And a damn good shot!'" In real life Denzel may not be a card-carrying NRA member or a true-blue Republican, but many of his values are conservative, suggesting that he saw much of himself in the traditionalist family man he here portrays. Denzel felt a need to deny that, insisting: "I had to relearn certain prejudices; I didn't feel I was that kind of person," though perhaps at some point in his life he was and drew on memories of the less enlightened man he earlier had been.

Indeed, by projecting the truth about the fictional Joe Miller and all he represents—for better or worse—did Denzel inadvertently discover certain truths about himself that he might rather have avoided? Did he discover a hidden residue of prejudice within his own decent but, by his own admission, flawed nature? "I think so," Denzel quietly admitted to interviewer Peter Richmond of GQ. "I... think so. Because I didn't think I was at all. I said, in general, 'I have no problems with homosexuals, and I want to do everything I can to end AIDS. . . .' I think that, much like the character, I think I got a chance to vent certain frustrations, maybe. It was a good education."

An education, for himself and for his audience, is what makes a film worth doing. In addition to an education about AIDS, there were also the aforementioned implications in favor of assimilation and against the politically correct idealization of minorities as morally superior to whites. Such attitudes, long held by Denzel and instrumental in guiding his previous choice of roles, makes it clear that *Philadelphia* was a collaborative effort, with Denzel a contributor who helped shape the material.

No wonder, then, that Denzel said: "One of my favorite scenes is with my wife and me, where I air my antigay discomfort. I like those kinds of moments because I know this is what people really say. Not just about AIDS or gay people; about a lot of things. About blacks, whomever, Jews—you know the particular prejudices. They haven't been examined quite this way before"—that is, having the ostensible hero/audience surrogate admit his own long-suppressed bigotries, the "hero" a black man at that. It would work just as well if he expressed resentment against Jews or a Jewish hero did so about blacks. Denzel pointed out: "This is not a movie about AIDS, really. It's more of an emotional self-examination [of the residue of prejudices still existing within normal, decent, educated people]."

Once again, Denzel won rave reviews. Anthony Lane of the *New Yorker* noted that the movie contained

> a rich, controlled performance from Washington, who has to cover a lot of ground as his character wanders into unmapped areas of experience. We know immediately that Joe will come round to Andrew's cause and stand up for him in court, and there are plenty of actors who would have milked that metamorphosis for schmaltz value, but Washington sets his face against any hint of fairy tale. He gives himself no gold stars for good behavior, deliberately making Joe every bit as sexy and relaxed in his bigotry—joshing around with his wife, doing his gay impression in the doorway of the kitchen—as he is during his ringing proclamation of constitutional rights.

Lane rightly pointed out the complexity of Denzel's character, noting that when Joe offers a glass of water, along with his own handkerchief, to a juror on the verge of emotional collapse, the action manages to play as a kind and gentle one, done on impulse by a decent man. Simultaneously, however, it is a cleverly exploitative gesture from a win-at-any-cost lawyer who milks every unexpected situation for everything it's worth. No other character in the film has such a double edge: Andrew's family members are too good, accepting, and understanding of his problem to be believable, while the vicious monsters at his law firm resemble sneeringly villainous Nazis from an old World War II propaganda film, virtually without redeeming human elements, which is why the movie is finally simplistic in a way his work is not.

As Lane said:

> The film badly needs Denzel Washington; without him, it could have collapsed under the weight of its own goodness." *Commonweal* reported that he certainly gets everything right on-screen with a performance of admirable economy and terse humor that nicely interacts with Tom Hanks's piquant blend of feyness and lucidity.... In his client and friend, Washington sees not just the devastation of AIDS, not only the pathos of one man dying too soon, but the innate tragedy of all mortality; the ascending spirit flailing in its crumbling shell. Once Hanks subsides, Washington can only excuse himself, hurry home, and embrace his wife and child. It's a magnificent scene in an often gripping but unfulfilled movie.

Philadelphia is to homophobia what, in the postwar years, *Gentleman's Agreement* (1947) was to anti-Semitism and *Home of the Brave* (1949) to antiblack bigotry: the first important Hollywood movie on a pressing social subject. Neither of those two films holds up particularly well; other, greater movies were made on both issues, just as other, greater films will ultimately be made about AIDS. But there is something to being the first, and *Philadelphia*—like those previous pictures—was the necessary initial step to pave the way. As such, it earns its place in movie history.

No matter how happy an experience a film may be, actors—in particular, perfectionist actors like Denzel—invariably wish they could go back and do something over again, to make it better. About *Philadelphia*, Denzel could comfortably say that was not the case: "This is one of the first films I've been in where I didn't see something I wish wasn't in there. I'm saying that quite honestly. I don't think I've been able to say it before."

16

Crimson Tide

1995

A BUENA VISTA/HOLLYWOOD PICTURES PRESENTATION

CAST: Denzel Washington (*Lt. Comdr. Ron Hunter*); Gene Hackman (*Capt. Frank Ramsey*); George Dzundza (*Cob*); Viggo Mortensen (*Lt. Peter "Weps" Ince*); James Gandolfini (*Lt. Bobby Dougherty*); Matt Craven (*Lt. Roy Zimmer*); Lillo Brancato Jr. (*Russell Vossler*); Rocky Carroll (*Lt. Darik Westguard*); Danny Nucci (*Danny Rivetti*); Steve Zahn (*William Barnes*); Rick Schroder (*Lt. Paul Hellerman*); Vanessa Bell Calloway (*Julia Hunter*); Jason Robards (*Court Martial Admiral, unbilled*).

CREDITS: Director, Tony Scott; producers, Don Simpson and Jerry Bruckheimer; screenplay, Michael Schiffer, from a story by Schiffer and Richard P. Henrick; additional dialogue, Robert Towne, Quentin Tarantino, and Steve Zaillian; cinematography, Dariusz Wolski; editor, Chris Lebenzon; music, Hans Zimmer; production design, Michael White; costumes, George L. Little; art direction, Donald B. Woodruff, James J. Murakami, and Dianne Wager; set design, Richard Lawrence and Nick Navarro; rating, R; running time, 115 min.

Y ou don't speak for six weeks except to say, 'Nooooooo! Aaaaah! Stop!'" Denzel said in good-natured, mildly comical disparagement of his *Ricochet* experience. Never again would he star in an action film; running around shooting at bad guys was a far cry from his motivation to become an actor. But if there's one thing more

179

important to Denzel than career, it's his family; family was the reason why he eventually ate his own words, agreeing to appear in a pair of back-to-back action flicks, *Crimson Tide* and *Virtuosity*. Denzel's ten-year-old son complained that his famous father didn't appear in movies his peer group wanted to see. As Denzel Washington would eventually recall: "He was like, 'Dad, my friends are talking bad about me because you keep doing these old-folks movies. You've got to do some action movies.' I said, 'All right. All right.'"

As luck would have it, the role of Ron Hunter, the young executive officer aboard a beleaguered nuclear submarine, came his way after Brad Pitt, Hollywood's fastest-rising heartthrob, turned it down. Originally, Warren Beatty had been the first choice of producers Jerry Bruckheimer and Don Simpson (*Flashdance* [1983]; *Top Gun* [1986]) to play the part of Frank Ramsey, the older, crustier, antagonistic submarine commander. (While living in the Bel Air Hotel following the Northridge earthquake, Beatty and producer Don Simpson were next-door neighbors, allowing Simpson time to try to convince Beatty to do the film.) But Beatty was never satisfied with the script. Simpson and his partner then approached Al Pacino, also a temporary Bel Air resident, whose interest was piqued by the "mature" role of Ramsey: a hardliner from the old school, frightful in his willingness to begin World War III by launching a preemptive nuclear strike, yet sympathetic, thanks to absolute adherence to a rigid, outdated, admirable code of honor. Eager to work with Pacino, Pitt readily agreed to play Hunter, but when Pacino dropped out, Pitt went with him.

Denzel came onboard after learning that one of his own idols, Gene Hackman, had agreed to do the Pattonesque part of Ramsey. Though Hackman had not been considered a box-office draw since his *French Connection/Poseidon Adventure* halcyon days of the early 1970s, he remains one of Hollywood's most highly respected actors and, as such, one of the most reliable "fallbacks" for producers who find themselves stymied in the search for a mature box-office star. The frustrated producers settled for a performer who would confer status, if not box-office insurance. The hope was that the high-profile project itself, with its techno-suspense plot, somewhere between *The Caine Mutiny* (1954) and *Das Boot* (1981), would click at the summertime box office. That was certainly the case with *Jurassic Park* the preceding year and *Twister* the following year. Thus, with Hackman in place, the need was for a strong, quietly dignified performer in the youthful role; at that point, the producers pursued Denzel. Simpson, since deceased, said at the time that the Hunter role demanded "a thespian who had the kind of heavyweight quality to hold his own with Gene Hackman for two hours—and that's Denzel Washington. It had to be a rumble in the jungle, Ali-Frazier." A rumble, incidentally, of words: Though there is much dramatic conflict in *Crimson Tide*, it is more psychological than physical. Importantly, the Hunter role was not race-specific, a situation which Denzel prefers.

Crimson Tide did not originate with the Simpson-Bruckheimer team, as had such loud, unsubtle moneymaking items as 1990's *Days of Thunder*. Since their glory days of the Reagan years, when the public was unaccountably overawed by simplistic stories told with state-of-the-art style but without substance, Simpson and Bruckheimer had fallen, with surprising swiftness, on hard times. For several years, the team failed to turn out a single movie despite highly publicized studio deals and potentially lucrative multiple-picture contracts. A tad humbled by their recent fallow period, Simpson and Bruckheimer were understandably happy to be contacted by Disney's Hollywood Pictures division, then assigned to the job of producing a submarine story that Disney had wanted to do for some time.

Such a project first took shape in the minds of several Disney executives when, as a goodwill gesture, the U.S. Navy ushered an entire group of the studio brass abroad just such a "hunter-killer" sub for a real-life undersea journey. The Disney execs were singled out for the invitation because of the lingering appeal of their studio's *20,000 Leagues Under the Sea* (1954) and the ongoing popularity of Disneyland's Nautilus ride.

The joy ride, which far surpassed even their theme park's thrills, left several Disney execs wondering if perhaps the world wasn't ready for yet another Disney submarine movie. The timing seemed right, since Paramount's 1990 release *The Hunt for Red October* (1990), adapted from a popular Tom Clancy novel, had been a box-office smash. The trick was to come up with another such project,

Clancyish enough to attract the already existing audience for such fare and just different enough from *The Hunt for Red October* in story and theme that the public would not fear it was the same movie all over again. So work began on what would eventually become a $50-million-plus blockbuster. One of those Disney executives, Michael Stenson, chose a forty-five-year-old writer whose work he admired, to pen the screenplay.

Michael Schiffer's previous screenplays included the gang-banger crime film *Colors* (1988) as well as *Lean on Me* (1989), a biographical film about a controversial conservative educator. Those reality-based movies had in common an old-fashioned professional whose traditionalist approach to his work is challenged by a younger, more liberal newcomer to the profession. Schiffer's natural instincts as a storyteller led him to create similar parts for the emerging *Crimson Tide* effort: the older, cynical Ramsey in conflict with the idealistic young Hunter. Practically from the inception, though, there was an ongoing debate and severe indecision as to just what the argument ought to entail. This would not have been a problem ten years earlier, at a time when the American president openly referred to the Soviet Union as the evil empire, reducing that entire nation to a cliché from *Star Wars.* So long as the Cold War was at its height, we were the good guys; "they" were the bad guys. The era of perestroika descended upon Hollywood; *The Hunt for Red October* had been softened for this new reality, carefully changed to replace the book's eyeball-to-eyeball confrontational tone between the American and Russian characters with one of cooperation between the two, with Sean Connery playing the Russian commander as a sympathetic ally rather than a menacing antagonist.

So, working away at his IBM Selectric in his ninth-floor office on Washington Boulevard in Venice, California, Schiffer (with help from novelist Richard Henrick in plotting out the story line) concocted motivation for what transpires when an American bombing of a Serb position in what had been Yugoslavia sets off a conflict between the two countries. This concept would be rejected, brought back, rejected, and then brought back again a half-dozen times and was being reconsidered just before filming began. In the end, though, Schiffer settled on what seemed a far more acceptable and plausible plot line considering the changed relationship between the world's superpowers. Schiffer drew his inspiration from then current headlines about the right-wing nationalist Vladimir Zhirinovsky, redubbed "Radchekno" for the film. In a breakaway region of Chechnya, this rebel fanatic seizes control of a Pacific Coast missile base, pointing the warheads toward the United States. Our country, now friendly toward and fully allied with Russia's "legitimate" government, must nonetheless protect itself from the warmongering demagogue, dispatching the U.S.S. *Alabama* to launch a preemptive strike, if necessary. This possibility appeals to Frank Ramsey, who—clearly at a loss for a clear-cut enemy since the end of the cold war—mutters, "*Now,* we're back in business."

Shortly, Lt. Comdr. Ron Hunter arrives onboard to serve as the ship's new executive officer; since Hunter has been educated at Harvard as well as Annapolis, the brass believes that he is a perfect choice for second in command. The *Alabama* does indeed receive orders to fire; Ramsey and Hunter are about to do just that when another radio message starts to appear, then is interrupted by a brief shoot-out with a rogue Russian sub. Ramsey, rigid and elitist, feels that they must, without hesitation, fire the nuclear missiles; the reflective, cautious Hunter denies his formal assent. Considering the worldwide implications of what they are about to do, he contends that they ought to wait for the radio to be repaired and learn for certain what the second message was—in case it rescinded the launch. (If that proves not to be the case, Hunter is perfectly willing to then help Ramsey with the codes to fire). Since the crew is not allowed to carry out such an order without the command of *both* officers, the sailors immediately fall into a state of confusion, splitting into two camps. What follows is, virtually, a mutiny. For the remainder of the film, fighting breaks out between the two groups, even as the radio repairman desperately attempts to fix the equipment.

Tony Scott had agreed to direct only if he was allowed to hire Quentin Tarantino, hot from the success of *Reservoir Dogs* (1992), to come onboard and add his unique twist to the endless succession of rewrites. The various pop-culture references (to Silver Surfer comic books, *Star Trek,* and previous submarine movies), which would come to permeate *Crimson Tide,* were Tarantino's doing. Additionally, he brought with him an interest in racial divisiveness, which the edgy young writer-director considers an essential, if awful, part of

184 DENZEL WASHINGTON: HIS FILMS AND CAREER

the real world. For that reason, both the good and bad characters in Tarantino-scripted movies—Scott's *True Romance* (1993), Tarantino's own *Pulp Fiction*—constantly employ racial epithets.

As one might suspect, tempers did flare during production. On Stage 16 of Culver Studios, Denzel confronted Tarantino, asking him why the "n" word appears so often in his films. Tarantino, taken by surprise, muttered something about the need to write dialogue that rings true to life. Denzel didn't back off, and voices were raised. At last, the writer and star were separated by production people, who realized that there is no middle ground on this issue: Those who defend the use of offensive language on the grounds of authenticity cannot reconcile with those who attack such language in art and its negative influence on society. Denzel later refused to comment on the rift to the press other than to insist: "He's a fine artist, and I told him my feelings. So he knows what I had to talk about."

Though Tarantino did not add a single "n" word to the *Crimson Tide* mix, he did play the race card. In Schiffer's original script there is no racial element to the conflict, since Hunter is generic. By having Ramsey and Hunter break out in open argument as to their course of action, with race being the only issue *not* raised (age, attitude, and orientation are all important), the movie's implied "meaning" (with an African-American cast as Hunter) is that it is possible to achieve a color-blind society; when two men slip into a deep, hostile conflict, race is not necessarily playing any part, even if one of those men belongs to a racial minority.

Indeed, part of what makes Ramsey so sympathetic through the preceding events is that he apparently does not care about (or even notice) Hunter's skin color; he opposes Hunter as ineffectual and inexperienced. Even a viewer who agrees with Hunter can't help but respect Ramsey for his commitment. This is particularly true when one watches the way in which Hackman plays Ramsey; rather than allowing the man to veer into the type of caricatured hard-line military martinet George C. Scott and Sterling Hayden portrayed in Stanley Kubrick's 1964 black comedy *Dr. Strangelove* (1964), Hackman insists on a fundamental decency. The guy clearly loves his dog and respects any officer—including the black Hunter in the early pre-conflict scenes—who holds to the navy's code of conduct and its reputation above all else.

Then, in the final moments—as everyone waits to learn if the second message is to rescind the initial order, justifying Hunter's decision, or to obey it, justifying Ramsey's—Ramsey suddenly embarks on a wild, out-of-nowhere anecdote about the famed Lippizzaner stallions, emphasizing the importance of their *whiteness* and the purity of their blood. Hunter's weary eyes suggest that he feared all along it might come down to this but hoped it wouldn't.

Fans of the scene defend it by arguing that Ramsey was never truly oblivious of Hunter's blackness, that he only pretended to be, just as he, symbolizing the old military mentality, affects accepting African Americans as equals in the service without ever actually doing so, such posturing finally falling apart at a moment of true conflict. But there are those who insist that the scene belies everything that has preceded it. This includes Hackman's acting at the very end, a stereotypical portrait of a racist, with mean eyes and a cruel mouth, contradicting Ramsey's body language in earlier scenes of the movie. As conceived by Schiffer, Ramsey represented everything that was best and worst about the old military men, his "ride to the sound of the guns," knee-jerk patriotism balanced by a respect for all other Americans of a like mind, whatever color or sex. There is no hint, in Hackman's earlier moments, of the racism to come; it's never set up, so we are unprepared for what we see. And having chosen the film in part because his character was racially non-specific, Denzel ends up playing a man whose blackness becomes the crux of the conflict.

Tarantino, who only a few years earlier was holding down a minimum-wage job as a video-store clerk, was paid $350,000 to work for two and a half weeks, almost as much as Schiffer had been paid for his year-and-a-half involvement with the project. But the rewriting did not end there; Robert Towne, of *Chinatown* (1974) fame, added the key sequence in which Denzel and Hackman discuss great moments in military history from their differing points of view and another in which the characters attend a courtroom hearing after the incident is over. No wonder Janet Maslin, in her *New York Times* review, complained that "so many word processors were at work here that there's talk about both von Clausewitz's theories on the nature of war and surfer comic books." She was referring to Towne and Tarantino, respectively, two writers who may be equal in talent but whose abilities are of very different orders, causing Maslin to complain that the film "was beefed up by so many script doctors that it now suffers from multiple-personality disorder."

Steve Zaillian, who adapted Thomas Kenneally's 1982 novel *Schindler's List* for Steven Spielberg, arrived to add more texture to the dialogue, in particular for the supporting characters, who were little more than a group of generic figures running through their routine submarine jobs. Denzel proved himself a full collaborator by adding an element of his character's background, later explaining that "the fact that Hunter gets punched [by Ramsey] is something I had a lot of trouble dealing with; taking a punch and not swinging back. So, to make it worse for myself, I said, 'Let me make [Hunter] a boxer. That will set it up more; people will know he could punch back in a second if he wanted to." Finally, Gene Hackman himself penned the finished film's final words when no one else could come up with a last line that worked. Rather than complain, Schiffer (who would, incredibly enough, receive sole screenplay credit following an arbitration by the Writers Guild) took a philosophical approach to the addition of other scribes. "This is a $50-million-dollar movie fueled entirely by words, so they're going to throw [other] writers in."

As to the contributions of those writers, Schiffer told the *New York Times:* "These three guys could punch up *Hamlet*." The Harvard-educated Schiffer, who, before hitting the high note in Hollywood, had worked as everything from a teacher to a roofer, kept his focus on making the movie's words as authentic as possible, thanks to interviews with retired commanders Malcolm S. Wright and Gar-nett "Skip" Beard, both former captains of the *Alabama,* as well as meeting with the personnel of the U.S.S. *Florida,* a craft similar to the film's *Alabama.* It was Schiffer who insisted that, at a pivotal moment, Hackman say to Washington: "You won't be able to get the T.S.O. He's at the conn. You can get to Weps." As journalist James Ryan noted, "Schiffer never felt it was essential that the audience understand what was being said. The important thing was to make them feel they were aboard a submarine, specifically the U.S.S. *Alabama*—which is an actual Trident sub, based in Bangor, Wash-ington." But such hoped-for authenticity was endangered when the Department of the Navy abruptly withdrew any and all cooperation,

"Speak to me as you would to an eight-year-old"; Denzel as homophobic lawyer Joe Miller, who learns about life and love from his AIDS-stricken client in *Philadelphia*. (courtesy Tri-Star)

Philadelphia: Tom Hanks as Andrew Becket, who puts his faith in lawyer Miller. Once more, Denzel played a part that was written as white, though his ethnicity gives the film a subtle subtext. (courtesy Tri-Star)

Hunter and the *Crimson Tide* crew find themselves thrown off balance when their sub is hit during enemy attack. Denzel was now in competition with actors like Tom Cruise for the best racially nonspecific roles. (courtesy Buena Vista)

Crimson Tide: Denzel's "Hunter" is in many ways reminiscent of Henry Fonda in *Twelve Angry Men:* the reasonable man who keeps his head while all about him are losing theirs. (courtesy Buena Vista)

Tony Scott shot his stars in artful ways, visually implying that *Crimson Tide* was something other that one more action flick. (courtesy Buena Vista; photo credit: Richard Foreman)

The *Next* Action Hero: Denzel Washington as Parker Burns, supercop of the future in *Virtuosity*. (courtesy Paramount Pictures)

Suited up for action, Denzel searches for a computer-generated serial killer. *Virtuosity* flopped, convincing Denzel that Schwarzenegger-Stallone-style violence was not his forte. (courtesy Paramount; photo credit: Sidney Baldwin)

Devil in a Blue Dress: Dewitt Albright (Tom Sizemore) draws the unemployed Easy into a spider-web of complex intrigue. (courtesy Tri-Star)

Devil in a Blue Dress: As Easy Rawlins, a private eye in the Sam Spade/Philip Marlowe mold, but with a far more richly detailed history. (courtesy Tri-Star)

Serling interrogates
Monfriez (Lou Diamond
Phillips) as to what actually happened during a
controversial combat sit-
uation. *Courage Under
Fire* reunited Denzel
with his *Glory* director,
Edward Zwick. (cour-
tesy 20th Century-Fox)

Courage Under Fire:
Denzel drew on his own
strong marriage for the
scenes between Serling
and his wife (Regina
Taylor); though the fami-
ly is black, there is no
specific mention of the
characters' race in the
script. (courtesy 20th
Century-Fox)

Courage Under Fire: As Nathaniel Serling, in dress uniform. Intelligent middlebrow dramas with strong action scenes rather than bone-crunching violent action flicks were "right" for the star. (courtesy 20th Century-Fox)

adding a touch of irony to the film's difficult navigation from inception to completion, since it had virtually instigated the *Crimson Tide* project, however unknowingly.

The navy had been most cooperative, offering all sorts of assistance (including the possibility of shooting on actual navy submarines, perhaps the U.S.S. *Alabama* itself) just so long as they believed that this was a film that would do for their branch of the service what *Top Gun* had done for the air force. But the moment that the evolving script included a mutiny, one ultimately deemed righteous, all support was withdrawn. That meant filming on Culver City soundstages, using huge mock-ups of the actual *Alabama* for interiors, when the shoot began in August 1994. There was still a need for exteriors in which nuclear subs are seen from afar, so the moviemakers kept their ears open for reports of maneuvers which could legally be filmed by anyone who happened to be around with a camera. Learning through the grapevine that a submarine was about to depart from Hawaii, Tony Scott put together a camera crew in time to capture that moment on film. As luck would have it, the sub was none other than the U.S.S. *Alabama*.

Disney executive Michael Stenson, who had kick-started the project, always hoped that the results would be something more than just another slam-bang shoot-'em-up for summer release: "We didn't want just another straight-up action picture. We wanted something classic, a really visceral drama about honor and betrayal." Similarly, Schiffer claimed: "I gave it all the adrenaline of a summer movie without a lot of violence." He's quite correct about that: *Crimson Tide*, like *The Hunt for Red October*, is about people attempting to halt a violent act before it can happen; it's a cerebral film about the threat of violence rather than an obvious film that exploits graphic violence, artfully or otherwise.

Critics who reflect a mass audience's enthusiasm were most appreciative, even when they paid the film backhanded compliments; Todd McCarthy of *Variety* tagged *Crimson Tide* "a boy's movie all the way, with enough expensive military hardware and tough-guy power ploys to appeal to teenagers of all ages," describing the film as "skillfully crafted" and "relentlessly paced." Though perceived as a "serious" critic, *New York*'s David Denby gave his nod, noting that despite his own trepidations about "a ferocious atmosphere of hype—thudding soundtrack, torrential rains, red and blue lights playing across the faces of actors—*Crimson Tide* is an absorbing and at times thrilling entertainment...a largely serious action movie with two grown-up actors." Noting the film's synthetic origins and creativity-by-committee approach, *Rolling Stone's* Peter Travers marveled at this well-designed machine, quipping that "*Crimson Tide* isn't art, it's jolting summer entertainment—a slick packaging job that works the audience over with tension and humor." Frank Bruni of the Knight-Ridder newspapers tagged it a "smart, tense, rousing crowd-pleaser."

The film did have its detractors. The *New York Times's* Janet Maslin, who dismissed *Crimson Tide* as mere second-drawer pseudo-Clancy, was also uncharacteristically rough on Denzel: "Mr. Washington, an actor of immense natural charm, has been shoehorned into a faceless good-guy role that could just as easily suit Tom Cruise. Brash, handsome, brilliant, loyal till he reaches his breaking point: anyone familiar with smash-hit Cruise films of the last decade knows this drill." In fact, anyone familiar with Sidney Poitier films of the 1960s also knows it, too; however much Denzel despises comparisons to that particular actor, Hunter is precisely the kind of superhero role that Sidney specialized in. Maslin's description could fit Virgil Tibbs and at least a dozen different Poitier parts, including *The Bedford Incident* (1965) an extremely similar story.

To *Time's* Richard Corliss, *Crimson Tide* was far more thought provoking than Maslin claimed, in particular Denzel's role, requiring careful and serious consideration, and intriguing for the very reasons Maslin chose to dismiss it: "Washington does nicely playing the company man as '90s hero, an African American who has learned when to speak up and when to shut up in the white world." Whether one appreciates Tarantino's insistence that the racial issue be overtly raised before the final curtain, Corliss makes it clear that the very casting of Washington raises an African-American theme, at least by implication. If Tom Cruise had indeed played the part, then Hunter's carefulness in addressing his superior officer would be interpreted as part of the characterization, as it was in *A Few Good Men* (1992). But Cruise did not play the part; Denzel did. And in so doing, he brought an agenda to the performance which Corliss effectively addressed, one that has been a theme in many of his pictures: the role of a black man who chooses to live in the white world, insisting on equality, often proving his superiority, yet finding himself singled out all the same.

In the film's opening, Hunter is pulled away from a birthday party for his little boy, enabling him to leave for the mission. At this moment, it's difficult to separate character from star: Denzel, by this point in his career, had become comfortable enough with his success to turn down projects, including potentially exciting ones, that would have taken him away from his family for extended periods of time. "I'm there for my children," Denzel said while doing publicity for the film. Realizing that he was, at that moment, with an interviewer rather than his kids, he corrected himself: "I mean, I'm not there today, obviously, but I talked to them this morning, and they know where I'm going and why I have to do it. I'll be home for dinner tonight." And that he was!

Denzel has also made it clear that he's now aware *Virtuosity* was a mistake, though *Crimson Tide* was not; he could compete with Tom Cruise but not Sly or Arnold for roles and worked best in thought-provoking movies that contained action; Cruise could have nicely played Hunter, just as Denzel would have been fine in *Mission: Impossible* (1996)—but not *Judge Dredd* (1995) or *Eraser* (1996). "It's quote unquote an action-thriller, but it's quite theatrical. Everything that happens is so that these two heads can come [crashing] together"—intellectually, morally, and emotionally, but not physically.

17

Virtuosity
1995
A PARAMOUNT RELEASE

CAST: Denzel Washington (*Parker Barnes*); Kelly Lynch (*Madison Carter*); Russell Crowe (*Sid 6.7*); Stephen Spinella (*Lindenmeyer*); William Forsythe (*William Cochran*); Louise Fletcher (*Elizabeth Deane*); William Fichtner (*Wallace*); Costas Mandylor (*John Donovan*); Kevin J. O'Connor (*Clyde Reilly*).

CREDITS: Director, Brett Leonard; producer, Gary Lucchesi; executive producer, Howard W. Koch Jr.; screenplay, Eric Bernt; cinematography, Gale Tattersall; editors, B. J. Sears and Rob Kobrin; music, Christopher Young; production design, Nilo Rodis; costumes, Francine Jamison-Tanchuck; art direction, Richard Yanez-Toyon; visual effects supervisor, Jon Townley; rating, R; running time, 105 min.

I was real reluctant about *Virtuosity*," Denzel admitted to *Movieline* in 1995, shortly before the film's inauspicious debut during the height of the frenzied summer movie season, when this high-tech, state-of-the-art action thriller opened with some fanfare, then quickly closed to mostly negative reviews and a notable lack of audience interest. "It doesn't bother me that they were talking to Michael Douglas for a long time. Maybe in my younger days it would have bothered me more. But, hey, you can't assume when you get the call that you're the first choice."

For an eternal optimist like Denzel, it was gratifying to know that now he was right up there on the "A list," a close second to Michael Douglas, who, after all, had been plugging away for a full fifteen years longer than Denzel. Douglas had, over the years, paid his dues, gradually establishing his reputation and reaching superstardom only after much long, hard work. Like Denzel, Douglas had proven himself a conscientious actor, his good looks aside; for both men sex appeal existed as a kind of happy side dish to the main course of talent.

The comparison with Michael Douglas was, then, as with Robert Redford previously, one Denzel could live with, even relish. What he still scoffed at was the fact that the relatively untried pretty boys, who came and went with grueling regularity, too often garnered the best parts. True, in his early days, Denzel—like Redford—was mistakenly considered just such a pretty boy by those industry observers who failed to look close enough to notice the acting ability lurking beneath the physical attractiveness. But over the years, Denzel had mitigated such a view, so it remained something of a thorn in his side to accept the fact that such newcomers could, however briefly, go to the head of the class and be given first shot at the best scripts over Denzel, Douglas, or Bob Redford: "I imagine Tom Cruise gets first dibs at everything, although maybe now Brad Pitt may be getting some of his thunder. Everything's probably coming to him first. But there's ten other guys there next to Brad, and they're not getting the call."

So ego wasn't what had given Denzel reason to pause. "But I *am* concerned with the fact that my butt's on the line, and I want a good product to come out. [*Virtuosity* director] Brett Leonard did another film called *Hideaway* [1993] which I think is pretty good. Still, it's *my* butt on the line with the product. Nowhere to hide." Denzel was, as he himself now acknowledges, a film star of the first order. If the film flopped, he would be held responsible. It did, and he was.

Virtuosity certainly would have seemed destined to be a box-office hit, if not necessarily a favorite of the critics. The story line proceeded from a trendy premise: a virtual-reality thriller and a violent urban-crime film that was very much of and for the nineties. The movie—set in 1999—took various elements in present-day society and caricatured them in order to create a near-future cautionary fable. In the opening sequence, Denzel's character, Parker Barnes, is depicted in "tomorrowland" police garb, pursuing an ugly villain across a city that appears not quite real, existing, rather, in the manufactured world of a computer. Indeed, as we watch, we realize that the event is not authentic, but a virtual-reality simulation of what could happen during a police chase, fabricated as part of an elaborate training program for police officers.

Barnes was, until recently, one such police officer himself. Now, however, he's in jail, doing hard time for becoming a vigilante, tracking down and killing the murderer who blew up his wife and child. In jail, Barnes gets into an all-too-real fight with a white supremacist, one of the film's rare fleeting references to the hero's color, though it's just as likely this heavy would have picked on Barnes if he were played by a Jewish (Michael Douglas) or Italian (Sylvester Stallone) actor. Though Barnes is, by virtue of his color, a member of a minority, he is not specific to African Americans, more on the order of an all-purpose ethnicity.

In that computer program glimpsed during the opening sequence, Barnes pursued Sid 6.7 (Russell Crowe), not an actual man but "the prototype of future humanoid nanotechnology." Sid is a computer-generated creation designed, by crackpot scientist Lindenmeyer (Stephen Spinella), to give police-academy trainees their greatest challenge. Lindenmeyer fabricated Sid 6.7 as a combination of nearly two hundred of the world's worst real-life villains, from Adolf Hitler to Charles Manson, so that the young recruits would—in the safety of their virtual-reality training zone—come up against the worst-case scenario out there. In fact, the villain who knocked off Barnes's family is also a component of Sid, explaining why Barnes is chosen to pursue this monster in the video and why he does so with such intensity. Following their bouts with Sid 6.7, anything the budding policemen later encounter in the real world—however terrible—should seem relatively mild in comparison to the crazed composite of everything evil that's ever passed through history.

Unfortunately, the modern Dr. Frankenstein will follow the course of his predecessor, unleashing his creation on the outside world. Unhappy with the way he's being treated, Lindenmeyer lets Sid loose from his virtual-reality prison, sending him off into the streets of futuristic Los Angeles. No one but Barnes can track him down, so the hero is freed from jail. The situation is much like spoiled cop Sylvester Stallone's being allowed to redeem himself by going after flamboyant madman Wesley Snipes in *Demolition Man* (1993), only with the color of hero and villain reversed. Barnes is teamed with a police psychologist, Madison Carter (Kelly Lynch), whose intellectual understanding of criminal behavior, coupled with Barnes's street-fighter strength, may just provide the right combination to end the ensuing chaos. She just happens to be a gorgeous blonde, the film closely following all the conventional patterns of such an action movie.

Indeed, such conventionality turned out to be the film's downfall. As in *Terminator 2: Judgment Day* (1991) the villain's constant escapes rely on the filmmakers' ability to provide morphing images for his chameleon-like changes. But the syndrome that social critic Alvin Toffler once defined as Future Shock negated any ability of these special effects to impress an audience. A mere five years earlier, when *Terminator 2* appeared, such images were new and exciting, able to make an audience forget the unlikely elements in a story by keeping everyone mesmerized with these previously unseen visuals. Quickly, though, morphing had been adapted for use by everything from TV commercials to music videos and second-rate movie imitations of *Terminator 2*. For morphing effects to have been of any value by 1995, they had to be incorporated into an original narrative with absorbing characters, and *Virtuosity* offered neither of those elements.

Rather, it repeated one of the silliest story elements from *Terminator 2*, which viewers had perhaps once been willing to overlook, but no longer. The hero is told that the bad guy, being synthetically made from silicon, cannot be killed by normal means, such as simply shooting him several times. However, whenever hero and villain come in contact, Barnes shoots at Sid, who bleeds a blue ooze and then rushes off to quickly heal. You would think that Barnes, supposedly bright, would "get it" and try some other means of attack. Instead, he continues shooting at Sid, always appearing surprised that his bullets have no impact at all. On the other hand, one of the best things about *Terminator 2* was the nicely developed relationship between hero Arnold Schwarzenegger and his female companion, Linda Hamilton, who emerged as an interesting and, in the context of such a genre piece, well-written character. Here the female (Carter) is nondescript and generic, supposedly accompanying the hero because she's so smart but rarely making any notable contribution to the pursuit, in actuality present simply for her good looks.

Again, a love story between Barnes and Carter might have sparked the ever-lamer goings-on a bit, but that element wasn't developed despite the attractiveness of the two stars. Though a special-effects action flick like *Virtuosity* may seem as far as one can go, genrewise, from *The Pelican Brief*, the same lack of romance for Denzel—clearly a romantic figure in the audience's eyes, certainly more so than an action hero—once again seemed a major miscalculation. His winning combination of gentleness and masculinity makes him more right to play a lover than a fighter, though here he fights all the time. While Denzel performs the scenes convincingly enough, it isn't necessarily what his fans want to see him do, any more than they want to see Robert Redford or Michael Douglas in such situations. Such stars are the opposite of Arnold or Sly, who have yet to play love scenes convincingly on-screen; Denzel here seems bound and determined to go against the grain of his own talent.

The biggest problem, however, is that despite a striking visualization by the production-design wizards at L2 Communications of a fully realized, heavy-metal future world, screenwriter Eric Bernt, having come up with a terrific concept, was unable to provide the variations on the theme so necessary to extend the movie beyond the hefty running time of 105 minutes. Instead of the ever-increasingly interesting and surprising elements of cyberspace adventure audiences hoped for, Bernt's screenplay tossed out its neat premise, then ran out of steam, swiftly degenerating into a series of clichés numbingly reminiscent of situations from other, earlier films of the genre, from *RoboCop* (1987) to *Terminator 2*. *Virtuosity* relies on all-too familiar car chases and crashes, plus that incredibly inane staple of contemporary action flicks, glass shattering in slow motion. *Virtuosity* even concludes with a duel between hero and villain high atop a skyscraper, a virtual replay of the similar scene Denzel had already performed in *Ricochet*.

Denzel received strong notices within the context of reviews that damned the film. In *Variety*, Godfrey Chesire panned *Virtuosity* for "scripter Eric Bernt's recurrent tendency to sacrifice dramatic sense to jolts of action" but did point out that Washington emerges an able action hero." *Rolling Stone* tagged the film "stillborn" but conceded that "Denzel Washington is a big help." David Hunter of the *Hollywood Reporter* found the film "stylish but often trite," mentioning that "Washington handles himself well in the action scenes and stays in the film's serious frame of mind for his many agonizing flashbacks and confrontations with authority." Janet Maslin, in the *New York Times*, dismissed *Virtuosity* as "increasingly shrill" and "numbingly frantic," noting that "Mr. Washington is usually an actor audiences will follow to any dimension. But here his role is limited, too often leaving him playing second fiddle to this film's weirdly hypnotic special effects."

Perhaps Kevin Thomas, in the *Los Angeles Times*, summed up better than anyone Denzel's true reason for having agreed to participate: "Forget all the technical stuff, for the film's real inspiration is in casting Denzel Washington as its star. He brings a crucial humanity to the carnage—and, in turn, gets to muscle most effectively into Arnold and Sly superman territory, doubtless a shrewd career move for a prestige actor." Well, yes and no. Fans of hard-edged action films, mostly teenage boys, are pretty particular about whom they accept in such roles, preferring actors who lack the very humanity Thomas found so appealing and even redeeming. No matter how popular Michael Douglas and Patrick Swayze may be with the mainstream audiences that crowded in to see *Romancing the Stone* and *Ghost*, they flopped when they tried to expand into urban-action territory with *Black Rain* (1989) and *Next of Kin* (1989). Acting range has nothing to do with it, nor do issues of race. A preconception on the part of audiences as to who, in their minds, appears right for any particular kind of film determines whether they will turn out for the picture.

And they did not turn out for *Virtuosity*. In addition to Denzel's being in what the public considered the wrong kind of movie, there was another reason why the film failed. Hollywood had long since convinced itself that to be on the cutting edge of entertainment, it must incorporate the evolving notion of cyberspace into films, even as computers became a household appliance rather than a corporate luxury, and computer games replaced the pinball machine as the favorite indoor pastime of America's kids. But when Disney tried to create a new kind of animated film with 1982's *Tron*, employing computer animation rather than their classical hand-drawn approach for a story about kids sucked into a popular game, the movie surprised everyone at the company—and industry observers—by flopping with the public.

It's one thing to play a computer game, quite another to watch other people play it. So it should not be counted against Denzel that his cyberspace film flopped: So, too, did *Johnny Mnemonic* (1995), with Keanu Reeves, and *The Net* (1995), with Sandra Bullock, despite the actors' strong drawing power in other films. Likewise, Michael Crichton's *Disclosure* (1994), with Michael Douglas and Demi Moore, did at best only decent business despite the industry's box-office expectations, perhaps because their sexual shenanigans in the office served only as a prelude to the real focus of the film as each character searched through cyberspace for important information with which they could destroy the reputation of the other. In the earlier, more innocent era of the 1950s, the public loved movies and baseball more than anything else, but baseball movies never made money. Films dealing with virtual reality can be seen as the 1990s counterpart; it appears that when people pull themselves away from their computers to go to the movies, they don't necessarily want to see films about other people using just such instruments.

How did Denzel feel after the experience of filming *Virtuosity* was all over? "I said after I did the first [action film], *Ricochet*, that I'd never do one again. And now that I've done it again, I'll say it again." Denzel laughed at his own self-contradiction, then admitted: "I don't like them. You gotta run and jump and you don't talk. It's not acting."

18

Devil in a Blue Dress

1995

A TRI-STAR RELEASE

CAST: Denzel Washington (*Easy Rawlins*); Tom Sizemore (*Dewitt Albright*); Jennifer Beals (*Daphne Monet*); Don Cheadle (*Mouse*); Maury Chaykin (*Matthew Terrell*); Terry Kinney (*Todd Carter*).

CREDITS: Director, Carl Franklin; producers, Jesse Beaton, Gary Goetzman, and Jonathan Demme; screenplay, Franklin, from the novel by Walter Mosley; cinematography, Tak Fujimoto; editor, Carole Kravetz; music, Elmer Bernstein; production designer, Gary Fruitkoff; rating, R; running time, 102 min.

*D*evil in a Blue Dress features a framing device that does far more than merely provide an opening and ending for the film's story. When Ezekiel ("Easy") Rawlins leaves his small but substantial home in the first scene, fearing he may lose his humble abode because he's out of work, Rawlins represents every working man who ever believed in the American Dream of owning a home of one's own, only to fear it might slip through his fingers through no fault of his own. The culprit, rather, is a system which promises rewards for work but doesn't always pay up. When, at the end, Easy relaxes on his porch, having undergone a bizarre journey for the sake of hanging on to that beloved piece of property, we see his belief in the American Dream reconfirmed, but only if one is able and willing to wrestle with a wide assortment of demons.

Filmmaker Carl Franklin later reflected on the film that he and Denzel made together: "Easy has to make a pact with the devil to save his house, which to him represents everything about the opportunities he was fighting for during World War II. By the end of the story, Easy has learned the world is a very complicated place, where you can't wait for things to come to you. You have to go out and get them."

Forty-six years old when he directed this critically acclaimed crime thriller, Franklin found himself seated in the director's chair following a long and often winding personal odyssey of his own. The trek included studying history at the University of California and working as a well-regarded but unknown actor, playing roles as diverse as a Greek slave in Joseph Papp's Public Theater production of *Timon of Athens* to a recurring part on *The A Team*, television's slam-bang action show of the 1970s. There was even a stint teaching at the American Film Institute before critics sat up and noticed the inexpensive but original film *One False Move* (1992), allowing Franklin the thrill of being discovered as a hot director in Hollywood.

"He's really a history professor trapped in a movie director's body," Denzel Washington said admiringly of Franklin. "You know he's always going to get deep into things." The film achieves precisely that, delving deep into the history of racism in Los Angeles while on the surface appearing only to tell a highly involving detective yarn, and tell it well.

It was such a sense of history—as well as the realization that, as a black film director, he had an opportunity to make millions of people see the way things once were rather than merely summing up history in words for a single classroom full of students—that led Franklin to arrange for a special preproduction lunch at the ancient Harold & Belle's restaurant on Jefferson Boulevard. There, surviving jazz musicians from the late forties were encouraged to describe at length their most personal memories of those times. Victoria Thomas, Franklin's casting director, meanwhile found old family photos, bringing them into the office in the hope that they might be useful for research purposes. Franklin shared them with Denzel, knowing that the actor was as dedicated as himself to the task of bringing truth rather than movie mythology to the screen.

One particular photograph caught Denzel's attention: In it, a pair of black teens stood on the front porch of a shingled house, smiling optimistically, as if the world were their oyster. The image never left Denzel's mind: "It's hard to say what's so powerful about a photo like that," he would later reflect. "It's just a vibe you get. But when I saw those kids, I ran over to Don Cheadle, who plays Mouse, and I said, 'Man, look at this picture. This is us!'" It could also be the "us" of Denzel (as Malcolm X) and best pal Shorty (Spike Lee) in the opening sequence of Lee's *Malcolm X;* it is any pair of young black friends who early on believe in the American Dream and set out to achieve it, all too often having such positive attitudes kicked out of them, step by violent step, by the realities of an unjust system.

A key character in the story, "Mouse" is the psychopathic sidekick who saves Easy's life on several occasions. Perhaps unconsciously, novelist Walter Mosely had fashioned Mouse as a precursor to today's gang-bangers; Franklin's conception was to take that suggested notion of the character and make it a major metaphor in the film, so he toyed with the idea of casting gangsta rapper turned actor Ice Cube in the part. Eventually, Franklin settled on the highly respected performer Don Cheadle, who pumped up the volume on that particular slant to the character. The result is a film that offhandedly comments on the present while masking its story in the nostalgia-drenched mists of the dimly remembered past.

When we first meet Easy Rawlins—in Mosley's 1990 novel, as in Franklin's film—he has no intention whatsoever of becoming a "private eye" despite the fact that this is 1948 and Los Angeles is filled with such fictional fellows, ranging from Dashiell Hammett's Sam Spade to Raymond Chandler's Philip Marlowe. Rawlins is an ordinary, everyday working man, a World War II veteran who joined in that mass migration of African Americans from the Southland following "the big one," the war during which the military was at last integrated. The promise is that integration in America's mainstream will shortly follow suit, though this didn't really begin until the turbulence of Selma, Alabama, and Memphis, Tennessee, during the mid-1950s. Meanwhile, Easy has taken a job at an aircraft plant and begun paying for the mortgage on his home; then the American Dream that seemed within reach turns out to be a carrot dangled in front of his face, for the postwar recession leaves Ezekiel Rawlins without a job.

Sitting in a bar, reading the want ads, he's approached by Dewitt Albright (Tom Sizemore), a gregarious but faintly menacing white man who offers the desperate Ezekiel an opportunity to make fast, easy money. Daphne Monet (Jennifer Beals), the gorgeous, mysterious fiancée of a well-to-do local politician, has disappeared. Ordinarily, this would be a task for the police, but Daphne has been known to slip away and lose herself in black neighborhoods; she loves the jazz that's barely accepted by mainstream white society and apparently also has a taste for the black men who create that soulful music. Since a mayoral race is currently under way, any possible embarrassment for the candidate must be skirted. Daphne must be quickly found and brought home, and a black man like Easy—quiet, charismatic, unobtrusive, formidable—would be perfect for the job. There's a hundred dollars in it, a piece of change Easy sorely needs.

So Easy becomes a reluctant detective, one who discovers—as J. J. Gittes (Jack Nicholson) previously did in Roman Polanski's *Chinatown* (1974)—that nothing is as simple as it first seems. The bright L.A. sunlight provides a golden veneer for an all-encroaching moral darkness lurking beneath the shimmering surface. Like other dectective heroes before him, Easy Rawlins is a middle-class man who finds himself straddling the heights and depths of society, a cross-cultural journey which makes him fully aware of the class warfare in America, where ugly foibles of the very rich impact on the daily lives of the very poor. It is only through the violent efforts of his pal Mouse, who started out on the same road in life as Easy but took the alternative road—as an unconscious anarchist rather than a slave to the system—that Easy survives, a plot structure that has underlined other Denzel vehicles as varied as *The Mighty Quinn* and *Ricochet.*

Producer Jesse Beaton, who collaborated with Franklin on several earlier projects, read the book shortly after its release and passed it along to the director, suggesting that it would be a strong possibility for them to develop. In 1992, Jonathan Demme acquired the rights to the piece; as luck would have it, he'd just seen *One False Move*, and called Carl Franklin to let him know he'd like to work with the budding talent as soon as possible, never realizing he'd just locked on to the same project Franklin hoped to do. Demme added ideas of his own but chose to remain in the background. At this point, Franklin wrote a draft, "streamlining" the story by eliminating superfluous characters and combining others, attempting to remain true not so much to the letter of the novel as its spirit: the tone and intent that are essential to Walter Mosley's vision.

Precisely what is that vision all about? Less about racism than one might assume if the author himself is to be believed: "There's racism in *Devil*," Mosley commented, "but it's not about that; it's about Easy. Overcoming racism is just one of Easy's problems." What are the others? "I write about poor people," Mosley continues. "Poor people have few outlets in life in America. They have sex, intoxicants, and storytelling. And that is what my characters do." Understandably, Mosley was drawn to doing a black variation on the detective tale, the only genre that easily allows a writer an effective canvas to paint a portrait of a decent, if flawed, man attempting to cling to a belief that life has meaning and morality remains possible in a universe careening toward nihilism. "I'm interested in a kind of world that's slightly cracked. You're trying to figure out what's good, what's bad, what's true and not true. Trying to hold on to your own memories and sense of yourself. Trying to do the right thing in a world where doing the right thing means you have to do something wrong."

Devil in a Blue Dress had been lingering in preproduction purgatory over at Universal, where Mosley himself had taken a stab at scripting, though he admitted that screenwriting was not his forte. There is a tradition of great crime novelists who cannot get the hang of the film medium, with its unique storytelling demands; Raymond Chandler himself, having happily completed the book *The Big Sleep,* was miserable when working with Alfred Hitchcock on *Strangers on a Train* (1951). Compounding the problem was that, at Universal, the project suffered from the desire of that company's execs to make the film version as simple a murder mystery as possible.

Everything changed when Demme entered the mix, proving to be the catalyst the simmering project sorely needed. No sooner had Demme brought *Devil in a Blue Dress* to Mike Medavoy, then chairman of Tri-Star, than everything began rolling. At Universal, those assigned to develop the project had been told to turn Easy, the laconic observer, into a more traditional tough guy via action-oriented sequences. "They wanted Easy to be a stronger character," Franklin said. "But that's not who Easy is. Easy's dilemma is that he's a guy who's fighting fear: the basic fears of a black person in 1948—

problems with the police, being in the wrong neighborhood at the wrong time, afraid because he's been in the war and has killed, afraid of becoming like that again; afraid of *being* killed, afraid of becoming like Mouse."

Franklin was anything but shy about altering the plot, changing the ultimate identity of the killer and, midway through, eliminating the steamy bathtub sex scene between Daphne and Easy. Mosley was relatively comfortable with Franklin's decision to alter the identity of the murderer. "When I look at the movie," he claimed, "I don't think about the book. The ending is different, but I'm not unhappy about that, because the movie needs to be a little more uplifting. The book is darker. Easy is carrying a lot more baggage."

Mosely was more critical of the director's decision that Easy and Daphne would not become lovers: "I love their relationship in the book." In fact, there are some feminist critics who claim that Mosley's depiction of this lustful romance, much like other man-woman bouts in his books, is sexist in nature; he has been criticized by black female critics for his portraits of black women, perceived from the perspective of a male artist, just as Alice Walker (*The Color Purple*) has been criticized by black male critics for the largely negative portraits of African-American men in her books. In his defense, Mosley states: "You have to be careful not to become a victim of political correctness. There's something wrong if you can't talk about the problems, if you can't risk being unpopular in order to try to cause a deeper understanding. Easy's as much a victim of women as they are of him. . . . If you don't talk about the kind of mistakes people make, then you can't talk about the things they do right." As in the film adaptation of *The Pelican Brief,* the romance between Denzel's character and a white woman, so essential to the novel, was dropped; in each case, it seemed the biggest mistake the filmmakers made.

When, for a *Movieline* interview, Stephen Rebello asked Denzel about the excision of this scene, he received a hard, cold look and one single statement: "It's Carl's vision, it's his film. Those [sex] scenes you talk about were never in the script," insisting he had nothing to do with the decision at all, his body language broaching no further discussion on the matter.

At any rate, everyone involved with the project—Mosley, Franklin, Demme, et al.—knew that *Devil* would sink or swim depending on the casting of the lead. Danny Glover and Wesley Snipes were both mentioned; Tim Reid expressed interest. Denzel, always on their short list, seemed so right for Easy that some people wondered if Mosley had created the part with him in mind, though the author insists that was not the case: "A lot of people you talk to, they say, 'Who do you see as Easy?' But I come from the theater, where if someone tells you Laurence Olivier is going to play Hercules, you say, 'Gee, I wonder how he's going to do that?' That's the way I think." But if Mosley thinks theatrically, Franklin necessarily thought cinematically. Despite the marquee talents interested in the part, he honed in on Denzel almost immediately.

As Franklin put it, "Denzel is deceptive. You always see him play these highbrow guys—doctors and lawyers—but he's actually a very down home guy. And I think he brought a lot of that earthiness and charm to Easy's character." Glover is more of a father figure, at his best when (as in the *Lethal Weapon* films) playing highly dependable, less than charismatic men; Snipes projects a risible contemporary anger at racial injustice that's always appealed more to black audiences than to whites. Denzel was the one performer who could convey both sides of the Easy Rawlins coin: at once a black man and a universal man. At the heart of what makes the script so rich is this double-edged element. Easy's racial identity and his human identity exist in precarious balance, an unacknowledged but always present internal duel.

Denzel had his own reasons for wanting to play the role. "We'd never really seen South-Central Los Angeles from that time, so it was fresh territory," he explained to visitors on the set, making it clear that among his ambitions as an actor was to involve himself with projects that vividly brought to life various periods in black American history previously overlooked, as *Glory* had done for the Civil War. This approach allows ethnic audiences an opportunity to experience a surge of black pride while also giving white audiences an entertaining education that would leave them with a new awareness of the key role African Americans played in diverse historical periods.

But Denzel's involvement went further; his comments on the character of Easy reveal as much about himself as they do about

Rawlins: "It was *real*! Easy's a regular guy who's in over his head in a crazy situation. When I'm down at the station, being questioned by the police, I'm scared. It's how you react in real life—you're not so tough when you got a billy club up the side of your head." That key scene can be interpreted racially, with Easy viewed as a black man being beaten by white police officers. But Denzel did not specifically refer to Easy's blackness, though that can be inferred. The openness of Denzel's phrasing allows for a broader interpretation of the scene and of the movie. Easy is a human being who belongs to a particular minority group that has been kept powerless. While the identification with that scene may be strong among black moviegoers, it also works for anyone who has ever felt vulnerable for any reason—race, religion, length of hair, etc.—taking on a more generalized significance.

Critics largely agreed that the casting proved as perfect as Humphrey Bogart as Sam Spade, Paul Newman as Lew Harper, or (lest we forget) Sidney Poitier as Virgil Tibbs. David Denby of *New York* wrote that "Washington conveys just the right measure of necessary deference and implacable male pride" to suggest a man both true to the historical reality of black males in the segregated society of that time, and a possible role model for African-American audiences of today. Stuart Klawans of the *Nation* wrote:

> The role calls for an actor who has more than star power. It needs someone with such an innate sense of dignity that he wouldn't even *think* of swaggering; maybe even someone who's a little self-involved, therefore credible when he talks back to a white cop or strides uninvited into a rich man's domain, as if he doesn't notice the other people there, who might object to his behavior or simply shoot him. Denzel has always tended to give just that impression of being intact—so much so that in this film he seems rather offended, for both Easy Rawlins and himself, when Jennifer Beals's character gives him a classic B-movie come-on.

This comment is particularly apt, considering the fact that in the book Mosley's Easy Rawlins quickly succumbs to Daphne's lurid charms. Mosley could write it that way because, by his own admission, he did not have Denzel Washington in mind while crafting the book. But Franklin, when penning the script, did.

Thinking cinematically, Franklin was aware, consciously or not, that when tailoring a script for a particular star, it's important to keep in mind the things an audience will or will not accept that star doing: John Wayne, Paul Newman, Sidney Poitier, and now Denzel are all approached by audiences who harbor expectations about what each will or will not do in a film. What Klawans rightly describes as Denzel's being "offended," violates Mosley's original conception of Easy Rawlins, but it accommodates Denzel as a star, who previously *had* been offended by just such an attempted come-on by a white woman in *The Mighty Quinn.*

"It helps his performance," Klawans continued, "that the story sends Easy Rawlins into so many different places, from an after-hours club to a mansion, from a shack on the outskirts of town to a pier at Malibu; as the situation varies in each place, Washington gets to show off a range few other actors can claim." Denzel is a canny *reactor* as well as a highly effective actor, allowing his observant eyes, body language, and vocal inflections to transform in keeping with whatever demimonde Easy finds himself in.

Terrence Rafferty of the *New Yorker* further analyzed another key theme. Denzel here takes a modern perspective on a historically accurate character and situation without condescending to what is clearly a bygone way of behavior for an African American. Nor, on the other hand, does he "update" a period story by having the character operate as if he were a modern, dropped back into history as far as costuming is concerned, though not in attitude.

Washington's . . . work in *Devil in a Blue Dress* is deeply satisfying, because he's playing a character whose worldview doesn't jibe with contemporary notions of how black men should operate in white society, and he explores Easy's wary, essentially non-confrontational personality with genuine curiosity and sympathy. Washington finds the humor and quiet heroism in the character's adaptability, and the practical intelligence in his cautious manner. The actor's relaxed star presence works unobtrusively to dispose of any lingering impression that Easy's fear is a sign of weakness, with himself so assured that he doesn't need to swagger. When he's afraid, we feel instinctively that he has good reason to be—that he's careful because he's not stupid.

Janet Maslin, commenting on how fashion-magazine-cover handsome Denzel appeared in the period costumes, commented: "The role of Easy looks as tailor-made for Mr. Washington as his suit, and it shows off the full effect of this actor's movie star dazzle. In a career dotted with generic roles and noble ones, he's never had a part that fit him better." Intriguingly, though, this element of costuming was not what it appeared to be (an extremely expensive suit worn by a supposedly out of work regular Joe, done strictly for purposes of Hollywood glamour), but a case of class shining through. "Look at Denzel," one crew member whispered to cinematographer Tak Fujimoto while the scene was being filmed. "That's actually a cheap suit he's wearing because that's what Easy would be able to afford, but on Denzel it looks *GQ*."

If that suit is "real" to the period, so was everything else about the picture. The story is set in the area today referred to as Watts, though at the time, Central Avenue, and the environs where it dissects 103rd Street was by day a burgeoning business area filled with crowded shops and busy companies, at night a home for blues and jazz artists and the fans they attracted, ranging from lowlifes on the make to high-society types out slumming. It was impossible to shoot the film where the story took place, since today's burned-out Watts bears little resemblance to the magically menacing territory of the past. Instead, the company scouted the greater Los Angeles area for locations, finding what they needed downtown, where a four-block section of Main Street, near Pico, could, with some careful disguising of modern "conveniences" like parking meters and the restoration of the famed Red Car trolley, be transformed into a believable facsimile.

Likewise, the foundation offices of Todd Carter, the political bigwig, were shot in Pasadena, where the formidable white-stone main structure of the private Mayfield Senior School came so close to being what Mosley had described in his book that the author, visiting the set that day, proclaimed: "I'm looking at the office that I wrote." While shooting, Denzel and director Franklin developed an odd method of relating, referring to each other through a series of eccentric nicknames that included "Pain," "Hurt," and "Slice," throwing these epithets back and forth in place of their actual names.

This organic system, which worked well in the context of what the two mutually agreed on as the essential integrity of their project, derived from the work of yet another black writer of detective fiction, Chester Himes, whose thrillers *Cotton Comes to Harlem* (1970) and *Come Back, Charleston Blue* (1972) had been brought to the screen in the early seventies, with Godfrey Cambridge and Raymond St. Jacques as detectives Coffin Ed Johnson and Gravedigger Jones. By the mid-eighties, Himes had been virtually forgotten, dying alone in exile, though not before penning his searing, unsparing autobiography *The Quality of Hurt*, articulating the unique pain of being a black artist, the stigma of racism mixed with the pangs of creativity unappreciated.

"We had this ongoing Chester Himes thing where we'd try to find new ways to hurt each other's feelings," Denzel recalled. "I'd say to Carl, 'Brother, I saw some of your work yesterday, and it was terrible!' And then he'd say to me, 'That's just what I was thinking about your work, brother!'" In fact, actor and director—self-consciously "performing" a dark comedy skit in tandem—had only the greatest admiration for each other's work. But the running off-camera gag allowed them to inject a certain texture of honest emotion into what was always in danger of degenerating into a glib and clever period piece, a "black *Chinatown*," as industry wags superficially tagged the film.

Nevertheless, Patrick Goldstein of the *Los Angeles Times* raised a pertinent question: Would Denzel have been comfortable engaging in such eccentricities had a white director been guiding him through the project, and would *Devil in a Blue Dress* have in fact turned out quite differently if that had been the case? "I think that being black, Carl definitely brings things to the movie that a white director couldn't," Denzel explained, making clear that this or any film about a gripping moment in black history is going to feature a special aura if an African-American auteur is at work behind the camera. Nonetheless, Denzel would not take the attitude that such a film would be invalid if a white director helmed the project: "But I'm sure someone like Jonathan Demme could've brought his own set of special things, too. Having Carl make the movie made it unique, but I don't know if that's Carl being black or just being Carl. I think the theme of the movie was really personal for Carl. He really understood that it was a story about a man overcoming his fears."

A man overcoming his fears: specifically, a black man overcoming the fears unique to a black man in Los Angeles, circa 1948; then again a human being, somebody anyone can relate to, a man who overcomes universalized fears, as we all must. For that reason, the period decor could not be allowed to dominate the film, transforming this into one more cold, clinical exercise in *noir* sensibility. Washington and Franklin agreed, from the start, that they must create well-rounded, fully motivated, completely believable human beings who happened to live in the past, portrayed as a vivid period in history rather than a fabled era of myth: "Film noir is one of my favorite genres," Franklin explained, "although I don't think you need to approach it as a genre when you do it. I like the forties; I like detective kind of things. But what I never liked about them is the inaccessibility of the characters. Usually they're people that you never run into in real life. You know, where does [Philip] Marlowe live? Who's his mom? Where did he come from? Same with... Sam Spade. The thing about *these* people is that they were all people I had seen before. Easy lives in a neighborhood."

Richard Alleva expressed this element beautifully in his *Commonweal* review, describing his own reaction when Easy is beaten by bigoted cops and literally yelps rather than screams. As Alleva noted, this was

> something no movie private eye, white or black, has ever done.... That yelp, that stutter, that flurry of fists [which follow the 'yelp'] express so much of Rawlins's character—his daunting knowledge of what white men feel free to do to blacks, the courage that persists in defiance of that knowledge, his surprisingly unquenched capacity for being outraged by the world's injustice—that, days after seeing *Devil in a Blue Dress*, I am still struck with admiration at the way Washington managed to show so much of Easy Rawlins in a few seconds.

Easy the individual human being rather than the black Sam Spade that might have emerged had this been played as a tried-and-true genre piece.

Though well received by critics, *Devil in a Blue Dress* did surprisingly disappointing business; budgeted at $20 million, the film only brought in $16 million at the box office—a particular disappointment to Denzel, since it had been the first film produced by the star's own company, Mundy Lane. The following summer, Denzel shrugged the situation off while being interviewed for *Entertainment Weekly*: "They say period pieces are [a] hard [sell]. We also opened the weekend of the O. J. Simpson verdict, which didn't help. But making fifty million dollars the first weekend is not the criterion for whether it's a good film."

19

Courage Under Fire

1996

A 20TH CENTURY-FOX RELEASE

CAST: Denzel Washington (*Lt. Col. Nathaniel Serling*); Meg Ryan (*Capt. Karen Walden*); Lou Diamond Phillips (*Monfriez*); Michael Moriarty (*General Hershberg*); Matt Damon (*Harlo*); Seth Gilliam (*Altameyer*); Bronson Pinchot (*Bruno*); Scott Glenn (*Tony Gartner*); Regina Taylor (*Meredith*).

CREDITS: Director, Edward Zwick; producers, John Davis, Joseph M. Singer, and David T. Friendly; screenplay, Patrick Sheane Duncan; cinematography, Roger Deakins; editor, Steven Rosenblum; music, James Horner; production design, John Graysmark; rating, R; running time, 120 min.

W hat is heroic about this guy?" Denzel asked in response to reporters who, interviewing him in Washington, D.C., for a story about the upcoming *Courage Under Fire*, continuously referred to his character as the film's "hero." Insisting that Nathaniel Serling is too average, fallible, and confused a man to be slapped with such a stereotypical label, Denzel sounded nearly as insulted as he had been when, years earlier, other such reporters likewise tried to compliment the then young actor by referring to him as "the new Sidney Poitier." "He trips and falls big time," Denzel said of Serling, a man who, as Denzel perceives him, is merely trying to survive. "He becomes a slobbering, wandering drunk."

Serling does indeed become just that following the Gulf War. As a tank commander during a midnight attack on Al Bathra, one part of the larger Operation Desert Storm, Serling hurriedly orders his crew to fire at what he perceives as an approaching enemy vehicle, the T-54, inadvertently killing some of his own companions via "friendly fire." Perhaps he could live with this, however haunted he might be by nightmares, were it not for the fact that his mentor, General Hershberg (Michael Moriarty), orders a cover-up so that the reputation of the outfit, as well his favorite officer, will not be tarnished in the context of a brief, media-monitored war fought in large part to make America feel good about itself again. But Serling does not merely pay lip service to the military code of honor; rather, he lives it out to the fullest every day. So he turns to drink, even leaves his loving family, after being forced to lie to the parents of a deceased boy, telling them their son was killed by the enemy.

To help Serling recover, then move on with his promising career, Hershberg assigns him a seemingly routine paper-pushing job. Karen Walden (Meg Ryan), a medevac pilot killed in combat, has been nominated for a Medal of Honor, her country's highest award for bravery. Apparently, she saved a group of American soldiers by dropping a fuel tank on the Iraqi tank that had those men pinned down; then, after her chopper fell, Karen kept the enemy at bay all night long by firing her M-16, eventually dying while providing cover when a rescue vehicle arrived.

The military brass is excited about the possibility of demonstrating their new "enlightenment" by making Karen the first female Medal of Honor winner, while the White House is so high on the idea that they've assigned a media hack (Bronson Pinchot) to steer the process through quickly. At first glance, Serling agrees that Karen does appear to be a perfect contender, taking the attitude that interviewing the survivors from Karen's unit is a mere formality. Then, as their individual memories of the event begin to conflict in at first subtle, then ever more obvious, ways, Serling has doubts. One thing begins to gnaw at him: If the survivors insist that they ran out of M-16 ammunition during the night, then why do members of the rescue team say they heard the M-16 firing moments before Karen died?

Serling, believing in "honor" in the fullest sense, becomes more intent on learning the truth, whether it qualifies Karen for the medal or denies her posthumous receipt. Though Hershberg, hoping to wrap this business up swiftly, grows frustrated, Serling continues to prod and push witnesses, particularly the belligerent medic Monfriez (Lou Diamond Phillips), in part because Serling is dedicated to the idea that the medal's reputation should remain a graillike object of purity in a morally graying world, in part because he's unconsciously searching for some way to redeem himself, to reclaim some sense of his own lost honor.

Courage Under Fire reunited Denzel with Edward Zwick, the director who, with *Glory*, had guided Denzel to his first Academy Award. But the inspiration for this picture began with Patrick Sheane Duncan, a former serviceman himself turned Hollywood scriptwriter (*Mr. Holland's Opus*, [1996]). Duncan became intrigued by the Medal of Honor and its symbolic significance while writing and directing a cable-TV series about the esteemed decoration. Meeting a number of real-life medal winners for the show, Duncan was surprised to realize that none appeared, in any obvious way, to be heroes. Rather, they were "ordinary people, regular folks who did something really extraordinary" at a moment of great pressure. Furthermore, Duncan said, "when I would ask people to talk about the Medal, they would often tell totally different stories about the same events." (Interestingly, Duncan's favorite film was the Japanese classic *Rashomon* (1951), Akira Kurosawa's study of a single event as varyingly recalled by four different participants.)

When Duncan pitched the idea to Zwick, the director—fresh from the commercial success of *Legends of the Fall* (1994)—was intrigued for his own reasons: "I liked the notion that a story set amidst a popular war—a media event—should also be a meditation on the nature of truth." Though Harrison Ford, Tom Hanks, and a number of other A list names were bandied about to play Serling, whose race is not specified in the script, Zwick—a former next-door neighbor of Denzel's as well as a close friend eager to collaborate again—soon seized on the idea of the film reuniting them professionally. "Having once told a story with [Denzel] of a man struggling to *find* his dignity in *Glory*, I was fascinated by the notion of him portraying a man who has *lost* that very thing and must now find a way to regain it."

Denzel, who initially felt that the character, as scripted, was a bit thin, finally agreed to sign on following a four-hour dinner discussion at a Chinese restaurant in Pasadena with Zwick and the producers. Then it was time to throw himself into the work of preparing for the part with his usual diligence. At the army's National Training Center in Northern California, Denzel joined a M1M1 tank group, quickly becoming one of the first civilians to ever fire a high-tech Abrams accurately. The actor observed the way military men move, speak, carry themselves, and relate to one another, filing away such surface information in his mind to make the character as true to life as possible. More important, though, was the essence of the military mind: "The research I did made me understand the importance of integrity. When you ask men and women to put their lives on the line for you, you have to prove that you're worthy for them to say, 'Yes, I'll go.' It's a tough job. There's no middle ground in war."

Initially, the Department of Defense planned to cooperate with the film crew, apparently believing that *Courage Under Fire* would essentially take a pro-military stance. At the last minute, though, all such cooperation was withdrawn. The military brass apparently believed, after reading the script a second time, that the portrait of military people as flawed, willing to play games with the truth, was basically negative. In fact, the movie's sensibility is neither hawkish nor dovish, instead assuming an unbiased, nondidactic middle-ground approach, as David Ansen would eventually state in his *Newsweek* review: "Duncan's take [is] neither a knee-jerk put-down of the military nor simply a patriotic salute. He has his bones to pick with the army's duplicitous protection of its own image, but it's the critique of an insider who believes in military values."

At the time, though, this loss of support created a major problem for the filmmakers, who, upon learning that the needed equipment would not be loaned to them, had to literally search the world for tanks and other material they could use. Forty-year-old British Centurions, carted across the ocean on a ship from Australia, had to then be modified so they would look like Abrams and T-54s. To achieve a strikingly original effect for the aerial shots of battle, cinematographer Roger Deakins employed a new camera from Otto Nemitz, called the Moviecam, the lightest, smallest 35-mm camera ever to be used to shoot a feature film.

"I think there's the kind of courage that has to do with the explicit courage under fire," Zwick said of his project. "And there's a very different kind of moral courage to overcome the demons in one's own life. *Courage Under Fire* juxtaposes those two kinds of courage" in its parallel story lines; Denzel and Meg Ryan never worked on the set together, since their characters are featured in separate but equal stories. Eventually, Serling learns the truth about Karen: She is not the pluperfect hero some make her out to be or the coward others dismiss her as, but an imperfect, worthwhile human being who excelled under pressure. As such, he concludes, Karen is indeed worthy of the medal. In reaching that conclusion, he finds the courage to tell the truth to the parents of the boy he killed, thereby rising to a kind of quiet heroic stature himself.

Denzel once again assumed a role as collaborator. During his research period, he spoke with a soldier who had lost a man in combat. "The man's wife and family blamed the soldier for that," Denzel recalled. " 'Why did you send him? He was your friend!' " Denzel wanted to know how the man lived with such questions, how he lessened his pain. The man replied that he did so by dealing with the family, even if it meant just being the whipping boy for them or setting up a scholarship fund for the child—whatever it took. "And then it clicked," Denzel explained; the actor understood, from the inside out, the character he had agreed to play. So he would not be playacting or faking some emotion for the camera but living it out entirely. Once this acting epiphany happened, Denzel induced Zwick to change certain scenes in the script, including the final moments, so that he could draw more directly on what he'd learned.

The movie, then, is as much Denzel's "truth" as anyone else's. He was also responsible for beefing up his character's traditionalist beliefs, ranging from religion to family values, making them a larger part of the dramatic fabric, while bringing the movie more in line with his own beliefs. It was Denzel who actually wrote the lines that immediately suggest the contradictory sides to Serling, who pauses to pray before the big battle, then immediately turns to his men, imploring them: "All right, let's kill 'em all!"

Another intimate moment that Denzel created, without relying on either the script or his director, was the final shot; here, once again, it is the actor who paints his character's key strokes of human coloring. Zwick had already filmed the sequence in which Serling returns to his estranged wife and felt relatively happy with it. Then he considered the front of the house and decided he wanted to do it again, this time with some visual evidence that the children were inside. So he took a bike and moved it up onto the steps. "I said, 'Let's go again,'" Zwick recalls. Denzel nodded affirmatively and then, in Zwick's words, "as he got to the steps, he tucked one bag under his arm and with the other arm he righted the bike. In that moment, he was a father cleaning up; he was a man resuming his duties in that house. That moment breaks my heart." And, in a quiet kind of way, it does the same for an audience: Such nuances, barely noticeable on any conscious level, are what provide truly memorable movies with a rich, textural verisimilitude approaching that of real life.

Nearly fifteen years earlier, Denzel made his first great impression as a film actor with a supporting role in *A Soldier's Story*, also about a black military officer who interviews various witnesses to a controversial incident in order to arrive at the truth. Some industry observers now wonder if perhaps Denzel should have played the part that went to Howard E. Rollins, since that actor clearly lacked the special magic necessary to bring the character to full life on-screen. Denzel's significant but secondary part actually stole away much of the dramatic thunder.

In fact, though, Denzel could have done little with the part of Captain Davenport, essentially a cipher who exists to discover "the truth." From what we were allowed to see, Davenport was as perfect as any of those role-model-type black heroes previously portrayed by Sidney Poitier, an actor who might have brought more oomph to the role than Rollins did but who couldn't have made the character any more interesting due to limitations in the writing. How much more worthwhile for Denzel, then, was the part of Serling in *Courage Under Fire*, who has his own inner journey to complete, his own arc to travel, even as he charts out the truth about the incident he's assigned to cover. Serling isn't, like Davenport, immediately identified as a black man; Denzel has always insisted, in his personal life, that he wants to be treated in a color-blind manner, while professionally he has always been on the lookout for just such film roles.

Although Serling is a black man who has achieved an exalted

status within the military, he is not some idealized role model. Though there is nothing about the man, as portrayed, that would embarrass black audiences—something Denzel has insisted he would never do—Serling is a human being who, like the actor playing him, achieved his position of respect through diligent hard work, though he is not incapable of making mistakes. Denzel has made mistakes, too: *Ricochet*, *Virtuosity*, and *Heart Condition* among them. Then again, every actor has his share of turkeys hidden away in his cinematic closet.

During the July 12–14 weekend, *Courage Under Fire* opened in the number-three position at the box office, behind the staggeringly successful sci-fi action epic *Independence Day* (1996) and *Phenomenon* (1996), with John Travolta as a Forrest Gumpish idiot savant. Certainly a "serious" drama—even one with a few well-placed explosions—can't be expected to compete with special effects and outright sentiment, though *Courage Under Fire* did win that audience which opts for a story featuring substance and characters boasting complexity. No wonder, then, that some critics tended to overpraise the picture. "Yes," Susan Wioszczyna wrote in *USA Today*, "it's safe for adults to go back to the movies," hailing the film as "Thoughtful. Intelligent. Moving. Provocative." To a degree, it was all those things, yet Janet Maslin of the *New York Times* seemed more to the point when she said that, like *A Few Good Men* (1992), *Courage Under Fire* is a skillful recycling of military-drama conventions that have been around at least since *The Caine Mutiny* (1954): "Mr. Duncan's plotting is impossibly neat, but he demonstrates the rare ability to shape a clichéd story in newly affecting ways."

About Denzel, Maslin was far more affirmative, hailing the film worth watching "thanks to the foolproof magnetism again shown by Mr. Washington in a potentially thin role. This unassumingly wonderful actor, so often the most valuable player in projects far less subtle than his own talents... brings substance and humanity to the story's conscience-stricken military man." Similarly, Wioszczyna stated: "*Fire* is also a reveille call that Denzel Washington has risen to the top-notch ranks in Hollywood.... Washington eschews histrionics and focuses on the more fleeting nuances of a good man torn apart." Ansen, arguing he'd "like *Courage Under Fire* more if it weren't quite so sure of its own importance," pointed out that

"Washington, subtle, moving and charismatic, anchors the movie."

Near the end, Serling takes a medal of honor, possibly his own (the film is ambiguous on this point), and places it on Karen's grave. The theme of acknowledging great work with a sought-after award can't help but make one wonder how Denzel (who, upon the film's release, was immediately touted as a possibility for the year's Best Actor Oscar) feels about awards. He was, after all, a presenter at the previous year's Academy Awards, though numerous African-American actors boycotted the ceremonies owing to the minuscule number of nominated blacks. Why and how had Denzel been able to participate in the ceremony under those circumstances?

His answer was consistent with everything he has ever said about race, acting, individualism, and identity. The solution is not how many award nominations minorities win but how much hard, diligent, high-quality work they do; one's own satisfaction at achieving such results are enough for him and, he believes, everyone: "They had a dinner the night before the Oscars for the African-American artists who'd been nominated. Well, there weren't any, but they had the dinner, anyway. And what I said that night, and I still say, is that we need to concentrate on making the best films we can and not concern ourselves with who's giving us an award for it. My concern is raising the standard of the work, not complaining about somebody not voting for me."

20

As We Go to Press...

Denzel's latest film, *The Preacher's Wife*, is in postproduction for a Christmas, 1996, release. A remake of the 1947 classic *The Bishop's Wife*, it stars Denzel in the part played by Cary Grant, an angel who helps the title character and her husband build their church. Besides allowing Denzel to return to comedy, a genre he has always admired, the story also is, in its quiet way, one that says something serious, with its positive theme about the need for religious guidance, even (particularly!) in our jaded world. Samuel Goldwyn Jr., whose father produced the original, did the honors for the remake, to be distributed by Disney.

As in Shakespeare's ostensibly "comedic" plays, the characters in *The Preacher's Wife* come perilously close to seeing their dreams destroyed. "A comedy in *theory*," Denzel says. "It could be a tragedy." About his ability to pull off such stuff, he admits: "Do I have the timing? It's new territory. It's not the comfortable things I'm used to." That, of course, makes it a challenge worth taking on.

Whitney Houston plays the Loretta Young role. Hollywood is so excited about the teaming of the two stars (Houston essentially is Denzel's female counterpart, a black performer with equal appeal to black and white audiences) that other possible screen vehicles for the two have already been suggested, including an umpteenth remake of *A Star Is Born* (1937; 1954; 1978), to be produced by Quincy Jones for Warner Bros., and a screen version of Michael Bennett's musical *Dreamgirls*.

Spike Lee, meanwhile, has optioned the rights for a Jackie Robinson biopic, about the black athlete who broke the color barrier in baseball during the early 1950s. The director has made it known that Denzel is his first choice. Like women, Spike "love him some Denzel!" Since Robinson was a hero of the integrationist movement, paving the way for the desegregation of American sports, this project would certainly seem compatible with Denzel's outlook and could provide ample material for another of his uneasy but rewarding working relationships with Lee.

There's also endless talk about pairing Denzel with Susan Sarandon in a film version of Chris Darden's book *In Contempt*, about his and Marcia Clark's prosecution of the O. J. Simpson case. The role of Darden would seem tailor-made for Denzel: a handsome, upscale lawyer—flawed but with great dignity—who is black and has achieved his status through hard work; he approaches the trial without concern for the accused's racial identity, then watches as the defense raises the race issue, painting him as an Uncle Tom for having been assimilated into the Establishment.

Denzel is scheduled to begin filming *Fallen*, in which he portrays a cop who discovers the fugitive he's after is possessed, during mid-Autumn of 1996. His paychecks continue to grow in leaps and bounds; the reported $8 million for *Crimson Tide* was followed by $10 million for *Courage Under Fire*, and now a whopping $12 million for *Fallen*. In the film, Denzel will play his share of action scenes, but he has appeared gun-shy about working in simplistically violent movies ever since flopping with *Ricochet* and *Virtuosity*: "I don't know if I have what a Stallone or a Schwarzenegger has to turn out blockbusters. I'm not that kind of action-hero type. I could be a [Tom] Cruise, maybe. I'm not complaining. None of these guys I've mentioned has an Academy Award, and I know all of them want one. I looked out at all those big stars the night I won and thought about that. I thought that you can't have it all. . . . But you can try. And you know I will!"

Fizzled film projects, like his stillborn action flicks, allowed Denzel to realize that his combination of intelligence and masculinity would serve him best in the likes of *Crimson Tide* and *Courage Under Fire*, character-driven movies with action along the way. Indeed, learning by doing, Denzel has gradually discovered the kind of role he was meant to play—one he's most comfortable with and his audience is happiest seeing him in. A few critics have suggested that

Mr. Decency ought to stretch by doing an outright villain; lest we forget, when he tried that with *Richard III* on the New York stage, Denzel received some of the worst notices of his career. The experience suggested that pure, unredeemed villainy is not his forte (even brilliant actors have their limitations) any more than are idealized, heroic role models.

Such idealized parts were as anathema to him as the caricatures of drug dealers and black pimps offered him—but refused—early on. What Denzel gradually honed in on is something else altogether, something far more valuable. He is the first black actor to ever portray on-screen a series of highly questionable, deeply flawed, ultimately worthwhile and decent people who are black. Like Denzel himself, any one of them could claim: "I am proud to be black, but black is not all I am."

Recall that a 1990 *L.A. Times Calendar* article hailed Denzel as "a leader among a handful of actors who are redefining how black Americans are portrayed on film." Though this claim was made a mere six years ago, it's worth noting that during the first half of the decade—largely through Denzel's quietly pervasive influence—such a "redefinition" has been achieved.

"People say, 'You're the guy that's gonna carry the torch for history,' he once scoffed, "but I'm *not* that guy." Surprise, Denzel: Yes, you are! His desire is to be an actor who assumes the most challenging, complex parts—doing roles written for whites and demonstrating that such parts can indeed be successfully played, critically and commercially, by an actor who is black—rather than self-consciously setting himself up as a role model. Ironically, this is what makes him such an effective role model against artistic Afrocentricity and in favor of assimilation. As a result of the image-altering work he has achieved, the perception of African Americans in film (and, subsequently, in life) has changed.

As Tri-Star's Mike Medavoy put it, "Denzel is a great actor who can do comedy, do drama, and who can carry a film. All kinds of films. To categorize them as appealing to a black or white audience is ridiculous. He is making movies about the human condition." If the O. J. Simpson trial, and its verdict, took a terrible toll on race relations in America—driving a wedge between blacks and whites and undoing so many civil rights gains put in place since World War

II—then the experience of attending a Denzel Washington movie serves, in some small way, as a healing process. Audiences—mixed audiences—don't consciously think of Denzel's characters as black. This is a person, a human being; color has little to do with our reactions to his characters, and by ritualistically watching the endless variations on a single theme, our national view of the importance of color is to some degree diminished through drama.

How great an influence has Denzel had? Note that, back in 1988, Denzel's friend and sometimes costar Robert Townsend observed the over-the-top histrionics Stallone and Schwarzenegger engage in, complaining: "No black man has ever saved the world." Yet one week before Denzel's *Courage Under Fire* opened, *Independence Day* premiered, starring Will Smith as a flyboy-hero who is black (no big deal) and does indeed save the entire world from aliens. Though a silly sci-fi-movie-cum-special-effects extravaganza, *Independence Day* broke all box-office records, thereby proving—as did Denzel's solid, if less spectacular, hit of a week later—that the emerging general audience of the mid-1990s can still root for a hero, his color being a nonissue. Smith was fortunate to ride in on the coattails of what Denzel diligently worked for fifteen years to achieve; Robert Townsend would be pleased.

And proud of the fact that Denzel, like Townsend himself, plans to direct. DreamWorks—the new studio created by Steven Spielberg, David Geffen, and Jeffrey Katzenberg—is wooing him to do so under their auspices, as are many other studios; Denzel will clearly have his choice of places to work when he finds the proper material. Directing is what the most creative film actors eventually turn to: Paul Newman and Clint Eastwood do it regularly, and Denzel's chum and *Philadelphia* costar Tom Hanks has now gone that route.

As did (lest we forget) Sidney Poitier.

Index

223

About the Author

Douglas Brode is a screenwriter, author, film historian, and college professor who makes his home in upstate New York. Over the years, he has also been employed as a radio announcer, TV-talk-show host, theater critic, and regional-theater actor. Currently, he teaches film courses at the Newhouse School of Communications at Syracuse University, Onondaga College, and Le Moyne College. His books include the 1970s college text *Crossroads to the Cinema* and, for Citadel Press, *Films of the Fifties; Films of the Sixties; The Films of Dustin Hoffman; Woody Allen: His Films and Career; The Films of Jack Nicholson; Lost Films of the Fifties; Films of the Eighties; The Films of Robert De Niro; The Films of Steven Spielberg; Money, Women, and Guns: Crime Films From Bonnie and Clyde to the Present;* and *Once Was Enough*. His articles have appeared in such popular magazines as *Rolling Stone* and *TV Guide*, as well as more esoteric journals, including *Cineaste* and *Television Quarterly*. Brode's original play *Heartbreaker* has been professionally produced; his original script *Midnight Blue*, produced by the Motion Picture Corporation of America and starring Dean Stockwell, is now available on home video.